SCARCE NATURAL RESOURCES

SAGE YEARBOOKS IN POLITICS AND PUBLIC POLICY

Sponsored by the **Policy Studies Organization**

Series Editor: **Stuart S. Nagel,** *University of Illinois, Urbana*

International Advisory Board

Books in this series:

1. What Government Does (1975)
   MATTHEW HOLDEN, Jr., and DENNIS L. DRESANG, *Editors*

2. Public Policy Evaluation (1975)
   KENNETH M. DOLBEARE, *Editor*

3. Public Policy Making in a Federal System (1976)
   CHARLES O. JONES and ROBERT D. THOMAS, *Editors*

4. Comparing Public Policies: New Concepts and Methods (1978)
   DOUGLAS E. ASHFORD, *Editor*

5. The Policy Cycle (1978)
   JUDITH V. MAY and AARON B. WILDAVSKY, *Editors*

6. Public Policy and Public Choice (1979)
   DOUGLAS W. RAE and THEODORE J. EISMEIER, *Editors*

7. Urban Policy Making (1979)
   DALE ROGERS MARSHALL, *Editor*

8. Why Policies Succeed or Fail (1980)
   HELEN M. INGRAM and DEAN E. MANN, *Editors*

9. Fiscal Stress and Public Policy (1980)
   CHARLES H. LEVINE and IRENE RUBIN, *Editors*

10. The Political Economy of Public Policy (1982)
    ALAN STONE and EDWARD J. HARPHAM, *Editors*

Volume 11. Sage Yearbooks in Politics and Public Policy

SCARCE NATURAL RESOURCES

The Challenge to
Public Policymaking

SUSAN WELCH
and
ROBERT MIEWALD
Editors

SAGE PUBLICATIONS
Beverly Hills / London / New Delhi

For information address:

SAGE Publications, Inc.
275 South Beverly Drive
Beverly Hills, California 90212

SAGE Publications India Pvt. Ltd.
C-236 Defence Colony
New Delhi 110 024, India

SAGE Publications Ltd
28 Banner Street
London EC1Y 8QE, England

Printed in the United States of America

Library of Congress Cataloging in Publication Data

Main entry under title:

Scarce natural resources.

    (Sage yearbooks in politics and public policy ;
v. 11)
    Bibliography: p.
    1. Natural resources—Addresses, essays, lectures.
2. Conservation of natural resources—Addresses,
essays, lectures.   3. Policy sciences—Addresses,
essays, lectures.   4. Scarcity—Addresses, essays,
lectures. I. Welch, Susan.   II. Miewald, Robert D.
III. Series.
HC59.S3435   1983   333.7'1   83-2898

ISBN 0-8039-1982-4
ISBN 0-8039-1981-6 (pbk.)

FIRST PRINTING

CONTENTS

Series Editor's Introduction
    STUART S. NAGEL   7

1. Natural Resources Scarcity: An Introduction
    ROBERT MIEWALD and SUSAN WELCH   9

PART I: Theoretical Approaches to Resource Policymaking

2. The Contest of Body and Soul: Resource Scarcity
Western Political Theory
    JOHN KINCAID   25
3. Liberty and Scarcity: William Ophuls Reconsidered
    R. MC GREGGOR CAWLEY   47
4. Resource Policy in Communist States
    SUSAN RIGDON   65
5. Social Responses to Protracted Scarcity
    ALAN BOOTH   85
6. Images of Scarcity in Four Nations
    LESTER W. MILBRATH   105
7. Political Responses to Environmental Scarcity
    HELEN M. INGRAM and DEAN E. MANN   125
8. Two Faces of Scarcity: Bureaucratic Creativity
and Constraints
    JEANNE NIENABER   151

PART II: Cases in Resource Policymaking

9. Water Scarcity and the Frugal Sustainable State
    MICHAEL W. BOWERS and DOROTHA M. BRADLEY   181

10. The Politics of Coal Severance Taxation
   UDAY C. DESAI and **OSBIN L. ERVIN**   203
11. The Sagebrush Rebellion: Utilization of Public Lands
   ALLEN R. WILCOX   227
12. Agriculture and Scarce Resources
   DON HADWIGER   243
13. Choosing Depletion? Soil Conservation and
   Agricultural Lobbying
   WILLIAM P. BROWNE and **KENNETH J. MEIER**   255
Name Index   279
Subject Index   282
About the Contributors   285

SERIES EDITOR'S INTRODUCTION

The specific problem of public policy toward scarce natural resources is particularly basic since it relates to the biology of human beings. Natural resources include air, water, and food, without which human life could not exist. Natural resources also include energy resources like oil, coal, natural gas, nuclear fuels, wood, wind, and animal power, without which the quality of human life would be greatly reduced. The same is true of natural resources that are used to provide materials for housing, clothing, and manufactured products. In a hierarchy of policy problems, natural resources are likely to be more basic than are policy problems that relate to technology, the economy, the polity, and other social institutions.

Without public policy, however, essential natural resources might be depleted, polluted, and or wasted. In the past, good quality air has been abundantly available except at high altitudes. Likewise, water has generally been available except in especially dry areas or in times of drought. In recent years, however, air and water pollution have created health-jeopardizing problems that cannot be resolved by relying solely on private action. Individual business firms have little incentive to incur the expense of pollution-reduction methods that add no income unless public policy provides an incentive. Recent years have also seen actual or threatened shortages of energy and material resources that have resulted in public policies designed to conserve existing resources or to promote the development of new resources. In the realm of food, there has never been an abundance approaching that of air and water. Ever since there have been human communities, there have been public policies on the allocation of food-growing land.

The problems of natural resources have grown worse in some ways, but they have grown better in others. They have become worse by virtue of the increase in (1) world population, which puts pressure on existing resources; (2) standards to which people are accustomed, which necessitates more energy and more materials especially for electricity, transportation fuels, and organic byproducts like plastics and fertilizers; and (3) pollution due to industrialization and urbanization. Natural resource problems can, however, be considered improved by virtue of the increase in our (1) food-growing capabilities, which have made it possble to abolish famines, (2) energy technology, whereby we can, if necessary, use solar energy and synthetic sources of fuels and materials, and (3) antipollution technology plus our willingness to use it. All six of those factors are influenced or are capable of being influenced by public policy including population growth, public demand, industrialization/-urbanization, food-growing capability, new technologies, and pollution reduction.

A key goal of public policy as it relates to natural resources should be to stimulate enough availability of essential resources so they never have to be rationed except by the marketplace. A related key goal is to keep the price of essential resources down or to subsidize limited purchasing power so the marketplace does not prohibit access by some segments of the population to minimum levels of food, energy, and other basic resources. If these minimums are not met, violent reactions can occur to the detriment of a smooth functioning, productive society.

This volume is concerned with such basic resources as water, energy, and food growing land. It is also concerned with more general aspects of policymaking in the realm of natural resources such as the role of governmental institutions and interest groups, public values, international relations, alternative economic systems, philosophical theory, and freedom from external regulation. The emphasis is on public policy, but with a recognition of the constraints under which public policy must operate relating to the environment, technology, the economy, other parts of the political system, and other social institutions.

The future availability of, and need for, natural resources is thus only partly dependent on nature. It is also heavily dependent on human values, particularly as collectively manifested through the governmental decision making of public policy. That kind of decision making needs to function well in terms of the effective, efficient, and equitable supply and distribution of resources in view of the important substance involved. That kind of decision making should function better as a result of insightful, informed analyses like those in this volume.

— *Stuart S. Nagel*
Urbana, Illinois

1

NATURAL RESOURCES SCARCITY:
AN INTRODUCTION

ROBERT MIEWALD
SUSAN WELCH

University of Nebraska

Things may not be so bad. Scientists in New York may be on the verge
of changing water into gasoline while researchers in Arizona are converting gasoline into water. Perhaps a clerk in Washington will discover
the misplacement of a decimal point and announce that the proven
reserves of coal, cobalt, and chocolate chips are much greater than we
thought they were. It is also conceivable that humans everywhere will,
as urged by economists, come to believe that the only scarcity is personal wealth and thus that there is no shortage of oil but instead a lack
of money to buy all that one wants. Any number of events could occur
to make the general concern with scarcity evaporate as quickly as it hit
us (and keep in mind that, twenty years ago, the title of this book
probably would have been "The Challenge of Abundance")

Enough evidence exists, however, to indicate that we are not now
poised on the cusp of a new age of endless bounty. Rather, we seem to
face a period of intensified sensitivity to the inevitable fact that there is

AUTHORS' NOTE: *The comments made on this chapter by Lynn White and Alan Booth
are greatly appreciated.*

9

never enough to go around. In turn, this sense of existing or impending deprivation should make a difference in policy outcomes if, as we have been taught by a generation of political scientists, the fundamental purpose of the political process is to make allocative decisions in the face of scarcity.

Scarcity seldom exists as an absolute fact. As has been noted often, for example, there is no scarcity of water on this big blue planet, nor is there any likelihood of ever exhausting such an abundant resource. The only shortage exists because people, for whatever reasons, insist on using water for the "wrong" reasons in the "wrong" places. In industrial societies, scarcity as a social or political problem is largely defined by people's perceptions of the lack of a resource in terms of their image of the good life rather than as a life-threatening deprivation. We will use the notion of scarcity to refer to a perception that the continued use of a certain resource, at a given time and place, carries too high a cost, either tangible or intangible.

In other words, we are not interested in entering into a discussion of resource scarcity solely in terms of economic efficiency. We are willing to concede that we could probably afford to sustain our economy, for a while anyway, at the level to which we have become accustomed. We could place oil rigs in Yellowstone; clear-cut the redwoods; turn the Grand Canyon into the world's largest landfill; wipe out the whales, snail darters, and several species in between; erect nuclear plants in every city; reopen hazardous mines; tear out our catalytic converters; and learn to live with acid rain, all in order to keep the gross national product at a preferred level. In the real world, however, politicians and administrators must confront that irony which Nathan Rosenberg (1982: 315), an economist, names as the major "debilitating concern": The attainment of affluence leads to an increased demand for material prosperity to be delivered in prettier packages. That is, the more we consume resources, the more misgivings we have about the way in which we approach nature. Answers might come more easily if Economic Animal were in charge of affairs, yet we must presume that, for better or worse, bumbling but lovable Political Animal will remain in control.

The contributors to this yearbook are not economists but instead come from those disciplines that Rosenberg suggests are rightful claimants to the title of "dismal science." They address the question of scarcity in making public policy, either in general terms or by case studies of specific policies issues. The volume begins with a consideration of the values underlying policy and the policy process when resources are seen as scarce (Kincaid, Cawley, Rigdon, and Booth). We then proceed to a discussion of the reaction of the public (Milbrath) and policymakers (Ingram and Mann, and Nienaber) to scarcity. Finally, we present several case studies of the policy process and outcomes in the areas of food (Hadwiger), soil conservation (Browne and Meier), land (Wilcox), water (Bowers and Bradley) and minerals (Desai and Ervin).

We can admit at the outset that the several articles do not add up to a definitive revelation about the impact of resource scarcity on the American political system. It would be far too presumptuous to claim to have developed special skills in interpreting the clues about what may be a new era in human history. What we can do with a little more confidence is describe the role of policy analysis in natural resources questions. The theme of this introduction, then, is not so much the challenge of resource scarcity to public policy, but instead, to public policy analysis. The art and science of policy analysis has several deficiencies when it comes to dealing with scarcity-related issues. Unless these deficiencies are overcome, analysts may wind up as historians, asking "What happened?" rather than as valued participants in the shaping of our future.

THE CENTRALITY OF VALUE

As several of our contributors note, discussions of scarcity have quickly entered the realm of social and political philosophy. A cynic might dismiss this development as a sign of how the elite will scramble in order to come up with an acceptable justification for the rich getting richer and the poor getting poorer. We prefer to believe, with Calabresi and Bobbitt (1978: 18), that "action in the context of necessary scarcity brings ultimate values, the values by which a society defines itself, into conflict." The pressure of scarcity reminds us that civilization depends on a moral basis for the question of who will get what. Without a philosophical explanation for the distribution of scarcity, there will be no legitimate base for the social order.

Policy analysts are poorly equipped to deal with this dimension of the political process. The deficiency is not hard to understand. Policy analysis, as a branch of social engineering, developed at a time when savants were proclaiming the "end of ideology" and that social science had "moved beyond ideology" (Waxman, 1968: 287). As tenders of the megamachine, analysts were concerned with regulating the outpouring from the cornucopia. Now, however, the allocation of negatives cannot be done so mindlessly.

Some analysts might rebel at the thought of still another "retooling" effort, this time not in computer hardware or in the latest econometrics formulae but instead, Platonic and Aristotelean philosophy. A thoughtful person might see this challenge as the salvation of analysis. As Fischer (1980) notes, analysis in many respects has degenerated into a series of sterile and pointless exercises, of little relevance to anyone except other analysts. The public and its politicians live in a world of conflicting values, and they want answers to, or at least intelligent guidance about, questions with considerable normative content. Ethical problems, exacerbated by scarcity, call for a reconsideration of the enduring questions of political theory.

In Kincaid's view (Chapter 2), scarcity makes us ask again whether it is better to feed the mind or the body. After all, the desires of the flesh (those "mad masters," as Plato called them) have pushed us to the edge of a crisis; the tyrannical "politics of the body" continues as the dominant ideology in both the East and the West. Although, as he concedes, we will probably wind up "muddling through," whatever policy answers we contrive will be rooted in fundamental theoretical issues. Analysts cannot afford to be ignorant of these issues.

Kincaid and several other contributors also carry on a dialogue, either directly or obliquely, with William Ophuls (1977), for that writer, in his seminal book on the "steady state," has reintroduced into our political discourse the awful figure of the Leviathan, the all-powerful state (see also Orr and Hill, 1978). Can the insatiable appetite of the individual be restrained by anything less than an authoritarian state? Cawley (Chapter 3) reviews the ongoing debate between Hobbes and Locke over the nature of political authority and concludes that Ophuls's vision of the control system in the "steady state" is based on a misunderstanding of both theorists. The Lockean tradition may allow for the manifestation of the spirit of community that avoids the need for control from above.

Advocates of a more powerful state face the difficult task of infusing in citizens a belief in its efficacy. Without a sense of will, Leviathan will be blurred in vision and palsied in limb. One would think that it is too late in the twentieth century for many to be deluded about the benevolence of the state. It would appear to require an especially potent political myth to convince the public to turn its well-being to any single group of stewards. In his review of evidence from less developed societies, Booth (Chapter 5) suggests that scarcity may tend to make believers out of us. It could be, that is, that the first victims of prolonged scarcity will be the philosophers and their fine ideals, which, after all, do nothing to feed the belly or keep fuel in the RV.

Scott and Hart (1979: 14) argue that Leviathan may visit us dressed in a three-piece suit and clutching an MBA. Fearing the loss of prosperity, "the American people have settled into a mind-numbing routine of trying only to preserve the status quo." We look to the managers for salvation, and for that group, whose training provides little awareness of ethical concerns, the only value is the strengthening of the organization. Scott and Hart fear that "the waltz of history will culminate in a totalitarian America, a monolithic society that is the logical culmination of the organizational imperative, unimpeded by any residue of the values of individualism" (1979: 210). In confirmation of this trend, White and Brinkerhoff (1981) found that those who expect scarcity are more likely to want government to play a larger role in the distribution of the scarce resources.

Those who would welcome the Leviathan as a way to deal with scarcity may learn much from a closer look at modern Communist states. Rigdon (Chapter 4) points out that although in some respects such states are better equipped than are those in the West to cope with resource scarcity, their record of accomplishment is not superior to that of the Western democracies. Although there are several reasons for this record, one can certainly conclude that in the area of resource scarcity, the dictates of an ideology ostensibly committed to social justice and equality are severely limited by human nature and tradition.

In any event, analysts can hardly continue to play the role of good, gray technicians, making sober scientific evaluations about the values decided by others. If they want to serve any useful purpose, they will have to become accustomed to the heat of ideological passion. Policy-making is not a spectator sport; effective participation requires some hard body contact, and that means analysts will have to make explicit their normative inclinations in suggesting alternative responses to questions of scarcity.

REACTIONS TO SCARCITY

As was said, scarcity seldom is a hard fact, posing an immediate threat to human life. It is a perception, often very vague, about some less pleasant future state. This polymorphic quality of scarcity is a great opportunity for policymakers, since it permits them much flexibility in the shaping of alternatives, as Ingram and Mann (Chapter 7) make clear in their inventory of possible responses to environmental scarcity. Still, because the definition of scarcity is locked away in people's heads and is almost never found in nature, the framing of solutions is a highly subjective business. We need more studies such as Milbrath's (Chapter 6) on the attitudes of citizens about a number of scarcity-related matters. While Milbrath's study does not tell us about the effects of these beliefs on behavior, others have investigated the importance of a belief in scarcity to the individual's attitudes about democratic values. Both White and Brinkerhoff (1981) and Ostheimer and Ritt (1982) found that those who believed that greater scarcity lies in the future also had less confidence in government, were less tolerant of inequality, and had a greater sense of alienation than did others. At the same time, the White and Brinkerhoff study showed that those who foresaw scarcity were also more likely to take an interest in government and to believe that government should allocate scarce resources. While Ostheimer and Ritt indicated that attitudes about scarcity have little association with actual political behavior, one might speculate that, without a vision of increasing personal resources, individuals may be reluctant to continue to maintain their share of the burdens of government. Thus, recent tax and spending limitation drives may be rooted in the general awakening to the possibility of coming restrictions on the availability of resources.[1]

Overall, the little empirical evidence we have provides some weak support for the arguments of earlier social scientists that democracy functions best when there are abundant resources (see Lipset, 1960; Cutright, 1963; for a counterview, see Neubauer, 1967). Visions of

scarcity seem to promote some antidemocratic and nonegalitarian attitudes but inhibit others. Certainly, however, the findings do not suggest
that Americans are running eagerly into the arms of the Leviathan
because of currently perceived resource scarcity.

Policy analysts, if they are to help guide developments, will have to
gain a sharper view of where society thinks it is going. At the present
time, that is a considerable challenge. Until recently, the Western view
of the political process was shaped by a belief in an abundant future.
Stemming in large part from the Enlightenment ideals that humans,
through the exercise of reason as expressed in science and technology,
could make progress toward an ever more materially abundant world,
this has had profound implications for the policy process and for the
outcomes of that process. This faith in an increasingly abundant future
has been shaken, but not entirely destroyed. Just as we do not have a
clear belief in an abundant future, neither do we accept our impending
doom. Since the gnawing doubts and formless little fears have not
crystallized into a widespread feeling that we face the "end of the world
as we know it," we are not mobilized by an urgent sense of having to do
something. We no longer have confidence in a bounteous future, but
neither do we believe that scarcity is inevitable. This confusion is
enhanced when we are told, on the one hand, that resource scarcity is
inevitable and that dramatic changes must be made to cope with it, if
indeed coping is possible (see Ward, 1979; Ehrlich and Ehrlich, 1972;
Eckholm, 1976; Heilbroner, 1980; Miles, 1976; Ophuls, 1977; Ehrlich,
1981), but, on the other hand, that the marketplace will allow us to
adjust to potentially scarce resources by substitution and diminished
consumption long before the resource runs out or causes serious hardship (Beckermann, 1974; Passell and Ross, 1973; Simon, 1980, 1981a,
1981b). With so-called experts in such vast disagreement, it is no
wonder that the public—both leaders and average citizens—are per-
plexed. Thus, as John Noble Wilford wrote:

> Everywhere we look there is a tension between the past and the future,
> between a pessimism we cannot shake and an optimism we cannot believe
> in. The present is thus a turmoil of understandable nostalgia, crippling
> indecision and bewildering prospect [quoted in Nisbet, 1980: 329].

For policy analysts, the main point about these perceptions is that
analysts cannot pretend to be disinterested observers. Analysis becomes

a large part of the environment to be perceived by the public. That is to say, if scarcity is primarily a social artifice, analysts may reify limits or potentials that simply do not exist in nature. It is likely that analysts could become an especially powerful band of doom-mongers (or, if Julian Simon's camp gains followers, pollyannas).[2]

There are objective reasons, for example, to support Stephen Long's description of the high plains as the Great American Desert. A prudent observer at the time might well have believed that mass delerium had seized those pioneers who flocked to the region in the 1880s because they were convinced that rainfall patterns had miraculously changed. However, it is undoubtedly to the benefit of the nation that those farmers overcame the facts to turn this "desert" into a highly productive agricultural center. Thus, "even though a new social reality about the use of natural resources may be desireable, it must be remembered that much of human progress can be understood as stubborn defiance of reality" (Miewald, 1978: 97). Analysts must be careful not to put a damper on the creative dissonance that sometimes occurs when people interact with their environment.

THE BENEFICIARIES OF SCARCITY

The very word "scarcity" has such an ominous sound to it that we may forget that it "is the peculiar condition of a business society, the calculable condition of all who participate in it" (Sahlins, 1968: 86). Shortages make the economy go round by conferring advantages on some people. If pure market conditions prevailed, the eventual distribution of scarce resources might reflect the true cost of extracting them from the natural world. As Hume (1739) pointed out, if all goods were free and unlimited, anyone could get as much as they wanted without harming others and would thus willingly share. That goods are limited produces the conflict and thus the means to regulate it.

While some are losers when resources grow short, others are winners. Just as the big winners in the Proposition 13 tax cuts may have been landlords, not tenants or small home owners, just as in times of famine those who control grain profit while others starve, so too does scarcity cause some to profit and others to lose. It seems apparent that while "more" is on the horizon, expanding the number of individuals and groups getting governmental largesse is a relatively small burden.

Although payoffs are not equal, everyone can be a winner. There will be more for everyone even thought the pie is being divided into more pieces. Visions of shrinking resources, on the other hand, make it less likely that those who hold power will invite new groups to share in either the decision process or in the benefits of government. Some must lose. Even former beneficiaries may find themselves cut out when times are hard, as many are now finding. Thurow (1980) has pointed out that at the heart of our economic problems is the fact that someone must bear the burden, must suffer an economic loss, if the economy as a whole is to prosper. Our political system has been unable to allocate the losses, at least on more than a short-term basis. We might expect, however, that images of future scarcity may allow these powerful groups in society to mobilize the public to reallocate burdens downward to those less well off. Reaganomics indicates that this phenomenon can work when the economic situation is bleak, and many people are willing to "try anything." Perhaps it is only the uncertainty surrounding our vision of the future that has prevented powerful groups from using scarcity as an excuse for even more dramatic changes.

Scarcity is a quite valuable natural resource for some political participants as well as for economically defined interests. Nienaber (Chapter 8) suggests that public agencies created to cope with this or that scarcity are frozen into a particular mode. While we thus have several agencies responding to parts of a perceived environmental crisis, no single one of them is really in charge of the problem of scarcity. All the bureaus have settled into a routine and, if one were of a conspiratorial frame of mind, it might be argued that they have an incentive to promote the idea that we are in constant danger of running out of whatever they are supposed to protect. Even if they tried to "solve" the scarcity problem, however, there are many impediments to doing so: They do not have a public mandate to take drastic action, nor do they have the resources. Many agencies have been captured by producer interests in those "iron triangles" political scientists are so fond of describing. This, along with the fragmentation, is enough to ensure that each bureaucracy continues on its isolated path, dealing minimally with the problem in its narrow area.

Elected political leaders have even less incentive to deal with scarcity. Alarming the public about a potential shortfall and possible future hardship is not a strategy perceived to win votes. And the more central the commodity to the citizenry and thus the greater importance of planning for scarcity, the less likely a political leader will boldly step forward to proclaim its impending scarcity and to suggest a plan to deal with it. Thurow (1980: 26) has argued that our failure to come to grips with future energy scarcity, for example, stems not from lack of solutions but from the fact that "each solution will cause a real income decline for some segment of the population." Given this likelihood, few elected politicians want to suggest solutions beyond finding more of the resource. Bowers and Bradley (Chapter 9) indicate what can happen when political leaders get too far in front of the public in implementing a solution to cope with future scarcity; raising Tucson water prices to reflect the real value of water led to a recall election in which those council members supporting the hike were voted out. Ironically, however, the policy remained essentially intact.

Nevertheless, with or without strong leadership, advantages created by scarcity will determine new winners and losers in the political struggle. In what may be called the "revenge of the Outback" against the industrial East, states such as North Dakota, Montana, and Wyoming have, as Desai and Ervin (Chapter 10) describe, added a new dimension to the integovernmental policy process. Whether they will be allowed to keep this advantage will depend upon a number of factors, including the justifications the energy-rich states have put forward for exporting the expenses of their local communities across state lines. In a report of another intergovernmental struggle, Wilcox (Chapter 11) describes the attempt of officials and citizens of Western states to wrest from federal control the public lands now owned by the nation.

In the final analysis, since there is no single scarcity issue, there is no scarcity policy. Instead, in a number of discrete areas, winners and losers confront one another. Consequently, little will be done about a general level of scarcity, and the burden of a reduced standard of living will be transferred to the politically weak. Each policy conflict creates a new policy and set of institutions dealing with a narrow segment of the problem. Institutional arrangements form around previous distributions of resources, thus making future adjustments more complicated. The result is often a layering of solutions, and the scholar may have to do an archeological exploration to get to the foundations of present policies. The end result is not a rational plan for the management of scarcity, and with each turn of the rachet, a coherent national policy becomes all the more unlikely. Of course, there were periods in our past—the Progressive and New Deal eras, for example—when the climate was favorable for a broader approach to environmental issues. The present time, marked by confrontations between Reaganites and environmentalists, does not seem to be one of those periods.

IMPLEMENTATION

The promise of policy analysis has always been that it will introduce greater rationality into the making of public decisions. More than any other policy area, resources policy illustrates the point that there is rationality and then again there is rationality. By what standard do we presume to define that noble word: individual rationality versus that of the collectivity, the locality versus the nation, short-term gain versus long-term benefits, the current versus future generations, political rationality versus economic rationality? There are as many definitions of rationality in resource planning as there are groups interested in the resources. Any plan for coping with scarcity, however rationally designed to take account of the larger interest and the welfare of future generations, must be implemented by individuals who, just because of their humanity, are not especially well qualified to serve as guardians of the larger good. The "general will" is not often apparent.

Attempted solutions to problems may have a number of unantici-pated and unintended consequences, as well as outcomes designed to benefit some at the expense of others. Hadwiger (Chapter 12) finds that second-order results in agriculture policy have had a positive effect for the consumer. Browne and Meier (Chapter 13) argue that, because of the configuration of individual interests in the policy process, the soil conservation program is not notably effective in conserving soil. This outcome, it must be emphasized is not because of the venality of politicians, the indifference of farmers, or the folly of officials; all would agree that soil conservation is an essential goal, even if no one is doing much about it. In the worst case, critics claim, there are no incentives to inspire among administrators a dedication to the public interest; as bureaucratic entrepreneurs, resource administrators are prone to pursue policies that, taken in their entirety, do nothing to ameliorate scarcity (Baden and Stroup, 1981: v). As Rigdon (Chapter 4) points out, this is just as true in Communist states, where bureaucrats are presum-ably more ideologically motivated, as in Western ones. Given these failures of bureaucracy, attention must be directed to the devising of incentives so that there is a greater likelihood of congruence between individual and collective rationality.

Until we have conclusive evidence to the contrary, however, it may be safer to regard resource administrators not so much as short-sighted wheelers and dealers but as reasonably dedicated public servants. Even reasonably dedicated people, of course, do not acquire omniscience by virtue of sincerity alone. They respond to a number of incentives and a number of information sources, the sum total of which may be nothing more than an awareness of the fact that "we have got to do something about this problem." Bowers and Bradley (Chapter 9) show that public officials, elected and appointed, can be moved to respond to a perceived scarcity crisis. Unfortunately, neither the City of Tucson nor the State of Arizona has solved the problem of a water deficit; their responses have probably only aggravated the condition.

In any event, rational choice is supposed to be the very special strength of the analytical profession. But how does one impose rationality on self-interested individuals engaged in a tense struggle with chaotic nature? And who defines rationality, anyway? It may not be too helpful to continue the quest for the ultimate analytical searchlight capable of cutting through the dense fog of conflicting values and perceptions. Unless one is willing to unleash the Leviathan, progress will have to be made in small steps.

CONCLUSION

With natural resources policy, we are surely in a situation "swept with confused alarms of struggle and flight, where ignorant armies clash by night." Too often, policy analysts have been in the front lines, engaged in hand-to-hand combat with narrow, technical questions. There is a need to retreat to higher ground in order to gain a better perspective on what the battle is all about. Nisbet (1980) has argued that, for the first time in centuries, we have lost our belief in progress, in a better future. In part he attributes this to a declining faith in the value of science and technology and the material prosperity they produce. Perhaps we are destined to live in an era of uncertainty as to whether future generations can look forward to lives resembling the poverty of Delhi's street people or the affluence of the middle-class European.

More optimistically, maybe this loss of faith in the limitless accomplishments of technology will be the beginnings of a new perspective on our relationship to this planet and to unborn generations.

If nothing else, the area of scarce resources policy ought to induce a great sense of humility among policy analysts. This is so not simply because the whole topic has been so little explored. Even when we know much more than we do now, little will be absolutely certain. Any specific issue is likely to remain an amalgam of confused values, distorted perceptions, uncertainty as to what the future holds, and individual self-interest. We can only hope that in a fit of impatience with human frailty the analysts do not invite the Leviathan in to make some sense out of it all.

Perspective and patience are difficult to learn and even harder to teach; most of all, they may be impossible to practice. But if policy analysis has any place in a democratic society, those qualities will have to be maximized.

NOTES

1. The lack of relationships found between support for tax cuts on the one hand, and standard individual socioeconomic status and fairly specific attitudinal characteristics of political trust, liberalism, and personal economic conditions on the other, offer the possibility that more general attitudes concerning declining resources in the future may be a partial explanation for this support (Lowery and Sigelman, 1981).

2. Simon (1980, 1981a, 1981b) has argued that resource scarcity is a myth and that increasing population size and consumption pose no threat to resource availability.

REFERENCES

BADEN, J. and R. STROUP [eds.] (1981) Bureaucracy vs. Environment: The Environmental Costs of Bureaucratic Governance. Ann Arbor: University of Michigan Press.
BECKERMAN, W. (1974) In Defense of Economic Growth. London: Cape.
CALABRESI, G. and P. BOBBIT (1978) Tragic Choices. New York: W. W. Norton.
CUTRIGHT, P. (1963) "National political development: its measurement and social correlates," in N. Polsby, R. A. Dentler, and P. A. Smith (eds.) Politics and Social Life. Boston: Houghton Mifflin.

ECKHOLM, E. (1976) Losing Ground: Environmental Stress and World Food Prospects. New York: W. W. Norton.

EHRLICH, P. (1981) "Environmental disruption: implications for the social sciences." Social Science Quarterly 62 (March): 7-22; rejoinder, 44-49.

——— and A. H. EHRLICH (1972) Population, Resources, Environment: Issues in Human Ecology. San Francisco: Freeman.

FISCHER, F. (1980) Politics, Values, and Problems of Methodology. Boulder, CO: Westview.

HEILBRONER, R. L. (1980) An Inquiry Into the Human Prospect: Updated for the 1980's. New York: W. W. Norton.

HUME, D. (1739) A Treatise of Human Nature (Frederick Watkins, ed.). in Theory of Politics. New York: Nelson.

LIPSET, S. M. (1960) Political Man. Garden City, NY: Doubleday.

LOWERY, D. and L. SIGELMAN (1981) "Understanding the tax revolt: eight explanations." American Political Science Review 75 (December): 963-974.

MIEWALD, R. (1978) "Social and political impacts on drought," in N. Rosenberg (ed.) North American Droughts. Boulder, CO: Westview.

MILES, R. E. (1976) Awakening from the American Dream: The Social and Political Limits to Growth. New York: Universe.

NEUBAUER, D. (1967) "Some conditions of democracy." American Political Science Review 61 (December): 1002-1009.

NISBET, R. (1980) History of the Idea of Progress. New York: Basic Books.

OPHULS, W. (1977) Ecology and the Politics of Scarcity. San Francisco: Freeman.

ORR, D. and S. HILL (1978) "Leviathan, the open society and the crisis of ecology." Western Political Quarterly 31 (December): 457-469.

OSTHEIMER, J. and L. RITT (1982) "Abundance and American democracy: a test of dire predictions." Journal of Politics 44 (May): 365-393.

PASSELL, P. and L. ROSS (1973) The Retreat from Riches: Affluence and its Enemies. New York: Viking.

ROSENBERG, N. (1982) "Natural resource limits and the future of economic progress," in B. Almond, M. Chodorow, and R. Pearce (eds.) Progress and Its Discontents. Berkeley: University of California Press.

SAHLINS, M. (1968) "Notes on the original affluent society," in R. Lee and I. DeVore (eds.) Man the Hunter. Chicago: Aldine.

SCOTT, W. and D. HART (1979) Organizational America. Boston: Houghton Mifflin.

SIMON, J. (1981a) "Environmental disruption of environmental improvement." Social Science Quarterly 62 (March): 30-43.

———(1981b) The Ultimate Resource. Princeton, NJ: Princeton University Press.

——— (1980) "Resources, population, environment: an oversupply of false bad news." Science (July 27): 1431-37.

THUROW, L. (1980) The Zero-Sum Society. New York: Basic Books.

WARD, B. (1979) Progress for a Small Planet. New York: W. W. Norton.

WAXMAN, C. (1968) The End of Ideology Debate. New York: Simon & Shuster.

WHITE, L. K. and D. BRINKERHOFF (1981) "The political consequences of the 'age of limits.'" NASIS-81 Report 3. Lincoln: University of Nebraska, Bureau of Sociological Research.

PART I

THEORETICAL APPROACHES TO
RESOURCE POLICYMAKING

2

THE CONTEST OF BODY AND SOUL: RESOURCE SCARCITY IN WESTERN POLITICAL THEORY

JOHN KINCAID

North Texas State University

Debates over scarcity in affluent Western democracies have moved quickly to considerations of ethics and philosophy. This is unusual. Public policy questions are not often elevated to the level of high principle. Yet within a decade of its appearance as a notable public issue, scarcity became widely construed as an integral feature of a global ecologic crisis so severe as to elicit basic reinterpretations of Western history (White, 1967), reexaminations of Western political thought (Ophuls, 1977), extensions of modern rights to nature (Stone, 1974; Singer, 1975), and numerous radical policy prescriptions (e.g., Schumacher, 1973; Bookchin, 1982). Even the language of discourse shifted from *conservation* and *environmentalism* to *ecology*, and from *shortages* to *scarcity*, to reflect conceptions of policy challenges held to be systemic rather than merely technical.

This turn to fundamentals was stimulated, in part, by a catastrophic imagery often employed by both proponents and opponents of a lean ecologic ethic. Such books as *Our Plundered Planet* (Osborn, 1948), *Standing Room Only* (Sax, 1955), *Silent Spring* (Carson, 1962), *The Frail Ocean* (Marx, 1967), *Famine, 1975* (Paddock and Paddock, 1967), *The Population Bomb* (Ehrlich, 1968), *The Doomsday Syndrome* (Maddox, 1972), *The Limits to Growth* (Meadows et al., 1972), *Models of Doom* (Cole et al., 1973), *The Coming Dark Age* (Vacca,

1973), *The Greatest Battle* (Glasser, 1976), *The Lean Years* (Barnet, 1980) and *The Zero-Sum Society* (Thurow, 1980) all convey a dire urgency, if not an international emergency.

The debates also spawned a brutal language of politics—imminent authoritarianism, lifeboat ethics, triage, claw-and-fang survivalism—as well as a lexicon of peculiar terms such as "eco-justice," "ecoanarchism," "ecodemocracy," and "ecofascism." At the same time, various spiritual movements emerged in response to, or found themselves rejuvenated by, this material crisis. These more pacific religious, holistic, and back-to-nature movements disputed the efficacy and propriety of purely secular, rational policy approaches to scarcity.

To an extent, these apocalyptic images can be attributed to the tradition of jeremiads and hyperbole to which American reformers are often given, particularly during reformist periods such as the 1960s and early 1970s. The presence of the mass media and a more literate population helped to disseminate and reinforce these crisis images.

For Americans, fears of scarcity also stemmed from a tradition of recurring doom as to an imminent close of the frontier and an end to American exceptionalism (Pickens, 1981). The prospect of a closed or contracting frontier has been viewed as a threat, not only to comfortable living, but also to virtue, democracy, limited government, and egalitarianism. Frederick Jackson Turner and Walter Prescott Webb, the great theorists of the frontier, feared the worst for the world from the closing of the frontier. With scarcity, they believed, freedom, democracy and civilization itself might be scattered to the winds or trampled underfoot by class warfare.

The possibility of global scarcity evokes apocalyptic concerns, therefore, not simply because it threatens the economic base of modernity, but because it undermines the ontological basis of modernity. If scarcity merely damaged modernity's economic base, the problem would be serious enough. But economists are accustomed to managing scarcities. Along with utility and transferability, scarcity is an intrinsic property of economic goods (Zinam, 1982).

The root cause of alarm is that the economic base of modern life, namely abundance, has become, in its essential respects, the ontological basis of modernity. Much of modern political and social science has come to regard the material conditions of existence as having the decisive, if not the only, influence on the course and character of human life. Human nature has been construed as an integral part of the economy of nature, not as something above or partly outside of it. The condition of the state of nature is the decisive determinant of expressions of human nature. Under conditions of scarcity, these expressions are generally held to be violent, beastly, and selfish. Under conditions of plenty, these expressions can be made more benign, or at least, less harmful.

As Karl Marx put it in the most severe modern idiom: "It is not the consciousness of men that determines their being, but, on the contrary, their social being that determines their consciousness" (Tucker, 1978: 4). If, therefore, as some have rephrased it "we are what we eat," then basic resource scarcities threaten to alter not only how we live, but who and what we are as well.

This problem is not new. Most people throughout most of history have lived in penury at the edge of scarcity. However, this is precisely what modernity has sought to escape through the conquest of nature. What is new is that modernity is peculiarly dependent upon nature's material abundance, and therefore, a continuing frontier capable of holding the Dark Ages and dark passions of mankind at bay.

This is especially true of the two great political ideas that have come to dominate the modern era: liberal democracy and socialist communism. While they are antagonists in many respects, they nevertheless share a critical dependence on material abundance for the success of their promise of peace and prosperity. This is why, no doubt, they have captured the allegiance so quickly of so many. These two political systems are arguments over how best to produce and distribute the abundance of nature elicited by modern psychology and technology.

SCARCITY AS A POLITICAL PROBLEM

Resource scarcity has always been a central problem in Western thought because most individuals seem to desire finite material goods more than they desire that which is Good, true, or beautiful regardless of its material status. Most individuals desire the good as well as material goods, but not with equal intensity. Chief Sitting Bull's observation about white Europeans at the Powder River Council of 1877 seems widely applicable: "The love of possession is a disease with them."

Humans can be made to love the Good, but only with great difficulty and at the risk of what modernity regards as excessive repression, as in the Platonic and Puritan commonwealths, or excessive idiocy, as in the noble savage. Hence, civilized humanity has tended to seek the Good through goods, with the latter serving as the criterion for the former. In the extreme case, this has become the relativism of certain sectors of modern thought. There is no Good or *summum bonum*, only competing goods. At best, the Good is the common good summed across individual goods or private utilities: in short, the transformation of private quantities into public qualities.

Human beings form political associations, said Aristotle, not merely to live, but to live well (Barker, 1962: 5). For most, according to Hobbes (1958), living well means a commodious existence free from external restraints. Indeed, when cultures of abundance confront cultures of scarcity, the latter tend to become disoriented and break down as cultural barriers to wealth getting, necessary under conditions of scarcity, are bridged by opportunities for accumulation. How to behave toward Stone Age societies has been one of the great ethical issues of modernity (Mead, 1967).

If living well moderately were the object of political association, the task of political science would not be so difficult. The more intractable problem is that human desires for material goods invariably exceed their bodily needs as well as their technical means of satisfaction. The irony of scarcity is that the conquest of scarcity merely regenerates scarcity because there is never enough; needs and wants have their own regenerative cycle when left to themselves. Hence the experience of scarcity is a permanent feature of human existence. That this experience is largely independent of the actual availability of resources is a crucial datum of political science.

Scarcity, therefore, is conceptually difficult to grasp, except at its extreme ends, and difficult to measure empirically, except in relation to specific desires. Even at that, scarcity can simply evaporate by changing desire. Basically, then, scarcity can be defined as any natural or human insufficiency of resources regarded as objectively or subjectively necessary to realize any given end valued by an individual, group, or society. Scarcities may be material (e.g., natural resources) or nonmaterial (e.g., knowledge, power, opportunity). It is this subjective character of scarcity that makes it so politically potent.

Essentially, there are two policy approaches to the problem: supply and demand. To alleviate scarcity, civil society may augment the supply of goods and/or reduce the demand for goods. The supply of resources may be increased by producing and discovering more or new resources, making more efficient use of resources, recycling resources, and substituting resources. These are, generally, the preferred options of modernity, and policies framed about them have many defenders.

The demand for resources may be lowered by increasing the costs of resource use through law, custom, command, or market forces; by rationing resources; and by substituting communal for individualistic means of end fulfillment (e.g., mass transit for automobiles). Demand may be reduced forcefully by the use of collective or superior power to deny the demands of whole nations, peoples, or sectors of a population; or it may be reduced voluntarily through appeals to lowered expectations. More drastic are policies of war, triage, and lifeboat ethics. Historically, population control has long been a major method of demand reduction, though not always a benign one. Migration has also been an important way of reducing pressures on regional resources. Finally, demand may be reduced by substituting ends rather than resources, by revaluing human ends, and by devaluing certain ends altogether, namely, those ends contingent on material resources. Generally, these latter policies are preferred by classical political theory.

These two policy choices, supply and demand, largely separate the mainstreams of classical and modern theory. Classical political thought generally emphasizes demand-side policies, while modern thought tends to emphasize supply-side policies. These differences are rooted in a more fundamental distinction that can be termed the *politics of the body* versus the *politics of the soul*. Classical political thought is concerned primarily with the goods of the soul and, therefore, with virtue and moderation. Modern political thought is concerned primarily with the goods of the body and, therefore, with prosperity and consumption.

By classical political thought, I will be referring mainly to Plato and Aristotle with occasional asides to Augustine. By modern political thought, I mean primarily Machiavelli, Hobbes, Locke, Rousseau, and Marx. These philosophers do not, of course, make up the entire tradition of secular political thought in the West, though they do constitute most of its core and, thereby, the tradition's most influential representatives. This is not to say that other philosophers ignore scarcity, but only that space constraints and economy of presentation make it necessary to limit attention to certain peaks of the Western tradition.

CLASSICAL POLITICAL THEORY

Scarcity presented both practical and moral problems for classical theory. On the practical side, most ancient polities were small by modern standards, and resource utilization was limited both technically and geographically. A number of civilizations had declined, in part, because they depleted resources within their fields of ecological support. Scarcity could be alleviated by expanding the territorial scope of political economy, mainly through trade and conquest; however, expansion encountered practical problems as well as more paramount moral objections on the part of classical theory, which regards the medium-size *polis* as the only basis for attaining a "rich" and virtuous political life based on informed dialogue and deliberation in a public arena laced with ties of friendship.

According to Plato and Aristotle, a "good" polity must be large enough to be autarkic—in the sense of being sovereign, self-sufficient, and able to provide the means for humans to realize their highest ends—but not so large as to break the bonds of friendship and dialogue, and thereby factionalize the polity or make government a distant abstraction or imperial burden (Barker, 1962: chaps. 4-6). As Cotton Mather wondered in 1690 how "at once we may Advance our Husbandry, and yet Forbear our Dispersion" (Kammen, 1973: 180), so too did the ancients believe that economic expansion dissipates the communitarian order of a virtuous *polis*.

Commitment to the medium-size polity requires classical theory to counsel moderation, lest citizen desires for abundance exceed supplies of local resources or the satisfaction of those desires actually deplete resources. Both possibilities disturb communitarian stability and awaken desires for foreign commerce, conquest, and colonization. While some commerce is necessary, foreign conquest and colonization tend to subvert good regimes and invite tyranny. Writing at the end of Athens' Golden Age, Plato and Aristotle were acutely sensitive to these problems.

However, the fundamental classical objection to material abundance is that it diverts attention from the truly good life. Abundance caters to the low passions of the body rather than to the high aspirations of the soul. The classical view is well summarized by the biblical rebuke: "For what shall it profit a man, if he shall gain the whole world, and lose his own soul?" (Mark 8:36). While Christianity attends to the soul's condition in this life for the sake of justice in the next life, classical theory attends to the soul in this life for the sake of justice in civil society. The concern, then, is not for the exploitation of nature per se, but for its harmful effects on human nature.

Classical theory, like modern theory, recognizes that humans differ from animals. Humanity is "in but not wholly of" material nature, standing instead, between the beasts and the gods, according to Aristotle (Barker, 1962: 6). The basic political question is whether humans shall behave more like beasts or gods. "The life of man is midway between that of Angels and of beasts," wrote Augustine. "If man lives after the flesh, he is on a level with the beasts; if he lives after the Spirit, he joins in the fellowship of angels" (Deane, 1963: 42).

Both classical and modern political theory agree that humans more often behave like beasts, although modern theory holds that man is only beast—the highest animal on the food chain—and classical theory holds that humanity is at once greater than the beasts and lesser than the gods. The leap from animal to human being is not an evolutionary mutation of quantity into quality, but a substantive transformation of nature made possible by a divinelike spark. Thus where man is simply body in modern theory, man is body *and* soul in classical theory.

In the classical view, each being has its own nature, and the best life is one lived according to that nature. This is easy for animals, but because human nature compounds the beastly and divine, humans must live according to two natures that pull in different directions: downward and upward. The two must be brought into some kind of balance, though the soul must be dominant, because the soul is the higher principle in human nature. The best life for man by nature is one lived according to the dictates of the soul. It is evil and unnatural, wrote Aristotle, for the body to rule the soul.

But the best life does not come easily because it must be determined by reason, not instinct. While animals are well programmed by instinct and habit to live according to their beastly natures, humans are not well programmed to live according to reason. Unlike the body, the soul is not a part of material nature; instead, its capacity for reason exists as a potential. To achieve the good life according to man's higher nature, reason must be cultivated independently of the body's needs, passions, and impulses.

Unfortunately, observed Plato, the body is the soul's prison. The body, so contingent on raw nature and sensory interactions with it, is chained to a "cave-world" of mere appearances, while the soul, which is not contingent on material nature, is potentially capable of apprehending the true nature of nature—the realities behind nature's manifold and transient appearances. Given the ease with which humans can follow the instincts of bodily pain and pleasure as opposed to the laborious efforts associated with reason, the body more often rules the soul and uses reason to serve its beastly desires. The worst life in the classical view is that lived according to man's beastly nature.

There are, then, two kinds of politics: the politics of the body, which is life according to man's beastly nature, and the politics of the soul, which is life according to man's almost divine nature. Each has its own kinds of goods and justice. The goal of classical theory is to help bring into being the politics of the soul.

All of this is well illustrated in Plato's *Republic*. The dialogue opens with Socrates being forced to attend a party associated with a religious festival. However, Socrates quickly takes command and transforms the party into a philosophic dialogue. The participants feast on this "food for thought" while neglecting the material food. Generally, in classical theory, there is an inverse relation between noetic and material goods. Justice, virtue, happiness, love, wisdom, beauty, and the like are goods of the soul whose apprehension requires a tempering and, perhaps ultimately for Plato, a transcendence of the body's goods. Indeed *The Republic* ends with a discussion of the soul.

The political question is directly addressed through the cities in speech. The first city, the city of necessity, is pacific, harmonious, and vegetarian. It seems perfectly just. But Glaucon rejects it as nothing more than a city of sows and, therefore, unjust because it denies humans the greater goods of which they are capable. At this point, however, Glaucon confuses his stomach with his soul. What he desires are "relishes and desserts," namely, a luxurious city (Bloom, 1969: 372e).

Glaucon's protest is a rejection of the city closest to nature in the simple sense. Although such a city in harmony with nature appeals to many as an easy, perfect justice, it is actually unjust because it is against human nature. Glaucon suggests that only weak, timid and less intelligent people seek refuge in nature. Anyway, a return to nature is impossible because there are too many Glaucons of varying degrees in the world, and one certainly cannot keep Glaucon down on the farm once he has seen Athens. The kind of rustic simplicity and even vegetarianism advocated by some contemporary environmentalists would have to be imposed on Glaucon, who is not about to give up meat without a fight. Ironically, then, the simple regime of nature can only exist by domination.

There being no return to nature, Glaucon's desire for a luxurious city raises all the hard questions of human justice. To quench Glaucon's desire, the second city must go to war to conquer men and nature. "Whence come wars and fightings and factions?" wrote Plato in the *Phaedo*: "Whence but from the body and the lusts of the body?" Glaucon delights in the conquest, not only because it brings him wealth and power, but also fame and glory—his first taste of the higher pleasures.

Socrates recognizes that Glaucon is what Benjamin Franklin called a "pest of glory." Since these pests often wreak havoc on civil society, their energies need to be redirected toward more publicly beneficial ends. However, where Franklin would have directed Glaucon toward commercial activity, and thereby toward the conquest of nature for the sake of human welfare, Socrates directs him toward philosophic activity, which will relieve both nature and man from the pressure of conquest. The remainder of *The Republic* is, in effect, devoted to the education of Glaucon and refinement of his soul. This, says Socrates, will bring Glaucon the greatest of all pleasures.

At the same time, it will rescue civil society from Glaucon's tyrannic desires. By diverting his erotic attention to the goods of the soul, which are good for everyone, Glaucon will lose interest in the goods of the body, which can be harmful to the soul as well as to the body (e.g., excessive wine drinking) and harmful to others because, ultimately, in a world of scarce resources, their possession can only be had by robbing man and nature. Hence, the politics of the body stops at the luxurious city, the *Civitas Terrena*, for Augustine; the politics of the soul transends it to the *Civitas Dei*.

Classical theory rejects the politics of the body for many reasons, but for our purposes, a principal defect is that the goods of the body are intrinsically scarce while those of the soul are not. The goods of the body are used up over time, leaving only, if anything, waste and memories. Oil and gas are finite, and their use leaves harmful byproducts. There is no end to wisdom, and its use is beneficial to the self and others. Similarly, bodily pleasures, even those not so directly contingent on material nature, are ephemeral. Sexual pleasures, for example, are transitory. The action must be repeated for repeated pleasure; even then, the ultimate orgasm seems unobtainable. Repetition may even reduce pleasure. But the love associated with a relationship not only enhances sexual pleasure; it also provides enduring gratification beyond it.

Another problem is that the goods of the body are not readily or easily shared with others. They are "divisible goods," in the classical view, namely, "those in which one man's gain is another man's loss" (Inge, 1948: 192). The goods of the soul are easily and infinitely sharable. They are "indivisible" goods "which many may possess at once, and no one is worse off in respect to them because another has them" (Inge, 1948: 192). A glass of water may slake the thirst of one person, not hundreds, but an idea may bring pleasure, justice, or relief to millions.

Because of this, the goods of the body have a possessive and selfish character. Many can be used by only one person or a few persons at one time. To give up such goods entails a substantive cost or loss. To share such goods is to risk their being used up or returned with diminished value. The goods of the soul, however, are naturally other-regarding. In certain respects, they can be acquired and enjoyed in solitude, but in most respects, goods such as love, virtue, wisdom, and beauty must be acquired and enjoyed in the company of others. In their sharing, moreover, they are almost always enhanced in value.

Since the goods of the soul can be shared freely and fully and "consumed" for eternity, there is no reason to fight over them or conquer nature to possess them. The politics of the soul is pacific, cooperative, other-regarding, and coincidentally ecologic. But because the goods of the body are scarce and divisible, a political life based on the body is invariably warlike, conflictual, and competitive. Violence may be sublimated through the jungle of the marketplace, but sooner or later, the resource base must shrink to the point at which all or some participants must sink in the lifeboat or fight to be the last survivor.

The politics of the body is also tyrannic. The body's desires are "mad masters," according to Plato, that take over a person regardless of the dictates of reason and welfare of others. They may become uncontrollable, and, thereby, harmful to the self and others. Plato would no doubt regard addictions to alcohol, cigarettes, and the like as enslavement to one's passions. Ironically, then, while the goods of the body are consumed "to make it feel better," they can destroy it instead. It is this self-destructive potential of the goods of the body that can be said to underlie our ecological crisis.

The politics of the body is also tyrannic because the body's desires are insatiable. Classical theory quite agrees with Hobbe's view that bodily felicity "is a continual progress of the desire from one object to another, the attaining of the former being still but the way to the latter" (Hobbes, 1958: 86). The body desires everything, according to Hobbes. The drive for satisfaction requires ever greater extractions or expropriations of the goods of nature, and of man, if necessary. Obstacles to gratification tend to become objects of conquest. Thus the politics of the body inclines humans to tyrannize nature. At the same time, nature comes to exercise its own tyranny over humans insofar as they become excessively dependent on it for happiness. Hence they are not truly free.

The politics of the body is also tyrannic because the "conquest of nature" leads inexorably to the "conquest of man." Given the inevitable scarcity of nature's goods, humans seek to gain from others what they cannot wrest from nature. The techniques of dominating nature are equally applicable to the domination of man, which is one reason why classical theory rejects the modern notion of technological freedom in favor of moral-political control over technology. As a result, the "many" are compelled to labor at the conquest of nature in service to the desires of the "few," as has been the case in virtually every civilization since the domestication of nature. Further, no matter how abundant the supply of resources, there will emerge those who, like Glaucon, desire ever larger shares at the expense of others. They will either have it by dominating others or be deprived of it by being dominated by the others (as in Hobbes's Leviathan). Either way, politics as freedom and justice for all gives way to domination. For all these reasons, therefore, the tyrant is, according to Plato, a person wholly devoted to bodily passions.

Lastly, the body (which is the public, visible manifestation of our being) is intensely private and individualistic, while the soul (which is the private, invisible engine of our being) is intensely public and communalistic. The body is private, selfish, and individualistic because, after all, it is one's own and cannot be shared with others. No one else can experience its mortal pain or death. In the body's world of scarce space, time and resources, all other bodies are potential threats. Indeed, it is the body's very mortality that impels individuals to defend it so fiercely against death. Thus it is the body, with its imperial desires and death-defying fears, that divides man from man, and man from nature, and uproots both nature and civil society. It is the politics of the body that is antipolitical, not the politics of the soul. It is the politics of the body that creates dissension and disorder in the universe, leading ultimately, in modern terms, to entropy.

The soul, however, is finally public, political, and "immortal." There cannot be a communion of bodies, only a comingling; there can, however, be a communion of souls. The soul must come out of its bodily prison, so to speak, in order to share love, wisdom, happiness, and justice with other souls. The soul is a part of that class of "things" that belong to everyone and exist forever apart from material nature. Its goods are necessarily public and can be passed on to future generations. By exercising the soul's capacity for participating in reasoned discourse about the best things for humankind (and not just for "me"), the speaking beast becomes a human being. This is what it means to live according to nature in classical theory, and this is what makes man, by nature, a political or public being. To attend only to the business of the gods or only to the business of the beasts is to be, like Cephalus and Thrasymachus in Plato's *Republic*, timidly senile or aggressively unjust. Justice, according to Plato, is minding one's own business—such is freedom and happiness.

Classical theory does not expect to found any actual regimes on the basis of the soul purely. Ultimately, such a regime can exist only by chance. In any event, even Socrates must eat, so politics cannot ignore the body. But classical theory does seek proximate solutions that place the body in proper perspective. In *The Laws*, Plato presents a more practical teaching of "the art whose business it is to care for souls—the art of politics." Aristotle is well known for his theory of the mixed middle-class *polis* based on the rule of the mean. Thus classical theory is not ascetic; instead, it seeks moderation in all things and looks to the medium-size polity of 50,000, perhaps even 100,000, citizens as being the best public arena for the cultivation of communitarian friendship, civic loyalty, and rational discourse. Furthermore, since few individuals can practice moderation by reason alone, the medium-size polity is conducive to the formation of cultural norms that induce moderation by habituation.

In the classical view, the ends and virtues of a polity are determined by the character of its ruling element. Therefore, any overriding drive to satisfy the material desires of citizens beyond their proper bodily needs is likely to change the character of a polity by bringing into prominence a new ruling element capable of expanding material resources. Like the rise of the Texas oil men or the "high-tech" professionals in Massachusetts (Peirce, 1982), new interests or classes may alter the configuration and use of power.

Given the usually selfish, acquisitive nature of bodily desires, classes whose power is rooted in material desires are not likely to have public-regarding conceptions of justice, nor are they likely to care for the virtues of the soul (e.g., the robber barons of *laissez-faire* capitalism). As Plato suggests through the story of Cephalus at the opening of *The Republic*, such individuals are likely to praise virtue only when nearness of death makes them fear for the fate of their souls. Having lied, cheated, and robbed others to acquire wealth during his lifetime, the elderly Cephalus suddenly becomes a philanthropist. He rushes off to pay his "debts" and make sacrifices to the gods. In the classical view, therefore, no polity can be justly ruled by such "lower classes" as merchants, laborers, military men or the wealthy. Military men are devoted to the virtues of war, merchants to the virtues of economics. While they may share in ruling according to Aristotle, the best political rule is provided by philosophers or aristocratic gentlemen.

Elevating civil society to new plateaus of material satisfaction increases the possibility that the political order will be absorbed by the economic order. The public realm of rational deliberation and citizen participation may be carved into private, segregated realms of material exchange such that economics may come to determine justice, while materially based desires may come to define the "good." Therefore, classical theory concludes that the greater the dedication of a polity to the exploitation of natural resources, the lesser its dedication to justice.

Even too great a commercial dependence on foreign resources can limit self-rule and expose a polity to undesirable influences. Like the recent U.S. campaign for "energy independence" or the drives of some Third World nations for modernization without Western enculturation, classical theory counsels a certain self-reliance and insulation. So fearful is Plato of the harmful effects of foreign influences that he recommends that a good republic be located at least ten miles from coastal waters. The sea "infects a place with commerce and the money-making that comes with retail trade," wrote Plato, "and engenders shifty and untrustworthy dispositions in souls; it thereby takes away the trust and friendship a city feels for itself and for the rest of humanity" (Pangle, 1970: 705a).

Yet scarcity is also a political challenge because of the historic problem of human penury. This is neither just nor desirable. People should live well. The noble savage romanticized by some Western writers is regarded as a poor beast and pagan by classical thought, chained to the necessities and vagaries of nature and quite vicious when deprived of natural resources. Thus one of the first tasks of political science is to free humans from the tyranny of nature so as to make possible a genuine political life. Aristotle especially regards leisure as a prerequisite for politics. In so doing, however, classical theory seeks a balance or "mean" between freedom from necessity and the overindulgence of needs stimulated by the desires awakened by this freedom. Too great an indulgence of desire reintroduces a dependence on nature's resources and opens the public door to political tyranny. The relationship is curvilinear, so to speak. At the farther ends of both scarcity and abundance, humans are overly dependent on material nature. Only near the high middle are humans relatively free from nature and, thereby, free to pursue the noetic ends of their unique nature.

The result is that nature cannot solve the human political problem; only humans can do that. Humans cannot look to the beasts or the gods for answers. They must look into themselves. By articulating a politics of the soul, classical theory seeks to set a direction for political life and a standard for judging political life, even if the realization of such a standard is ultimately beyond human capabilities.

MODERN POLITICAL THEORY

Modern theory largely concurs with the classical view of the consequences of the politics of the body, but nevertheless rejects the politics of the soul as being dangerous, nonsensical, and unjust. It is dangerous because it denies humans the best life and frequently costs them their lives. By teaching them to neglect the good of their own bodies, the politics of the soul encourages humans to suffer poverty and indignities for some future or common good. It is also dangerous because the politics of the soul, as classical theorists admit, cannot be implemented by the free-will exercise of reason by all concerned. It is not, then, democratic. The classical theory of the soul is also inegalitarian. It sees only a few being capable of reason and virtue. Since the many cannot love the Good voluntarily, they must be compelled to love it by sheer domination or by religion—which only defeats the very purpose of the politics of the soul.

The modernist assault on religion stems from horror at the civil deprivations of medieval Christianity, which became the institutional carrier of classical political theory in the form of what Nietzsche called "Platonism for the masses." By teaching humans to save their souls for the next life by being meek and poor in this life, Christianity, according to Machiavelli, allowed the Glaucons of civil society to impose a millennium of tyranny, what modernity has come to call the Dark Ages. The few imposed this pain on the many for the alleged benefit of their souls while, in reality, the pious elites were tyrants in the Platonic sense of being wholly devoted to their bodies. Critical images of corpulent clerics gorging themselves at feasts or dallying after women became popular caricatures. In practice, then, the politics of the soul, in the modern view, invariably dissolves into a vicious form of the politics of the body.

The politics of the soul is also nonsensical because the soul is a figment of imagination, a nonrational concept, according to Hobbes. The soul is invisible and unreal, and cannot be experienced by any of the five senses. Nor does it have behavioral referents. While classical theory attributes virtue, wisdom, and the like to actions of the soul, modern theory views them as emotive expressions. Hence modern theory sees selfish motives behind every noble or virtuous action. Hobbes asserts, for example, that compassion for the calamity of another arises not from an other-regarding orientation of the soul, but from the purely selfish "imagination that the like calamity may befall" oneself (Hobbes, 1958: 58). Likewise, wisdom is not acquired to be Good or to do Good, but to do good for oneself. Reason in the modern view is a mechanism for calculating how to satisfy desire and enhance self-preservation. It is the advance scout and spy for the passions according to Hobbes.

The politics of the soul is ultimately unjust, then, because it directs attention to a fantasy dream-world—"imagined republics," according to Machiavelli—while neglecting the real needs and wants of real men and women. It leaves humans, especially the many who are poor and oppressed, without effective solutions to their severe political problems. It condemns humans to a world of pain rather than pleasure, giving them instead the delusion of religion, which is only, according to Marx, "the sigh of the oppressed creature, the sentiment of a heartless world, and the soul of soulless conditions ... the opium of the people" (Tucker, 1978: 54).

The politics of the soul is supremely unjust because it is anti-political. Like the Trappist motto, "Leave your body at the gate," classical theory leaves out the only important thing needful in politics. As humans are simply body, not body and soul, the classical politics of the soul is absurdly fantastic because it really imagines a politics without people.

Consequently, modern political theory seeks to extirpate the soul from political life so as to build on the body as the only real or scientific basis for justice. Machiavelli, the founder of modern political science, refuses to mention the soul in *The Prince* and the *Discourses*. The body is also the only secure basis for justice because the body's needful self-interest is its own preservation. The soul's self-interest is indifferent to the body. The effectual truth of politics is that humans are "in touch with their bodies," not with imaginary souls. This may be a low view of life, but it is a safe one. The body's interests are self-evident, and humans will defend them against injustice because the body is life and it is the only one they will ever possess. If there is only one life and there is no life outside or after the body, then, in the modern view, one should "grab all the gusto" one can. Hence modern political theory aims low, not high, at man's beastly nature and its longing for peace, security, and prosperity. "Covenants not to defend a man's body are void" (Hobbes, 1958: 117).

If humanity is not suspended between the beasts and the gods, but is only beast, then there is no standard of justice or virtue outside the body's impulses. Political theory must take its bearings from pain, not evil. Indeed, pain is evil, not virtuous suffering in the classical sense, while pleasure is good. Every body must, therefore, be assumed to have a "natural" right to life and to be free from external restraints. Since each body is unique and autonomous, and no body can experience any other body's pain or pleasure, each body must also be the best judge of its own interests. Hence no body has a natural right to rule any other body.

Since each body has its own standards of commodious preservation, and the body is all that matters, each body must have an equal right to everything or, in conflicts over bodily goods, to participate in deciding which bodies get what, when, and how. Each body is also equal in the sense that every body experiences death and every normal body desires preservation. While bodies differ in the objects they desire, each body is equal as well in being a bundle of acquisitive desires.

However, because there are many other bodies in the world that bump into, and occasionally destroy, each other, and since no body is self-sufficient, these multiple bodies must voluntarily agree to create intersubjective meanings and common structures to secure their survival and comfort. It is in the rational interest of each body to enter into a treaty of peace with all other nearby bodies. This is the root meaning of the social compact in liberal democracy and the common consent of humankind in socialist communism.

This beastly view of human nature presents modern political theory with a spectacular problem: how to control the urgent, incessant, selfish, and infinite desires of the body as well as the violence unleashed and legitimated by removal of the restraints traditionally associated with the politics of the soul. Further, by construing man as beast and reason as experience, modern theory ties humanity inextricably to the vagaries and scarcities of nature and, thereby, to the violence likely to arise when, in the contemporary sense, the 4.8 billion human bodies that inhabit the earth are liberated by modern political theory from the politics of the soul and permitted to discover their natural right to everything.

Consequently, modern political science is preoccupied with violence and economics because, as yet, it has discovered only two basic policy resolutions to the dilemma of the politics of the body: the conquest of man and the conquest of nature. If the body and, therefore, political life cannot be regulated by the inner soul, they must be regulated by external coercion or simply permitted to run free through nature and, thereby, away from other bodies. The first requires the administration of humans, the second, the administration of things.

The early moderns, Machiavelli and Hobbes, who wrote during eras of civil violence and before the fruits of the scientific revolution were fully evident, counsel the conquest of man. Their portrayals of human nature are among the most violent, vicious, and beastly in modern thought. The violence unleashed by freeing the body from the soul must be regulated by authoritarian governments. However, these governments are not necessarily tyrannical because they are self-imposed insofar as every body realizes that it needs government to protect it from every other rapacious body. The people consent, directly or indirectly, to the Machiavellian Prince and the Hobbesian Leviathan. In this respect, the regimes are democratic.

The contemporary analogue is found in proposals for strong, centralized, but democratically elected governments capable of regulating the exploitation and equitable allocation of scarce resources. According to Machiavelli and Hobbes, such a conquest of humanity by strong government is the only effective policy for two reasons. First, the ability to conquer nature to satisfy bodily desires is limited; hence there will always be scarcities to engender violent conflict. Second, the conquest of nature only creates more desire and more conflict. Scarcity is primarily a subjective experience, not an objective condition.

This is the situation to which Rousseau responded in the eighteenth century. The development of material abundance did not free humans from dependence on nature and each other. Instead, it created tremendous inequalities and enslaved humans to a possessive individualism that prevented them from recognizing their common predicament and cooperating to free themselves from it. The greatest criminal, according to Rousseau, is the person who invented private property. Consequently, Rousseau proposes a reconquest of humanity in which individuals are forced to be free by being stripped of the layers of civilized habituation that make them selfish, possessive, and partial to their own so as to recover their essential nature, which, according to Rousseau, is basically benign. By being made utterly equal and utterly natural, humans will see everything from the same perspective and recognize their overriding common interests and, thereby, freely consent to the comprehensive rule of their General Will.

Unfortunately, Rousseau's scheme seems possible only in very small and perhaps rural polities and, in any event, a great legislator is required to force the people to be free. Rousseau is probably unjustly accused of fathering modern fascism, though his teachings can be bent in that direction. More benign contemporary analogues can be found in certain back-to-nature and "small-is-beautiful" movements as well as in radical egalitarian movements. Proponents of the latter argue that problems of scarcity can best be resolved by more, not less, participatory democracy. With greater equality and greater participation, humans will be better able to resolve distributive conflicts amicably. The problem, however, is getting to that point in the first place.

Although Machiavelli, Hobbes, and Rousseau temper their teachings with promises of moderate commercial prosperity, in the views of John Locke and Karl Marx, their teachings are inherently authoritarian because they counsel the conquest of humanity rather than of nature and because they require strong governments. Government is inherently dangerous and naturally inclined toward tyranny, according to Locke (and the classical liberal democratic tradition generally), while for Marx, government is nothing more than the executive committee of the ruling class. Humans must be freed, not only from the necessities of nature and its seeming scarcity, but also from the necessity for external government. Hence, Locke is the theorist of limited self-government, Marx, the theorist of no government, or spontaneous cooperation.

These versions of the politics of the body are made plausible by the assumption that material abundance can resolve the human political problem. Under conditions of abundance, human bodies are liberated from the bare necessities of nature. They need no longer fear for their self-preservation. There are enough goods for everyone's needs and most of their desires, plus a continual promise of more with the progress of science. "Science," wrote Marx, is man's "most solid form of wealth." It is the mechanism for man's emancipation from nature and, thereby, from the dark side of man's beastly nature.

At the same time, abundance frees humans from the necessity of robbing and depending on each other. Abundance has the effect of expanding the space between individuals, allowing each body to self-actualize without colliding with or harming other bodies. It also disposes every body to be more cooperative and reinforces such behavior with material rewards. Thus, as abundance progressively dissolves the causes of human conflict, and human life can become increasingly self-regulating, the need for government is reduced accordingly and politics becomes the administration of things. For Locke, the competitive drives of possessive individualists for the accumulation of private property and, thereby, expansion of the economic pie become well-nigh self-regulating and self-satisfying. This reduces the need for a strong government capable of managing scarcity and imposing solutions to problems of distributive justice that are so essential to the body. For Marx, the state finally withers away under conditions of egalitarian, communistic abundance.

Consequently, Locke and Marx advocate the conquest of nature. This has the additional benefit of diverting human energies from the conquest of man. It also has the advantage of converting substantive conflicts into procedural questions of how best to conquer nature and manage abundance. Since nature has no rights against humankind, one more reason for strong government—namely, moral control of technology—is eliminated as well.

This is why Locke and Marx hold a much more drastic view of nature and more optimistic view of human nature than do most Western theorists. They seek to teach humanity that nature, not man's beastly nature, is the real enemy. Hence they portray nature as fickle, penurious, intractable, and begrudging. It is the image of poor primitive man wrestling endlessly with nature that they hold up as the terror to be overcome by science and industry. As Locke wrote, a day laborer in England is better off than is a great Indian chief in the primitive New World. Nature does not give the body its goods; it compels humans to work hard for their bodily goods. Nature has no value then, except through human labor, and it is this labor theory of value in Locke and Marx which further justifies the conquest of nature. Thus through Locke and Marx, modern political theory promotes an extraordinary reconceptualization, not merely of human nature, but of universal nature as well.

There are, of course, vast differences between Locke and Marx, and each, in effect, accuses the other of tyranny, but the essential point is that abundance is a prerequisite for the practical success of the political traditions founded by these epic theorists. This would not be a great problem were it not that these traditions have become the leading political ideologies of the contemporary world, each imperfectly institutionalized by giant superpowers. If, therefore, the bounty of nature is about to be made scarce by depletion, pollution, and entropy—and it may not be, for this has been only a theoretical argument—the human political problem of limited resources and unlimited desires will indeed assume apocalyptic proportions.

CONCLUSIONS

In the final analysis, mainstream Western political theory has not yet solved the problem of scarcity. Indeed, modern theory may have exacerbated it. Either nature dominates humans and drives them toward penury, or humanity dominates nature and drives it toward penury. Although lessons might be drawn from the politics of the soul, a return to such teachings is undesirable because classical theory cannot resolve the problem of human tyranny. Efforts to institutionalize the politics of the soul in the modern world are likely to take the form of religious fundamentalism and another Dark Age. Yet it may not be possible to continue indefinitely along the courses mapped out by Locke and Marx. Institutionalizations of their teachings have given rise to their own forms of domination and inegalitarianism, and in the long run, they encounter the problem of scarcity. This leaves us with the authoritarian options of Machiavelli, Hobbes, and Rousseau. Indeed, Hobbes's philosophy has been undergoing a remarkable revival in recent years.

Fortunately, political life is not lived on a theoretical plane; civil societies muddle through on the basis of mixed and impure theories. Nevertheless, political theory throws into high relief the fundamental problems, issues, and choices that underlie "real" political life as well as the probable directions of public policies when carried to their logical conclusions. The historic tradition of political theory also shapes the ontological and epistemological contexts of public policy. One does not ordinarily take such issues down (or up) to human nature, yet all of the current policy debates over scarcity are ultimately rooted in theoretic fundamentals. By uncovering the fundamentals one can better understand the consequences of policy choices and possibly formulate, if necessary, a new political paradigm for resolving problems of scarcity.

REFERENCES

BARKER, E. [ed. and trans.] (1962) The Politics of Aristotle. New York: Oxford University Press.

BARNET, R. J. (1980) The Lean Years: Politics in the Age of Scarcity. New York: Simon & Schuster.

BLOOM, A. [trans.] (1968) The Republic of Plato. New York: Basic Books.

BOOKCHIN, M. (1982) The Ecology of Freedom: The Emergence and Dissolution of Hierarchy. Palo Alto, CA: Cheshire.

CARSON, R. (1962) Silent Spring. Boston: Houghton Mifflin.

COLE, H.S.D. et al. [eds.] (1973) Models of Doom: A Critique of the Limits to Growth. New York: Universe.

DEANE, H. A. (1963) The Political and Social Ideas of St. Augustine. New York: Columbia University Press.

EHRLICH, P. R. (1968) The Population Bomb. New York: Ballantine.

GLASSER, R. J. (1976) The Greatest Battle. New York: Bantam.

HOBBES, T. (1958) Leviathan. Indianapolis: Bobbs-Merrill.

INGE. W. R. (1948) The Philosophy of Plotinus, 2 vols. London: Longmans, Green.

KAMMEN, M. (1973) People of Paradox. New York: Vintage.

MADDOX, J. (1972) The Doomsday Syndrome. New York: McGraw-Hill.

MARX. W. (1967) The Frail Ocean. New York: Ballantine Books.

MEAD, M. (1967) "The rights of primitive peoples, Papua-New Guinea: a crucial instance." Foreign Affairs 45 (January): 304-318.

MEADOWS, D. H., D. L. MEADOWS, J. RANDERS, W. W. BEHRENS III (1972) The Limits to Growth. New York: Universe.

OPHULS, W. (1977) Ecology and the Politics of Scarcity: Prologue to a Political Theory of the Steady State. San Francisco: Freeman.

OSBORN, F. (1948) Our Plundered Planet. Boston: Little, Brown.

PADDOCK, W. AND P. PADDOCK (1967) Famine, 1975. Boston: Little Brown.

PANGLE, T. L. (1980) The Laws of Plato. New York: Basic Books.

PEIRCE, N. (1982) "High-tech boom brings new politics." Dallas Times Herald (June 13).

PICKENS, D. K. (1981) "Westward expansion and the end of American exceptionalism: Sumner, Turner, Webb." Western Historical Quarterly 12 (October): 409-418.

SAX. K. (1955) Standing Room Only. Boston: Beacon.

SCHUMACHER, E. F. (1973) Small is Beautiful: Economics as if People Mattered. New York: Harper & Row.

SINGER, P. (1975) Animal Liberation: A New Ethics for Our Treatment of Animals. New York: New York Review.

STONE, C. D. (1974) Should Trees Have Standing? Toward Legal Rights for Natural Objects. Los Altos: William Kaufman.

THUROW, L. C. (1980) The Zero-Sum Society: Distribution and the Possibilities for Economic Change. New York: Basic Books.

TUCKER, R. C. [ed.] (1978) The Marx-Engles Reader. New York: W. W. Norton.

VACCA, R. (1973) The Coming Dark Age. Garden City, NY: Doubleday.

WHITE, L., JR. (1967) "The historical roots of our ecologic crisis." Science 155 (March 10): 1203-1207.

ZINAM, O. (1982) "The myth of absolute abundance: economic development as a shift in relative scarcities." American Journal of Economics and Sociology 41 January): 61-76.

3

LIBERTY AND SCARCITY:
WILLIAM OPHULS RECONSIDERED

R. McGREGGOR CAWLEY

University of Wyoming

In 1968, amid growing concern for the environmental consequences of modern industrialized lifestyles, Garrett Hardin published his now classic essay, "The Tragedy of the Commons." Hardin's thesis was that as long as the belief in the right of the individual to extract personal gain from commonly held resources persists, those resources must eventually be destined to destruction through overexploitation. The "logic of the commons," and thereby the tragedy, is that the destruction of the commons evolves not from malicious intent, but rather, from rational people seeking rational ends within the ecodestructive belief system (Hardin, 1968).

From this thesis follows the argument that the ecodestructive actions that threaten the planet are the symptoms, not the disease. The cure for the disease lies in the realm of developing a new belief system that places the preservation of the commons above the right of the individual. In short, Hardin issued a call for the development of a new ideology on which future policy could be based.

AUTHOR'S NOTE: *The comments and suggestions made by Henry P. Caulfield and Robert W. Hoffert on earlier drafts of this chapter are gratefully acknowledged.*

Hardin's call has been answered by a school of writers who can be loosely grouped under the heading of "steady-state" advocates (Daly, 1973; Pirages, 1977; Sale, 1980). Although these writers differ on specifics, they find general agreement on two points: first, frugality rather than growth must be the future goal of society; and second, conquest of nature must give way to lifestyles that provide harmonious relationships between man and nature. Among these steady-state advocates stands one of particular interest—William Ophuls. The special interest in Ophuls's work results from two reasons. First, Ophuls has undertaken the most systematic investigation to date of the roots to the tragedy of the commons. Second, the conclusions derived by Ophuls represent a serious challenge to those who are devoted to the beliefs of individual liberty and freedom.

THE INDICTMENT

Ophuls begins his analysis by suggesting that Hardin's thesis can be viewed as essentially a restatement of the theoretical works of Thomas Hobbes. More specifically, Ophuls suggests that the "tragedy of the commons" is equivalent to Hobbes's "state of nature," and that Hardin's prescription for resolving the tragedy—"mutual coercion, mutually agreed upon"—is equivalent to Hobbes's great Leviathan. From this starting point, Ophuls issues his primary indictment:

> The external reality of ecological scarcity has cut the ground out from under our political system, making merely reformist policies of ecological management all but useless [1977a: 3].

Contained in Ophuls's indictment are two interrelated charges: first, that ecological scarcity is inevitable; second, that not only are our political institutions unable to deal with problems created by ecological scarcity, but in many important respects our institutions are also directly responsible for the inevitability of ecological scarcity, which according to Ophuls,

> . . .is a new concept, embracing more than the shortage of any particular resource. It has to do primarily with pollution limits, complex trade-offs between present and future needs, and a variety of other physical con- straints, rather than with simple Malthusian overpopulation [1974: 48].

In short, ecological scarcity is a condition in which there is not enough of anything to go around.

Ophuls's argument is more complex than simply the inevitability of scarcity in the future. He argues that scarcity has been predominant throughout the history of mankind. "For most of recorded history, societies have existed at the ecological margin, or very close to it. An equal division of income and wealth, therefore, would condemn all to a life of shared poverty" (1977a: 148). Politically, this natural condition of scarcity has produced inequality, oppression, and conflict. There is however, in the midst of this rather pessimistic view of history one deceptively shining exception:

> During the last 450 years, the carrying capacity of the globe (and especially of the highly developed nations) has been markedly expanded, and several centuries of relative abundance have completely transformed the face of the earth and made our societies and our civilization what they are today—relatively open, egalitarian, libertarian, and conflict-free [1977a: 148].

Therefore, impending ecological scarcity has an extra-bitter taste for us because we have been lulled into a false sense of security by abnormal conditions of abundance created by the discovery of the "New World" and embellished by technological innovation.

Among the various vestiges of this abnormal abundance that will experience fatal stress with the return of scarcity, none are more basic than our political and economic institutions. Ophuls argues:

> Our politico-economic system is based primarily on the tenets of Adam Smith and John Locke, and their philosophies reflected the existence of the Great Frontier. Thus, our government was set up not just to permit the ruthless competitive exploitation of the commons (via "development"), but actually to encourage it [1973b: 51].

Therein lies the real concern of Ophuls's work—not only will the return of scarcity produce crisis situations, but our political institutions based on Locke's theory are structurally incapable of resolving these crises. Thus Locke is portrayed as the author of the logic of the commons, which is driving us to the brink of catastrophe, and the institutions based on Locke's theory cannot, without complete revision, be modified to deal with ecological crisis. However, the history of Western civilization provides other theories that can be used to structure institutions capable of dealing with ecological scarcity. Paramount among these is the work of Thomas Hobbes, whom Ophuls characterizes as the great theorist of scarcity.

Within the framework offered by Ophuls we are left with few options. The two factors that might preclude the return of scarcity—technology and altruism—are either contributors to the problem or ineffective for solving it. On the one hand, technology has been responsible for extending the period of abnormal abundance. On the other hand, Ophuls argues that ecological scarcity will erect barriers that technology will be unable to cross. And of altruism, Ophuls suggests: "Real altruism and genuine concern for posterity may not be completely absent, but they are not present in sufficient quantities to avoid tragedy" (1973b: 52) Thus the Hobbesian vision is not merely the preferable direction for the future; it is the inevitable course of events. The only choice left to us in the matter is "determining the concrete shape of the Leviathan" (1973b: 52).

The attraction of the Hobbesian vision is discovered by recalling the essence of the problem—the destruction of the commons results not from malicious intent but from rational people seeking rational ends. Or in Ophuls's words: "The root of our problem lies deep. The real shortage with which we are afflicted is that of moral resources" (1974: 52). As will be considered later, a primary task of Hobbes's Leviathan is to instill morality in its citizens. For both Ophuls and Hardin, then, it is not possible to envision a world in which people *will choose* less. The demands and strains produced by the approaching ecological scarcity require that people be *forced to accept* less and it is only through the power of a Hobbesian Leviathan that sufficient force can be exerted.

THE STEADY-STATE

Having established the basic nature of the problem, Ophuls then provides a skeleton on which the steady-state could be constructed. This skeleton is composed of ten general characteristics. Although no specific ordering of these characteristics is offered by Ophuls, they could be grouped around three subjects—basic tenets, political structure, and the man/nature relationship.

BASIC TENETS

Two characteristics provide the basic tenets of the steady-state: "communalism" and "morality." Given the premise from which Ophuls begins, it is necessary that the steady-state be based on communalism rather than on individualism. Individualism is, after all, the logic of the commons that leads to the tragedy. The most prominent task for the steady-state, therefore, is to convince the citizenry that preservation of the commons, or community, supersedes the right of the individual to extract personal gain.

One way to effect this necessary change in attitude is through force. Another way is through the creation of a "new morality" or at least, through the renovation of an old morality. "Thus," argues Ophuls,

> the steady-state, like virtually all other human civilizations except modern industrialism, will almost certainly have a religious base— whether it is Aristotelian political and civic excellence, Christian virtue, Confucian rectitude, Buddhist compassion, Amerindian love for the land, or something similar, old or new [1977a: 232].

POLITICAL STRUCTURE

This new moral community base will require a new political structure. With the change from individualism to communalism will come the exchange of individual liberty for individual obligation. Individual obligation, in turn, provides the steady-state with the "authority" necessary to enforce its policies. Here the influence of Hobbes is most clear, for the steady-state must have *absolute power* if it is to preserve the community. Ophuls argues, however, that giving the steady-state such power does not necessarily mean submission to an arbitrary tyranny. "There seems to be no reason why authority cannot be made strong enough to maintain a steady-state, and yet be limited. The personal and civil rights guaranteed by our constitution, for example, could be largely retained in an appropriately designed steady-state" (1977a: 226).

In carrying out the mandate of the steady-state, the rulers will be required to place "certain restrictions on human activities" that "must be competently determined, normatively justified, and then authoritatively imposed on a populace that would do something quite different if it were left on its own immediate desires and devices" (Ophuls, 1977a: 227). In this light, we will no longer have the luxury to depend on random choice as in the political selection process. The rulers of the steady-state must constitute a "Jeffersonian aristocracy" selected on the basis of "competence and status." The potential that this aristocracy will oppress the ruled is precluded by the creation of "aristocratic principles designed to foster the common interest of the steady-state" (1977a: 227). This combination of an aristocracy guided by aristocratic principles creates, Ophuls argues, a society not unlike "the earliest days of the American Republic."

As to the ruled in the steady-state, Ophuls argues that the present system of politics must be replaced with a revitalized participatory democracy. The demands of dealing with ecological scarcity preclude the continuation of free competition in the open marketplace—what Ophuls calls "non-politics." Instead, the citizens in the steady-state must become "genuinely political animals in Aristotle's sense, self-consciously involved in designing and planning their community life" (1977a: 228).

Since a primary response to ecological scarcity is a shift from centralized, energy-intensive means of production to decentralized, labor-intensive ones, the steady-state will require a restructuring of society. A concentration of people in urban areas will give way to a redistribution of the population into small, fairly self-sufficient communities. Politically, this redistribution will give the steady-state the characteristics of "microautonomy and macroauthority" (1977b: 168). Each community would have wide latitude in the design of its politico-economic structure as long as it remained within the boundaries established by this macroauthority. As a result, the steady-state would possess considerable "diversity."

THE MAN/NATURE RELATIONSHIP

With a moral community base and new political structures must come a new attitude about the man/nature relationship. Ophuls characterizes this new relationship with the terms "holism, stewardship, and modesty." Holism is accomplished by "focusing on the interrelationships making up the whole system" (1977a: 231). The criticism of present scientific approaches is twofold. On the one hand, current scientific endeavors are trapped in reductionism, which focuses on the parts rather than the whole. On the other hand, reductionism has contributed to a feeling of alienation from nature. Thus holism will "go a long way toward making the average man feel once again at home in the universe" (1977a: 231). Of stewardship and modesty, Ophuls states, respectively:

> Quality will replace quantity, and husbandry will replace gain as the prime motives of economic life"; . . . "we shall abandon the tragic hero's deadly serious and angst-ridden quest for greatness . . . and learn instead cheerfully to enjoy the simple pleasures of ordinary life [1977a: 229-230].

Taken together these characteristics provide a strange mixture of authoritarian and democratic features that may appear contradictory at times. However, the strange and contradictory nature of the steady-state results from the fact that we are still locked into traditional—and erroneous—thinking. In actuality, the steady-state represents the essence of postmodernity in that it "combines the best of ancient and modern" (1977a: 232). That the steady-state represents a combination of ancient and modern features cannot be disputed—that it represents the best is a different question.

A CRITIQUE

The primary point of contention here is over the nature of Ophuls's solution, not his definition. Do we have to accept the inevitability of the Leviathan and the consequent loss of liberty? Or is it possible to respond to conditions of scarcity while safeguarding individual liberty?

Throughout his work, Ophuls has argued that Locke is the theorist of abundance and development while Hobbes is the theorist of scarcity and survival. The place to begin this critique, then, is with an examination of the role scarcity plays in Hobbes's theory. To provide an analytic framework for this task I must introduce two terms—*absolute scarcity* and *distributional scarcity*. Absolute scarcity is meant to indicate a situation in which there is not enough of anything to go around. As such, it is equivalent to Ophuls's concept of "ecological scarcity." Distributional scarcity, on the other hand, indicates a situation in which there are resources available, but in which conditions of social disturbance or technological immaturity exist that prohibit the distribution of those resources and hence create relative scarcity.

On the question of qualitative scarcity, Ophuls's position is clear: Hobbes bases his theory on an assumption of absolute scarcity, while

Locke, if concerned with scarcity at all, views it as relative scarcity emerging in one part of an infinitely abundant commons. There is no dispute with the fact that Locke's work contains language reflecting an apparent belief in abundance. However, we must question the notion that Hobbes bases his theory on an assumption of absolute scarcity.

In the early part of *The Leviathan*, Hobbes offers his well-worn passage on the conditions in the state of nature:

> From this equality of ability, ariseth equality of hope in attaining of our ends. And therefore if any two men desire the same thing, which nevertheless they cannot both enjoy, they become enemies; and in their way to their end, . . . endeavor to destroy, or subdue one another [1946: 81].

Thus, the classic dilemma of infinite appetites and finite means of satisfaction that leads to the "war of all against all" is suggested.

In Hobbes's framework, the war of all against all produces "continual fear and danger of violent death." This fear in turn creates an atmosphere in which

> . . . there is no place for industry; because the fruit thereof is uncertain: and consequently no culture of the earth; no navigation, nor use of the commodities that may be imported by the sea; no commodious building; no instruments of moving, and removing, such things as requires much force; no knowledge of the earth; no account of time; no arts; no letters; no society [1946: 143].

In short, an atmosphere that provides a "solitary, poor, nasty, brutish, and short" life. But what is the causal relationship here? Does absolute scarcity produce the warlike state? Or does the anxiety produced by the warlike state prohibit the development of resources and thereby lead to distributional scarcity?

The answer to these questions may be found in Chapter 24 of *The Leviathan*. It is important to remember that throughout his work Hobbes uses an extended organic metaphor that begins with the definition of the Leviathan as an "artificial man." This metaphor is important in understanding the full meaning of the title to Chapter 24: "Of The Nutrition and Procreation of a Commonwealth." Within the context of this organic metaphor it would appear safe to argue that discussions of nutrition would be directed toward providing the

Leviathan a healthy diet. A Leviathan suffering from malnutrition would undoubtedly lack the strength necessary to avert a return to the state of nature by its citizenry.

With these thoughts in mind, let us now consider Hobbes's definition of the nutrition of the commonwealth:

> The nutrition of the commonwealth consisteth in the *plenty* and *distribution* of materials conducing to life; in *concoction*, or *preparation*; and, when concocted, in the *conveyance* of it by convenient conduits to the public use. . . . For the matter of this nutriment, consisting in animals, vegetals, and minerals, God hath freely laid them before us, in or near the face of the earth; so there needth no more but the labour, and industry of receiving them. Insomuch as plenty dependeth, next to God's favour, merely on the labour and industry of man [1946: 160-161].

In this passage Hobbes offers two general concerns about the availability of nutritional materials for the Leviathan—"plenty" and "distribution." Although Hobbes suggests that "God's favour" may be a constraint on the amount and availability of necessary resources, the overwhelming tone of the passage is that the abundance of the nutritional resources is a direct function of man's willingness to expend the necessary labor to extract those resources from the earth.

This brings us back to the conditions in the state of nature. As will be recalled, the anxiety in the state of nature prohibits industry, cultivation of the earth, navigation, and building—in short, those activities necessary for the preparation and conveyance of resources to the commonwealth. Despite Ophuls's contention to the contrary, it appears that Hobbes begins with an assumption of distribution scarcity. That is, Hobbes views scarcity as the result of social disorder that prevents mankind from developing the abundant resources of the earth.

However Hobbes is interpreted on the question of scarcity, it is his more general view of the state of nature that Ophuls finds analogous to the demands of ecological scarcity. Besides violence and fear of death, Hobbes lists another condition extant in the state of nature. "To this war of every man against every man, this is also consequent: that nothing can be unjust. . . . Where there is no common power, there is no law; where no law, no injustice" (1946: 81). To remedy this situation, Hobbes would have the Leviathan create civil law for its citizens "to make use of for the distinction of right and wrong" (1946: 73). In short, a basic tenet of Hobbes's theory is that morality is a function of law.

On the surface, the tragedy of the commons—rational people seeking rational ends within an ecodestructive belief system—appears to parallel Hobbes's state of nature. In addition, a steady-state aristocracy creating aristocratic principles appears to parallel a Hobbesian Leviathan legislating morality. In this case, however, appearances may be deceptive.

Hobbes bases his theory on a fundamentally pessimistic view of human nature—a view in which people are likely to choose "wrong" over "right," even if they know the difference between the two. The mission of the Leviathan, therefore, is to bring order to the state of nature by controlling it. To accomplish this mission requires granting the Leviathan absolute personal power.

In defining the Leviathan Hobbes states:

> One person, of whose acts, a multitude, by mutual covenants with one another, have made themselves everyone the author, to the end he may use the strength and means of them all, as he shall think expedient, for their peace and common defense [1946: 112].

That the Leviathan is to act "as he shall think expedient" clearly vests it with personal power. Hobbes goes on to argue that "the sovereign of a commonwealth . . . is not subject to the civil law" and "no man that hath sovereign power can justly be put to death, or otherwise in any manner by his subjects punished" (1946: 173, 116). Thus Hobbes provides a lucid picture of an all-powerful sovereign who creates laws at will and who is largely uncontrolled by his subjects.

Realizing that granting the Leviathan naked power may be objectionable to some, Hobbes reminds us that

> . . . the greatest, that in any form of government can possibly happen to the people in general, is scarce sensible in respect of the miseries, and horrible calamities, that accompany a civil war, or that dissolute condition of masterless men, without subjection to laws, and a coersive power to tie their hands [1946: 120].

If nothing else, Hobbes is indeed honest in outlining the full implications of the Leviathan.

At this point, an apparent paradox emerges in Ophuls's argument. On the one hand, Ophuls argues that a Hobbesian Leviathan is our only salvation from the crisis precipitated by ecological scarcity. On the other hand, Ophuls suggests that the potential tyrannical tendencies of the Leviathan can be curbed by requiring it to "rule lawfully, give full explanation of his acts to his subjects, and heed their legitimate desires" (1973a: 220). But are these substantive protections if the steady-state Leviathan is truly Hobbesian in nature?

To explore this point, let us assume that the steady-state Leviathan is Hobbesian in nature. Ophuls suggests that the Leviathan must rule lawfully, but what does "lawfully" mean? In Hobbes's framework, there is no law other than that created by the Leviathan. Thus whatever the Leviathan does is lawful. Additionally, the steady-state Leviathan must heed the legitimate desires of its citizens. Once again, in the Hobbesian world the Leviathan, not the citizens, determines what constitutes legitimate desires. It is, after all, the legitimacy of all desires that produces the chaos in the state of nature. Finally, the steady-state Leviathan must provide full explanation of his actions. This may provide us with an understanding of why the Leviathan acts as it does; however, without the ability to "punish" the Leviathan, we have little recourse should we disagree with the offered explanation.

We are forced to conclude, then, that either Ophuls is misleading us as to the effectiveness of these "protections," or the steady-state Leviathan is not Hobbesian after all. When Ophuls suggests that the steady-state rulers will be "philosopher-king captains" (1974: 48), the latter conclusion becomes the more persuasive. Rather than an all-powerful, Hobbesian Leviathan, Ophuls offers us a Leviathan with limited power and imbued with Platonic virtue.

One possible resolution to this paradox, albeit somewhat cynical, is that the steady-state is more analogous to Plato's Republic than to Hobbes's Leviathan. That is, Ophuls's work is actually a justification for the steady-state advocates to become the new "philosopher-kings." A less cynical resolution is that the world that necessitates the steady-state is not Hobbesian, and thus, does not necessitate a Hobbesian Leviathan.

Whereas Hobbes begins with the assumption that the root of the problem lies in intrinsic human nature, Ophuls argues that external conditions are responsible for our plight. A period of abnormal abundance has given us a faulty "world view" on which we have constructed misguided political and economic institutions. As a result, the mission of the steady-state Leviathan is far more limited than is that of the Hobbesian Leviathan. The latter must force us to abandon our internal dictates, the former must simply reeducate and resocialize us to help cushion our return to scarcity conditions.

We have now arrived at the answer to the question with which we began this critique. Despite Ophuls's initial contention, in the end a Hobbesian Leviathan is neither an inevitable nor a preferable response to ecological scarcity within his framework. The task before us, then, is to assess whether or not the Lockean model is appropriate for dealing with conditions of scarcity.

LIBERTY AND SCARCITY: A THEORETICAL VIEW

In considering the applicability of the Lockean model to scarcity conditions, we must answer two questions. First, is an assumption of abundance an integral part of Locke's theory? Second, can the steady-state characteristics offered by Ophuls be implemented within a Lockean framework?

The answer to the first question is relatively simple. Locke argues: "The great and chief end, therefore, of men's uniting into common-wealths, and putting themselves under government, is the preservation of their property" (1980: 66). Therefore, if Locke's theory was in fact based on an assumption of an infinitely abundant commons, he would also have argued that there is little need for government. An infinite supply of property would produce a condition in which everyone could have all they wanted, and thus, everyone would be secure in their property. This is not, of course, the view offered by Locke.

To understand Locke's view on property, and thereby his view on abundance, we must return to the state of nature. Locke begins his discussion "Of Property" with the assertion: "God, who hath given the world to men in common, hath also given them reason to make use of it to the best advantage of life, and convenience" (1980: 18). Thus, in the state of nature the earth and its resources are common property to be used by all mankind. The natural reason that dictates the use of the commons is:

As much as any one can make use of to any advantage of life before it spoils, so much may he by his labour fix a property in: whatever is beyond this, is more than his share, and belongs to others. Nothing was made by God for man to destroy or spoil [Locke, 1980: 20-21].

Three points follow from this passage. First, we are presented Locke's labor theory of value. That is, the conversion of common property into private property is accomplished through the expenditure of human labor. Second, there is an interesting suggestion that Locke's state or nature is an ecological state in which nature is used but not abused. Finally, adherence to natural reason produces harmony in the state of nature.

And thus, considering the plenty of natural provisions there was a long time in the world, and the few spenders; and to how small a part of that provision the industry of any one man could extend itself, and ingross it to the prejudice of others; especially keeping with the bounds, set be reason, of what might serve for his use; there could be then little room for quarrels or contentions about property so established [1980: 21].

This passage places Locke's view of abundance squarely before us. Harmony in the state of nature does not result from infinite abundance. Rather, it results from a large supply of natural resources augmented by a small population with limited ability to use those resources and motivated by a modest view of what is needed to provide a convenient life. What disturbs this natural harmony and makes people insecure in their property?

As with his general observations on the state of nature, Locke argues that the disruptive factor relative to property is the perversion of natural reason by self-interest. More specifically, "the desire of having more than man needed . . . altered the intrinsic value of things" (1980: 23). Limited desires became voracious appetites, and the state of nature became a state of war that necessitated the creation of civil society and government.

The answer to our first question is that an assumption of abundance can be read into Locke's theory; however, it is not an integral part of that theory. More important, the problem offered by Locke is more complicated than is Hobbes's problem, and in fact, nearly identical to the problem defined by Ophuls. In a Hobbesian state of nature, people are *accustomed to scarcity*, and therefore, have much to gain and little to lose by submitting to the Leviathan.

In contrast, Locke offers a situation in which people who are *accustomed to abundance* (the state of nature) must confront scarcity (the state of war). Although Ophuls argues that the history of mankind is characterized by scarcity, his central problem is that we have become accustomed to abundance over the last 450 years and are now faced with scarcity conditions. Thus it would appear that Ophuls's argument is actually Lockean in nature. This conclusion, in turn, helps explain why an authentic Hobbesian solution is inappropriate within Ophuls's framework. However, it does not answer our second question: Can a Lockean framework support the steady-state as outlined by Ophuls?

There can be no dispute with the assertion that Locke sought to protect and maximize individual freedom. However, we must not lose sight of the fact that Locke's concern was for individual freedom within a communal context. The reason men quit the state of nature was that community provided a "comfortable, safe, and peaceable" environment in which individuals could have "a secure enjoyment of their properties" (Locke, 1980: 52). So important is community in Locke's framework that he argues that "the first and fundamental natural law which is to govern even the legislative itself, is the preservation of society" (1980: 69).

In the creation of community Locke requires that all individuals "give up all the power, necessary to the ends for which they unite in society, to the majority of the community" (1980: 53). Additionally, every individual must put "himself under an obligation, to everyone of that society, to submit to the determination of the majority, and to be concluded by it" (1980: 52). In compensation, individuals within community receive "a standing rule to live by, common to everyone of that society" and a liberty to follow their "own will in all things, where the rule prescribes not" (1980: 7).

Therefore, the basic Lockean model appears indeed consistent with the steady-state. It is based on communalism in which the citizenry has an obligation to preserve the community—an obligation that supersedes their individual liberty. The rulers are given sufficient authority both to preserve the community and to control the actions of the citizens. Because the citizens can follow their will where the rule prescribes not, the Lockean framework would even allow considerable diversity.

Admittedly, the Lockean framework does not prescribe a "new morality," nor does it advocate a "Jeffersonian aristocracy." The more important point, however, is that the Lockean model does not exclude these characteristics. The only requirement Locke would place on these matters is that they be the result of the consent of the majority. Finally, the most intriguing aspect of the Lockean model is the "natural reason" (law) that pertains to the use of the earth's resources. The injunction against spoiling or destroying those resources suggests that the steady-state characteristics of modesty and stewardship are consistent with the Lockean model; as with morality and aristocracy, it does not preclude a holistic view.

In short, the primary difference between the Lockean model and the Hobbesian model is the nature of the authority given the rulers: Hobbes would vest the rulers with absolute personal power; Locke would vest the rulers with limited impersonal power based on the consent of the majority. This is, of course, a vitally important difference, for limited impersonal power is the means by which individual freedom can be preserved and maximized within a communal context.

The reliance on the consent of the majority within the Lockean framework presents a potential problem. Can a majority of people accustomed to abundance agree on actions that are effective in dealing with scarcity? To answer this question we must shift from a theoretical level to a practical one.

LIBERTY AND SCARCITY: A PRACTICAL VIEW

If we adopt the Aristotelian perspective—the state exists for the sake of the good life—then it is inevitable that ethics, philosophy, and public policy become intertwined. Ethics and philosophy provide an abstract definition of the good life, and public policy provides the means by which the abstract definition is transformed into reality. Further, it is not at all surprising that the interrelationship between philosophy and public policy is most visible in the area of natural resources. As I argued earlier, most resource crises are actually lifestyle crises, and "lifestyle" is nothing more than our individual and/or collective definition of the good life. It is within this context that a brief account of the conservation and environmental movements becomes crucial to our argument. Although it may be debated as to whether or not the policies produced by these movements have lived up to our expectations, the real impact of both movements has been at the broader, philosophic level.

The conservation movement emerged in the late 1800s and early 1900s, during a period in American history analogous to Dickens's famous "best of times/worst of times" paradox. On the one hand, America was mesmerized by the Social Darwinists, who argued that through domination and exploitation of nature mankind gained freedom and liberty (Hofstadter, 1945). On the other hand, a growing number of national leaders believed that the United States was on the verge of a major resource crisis extending to timber, coal, iron ore, oil, gas, and soil—in short, all the resources that provided prosperity and security for the American society.

In response to this pending resource crisis, the early conservationists advocated public policy principles that are strikingly similar to the characteristics of the steady-state. For example, the basic principle of the conservation movement was that "the right of the public to the natural resources, outweigh[s] private rights" (Roosevelt, 1958: 216), and the way to protect the public's right was to place the nation's resources under federal management. The federal managers, in turn, were to be trained professionals who would regulate the use of those resources on the basis of scientific principles rather than the dictates of politics and economics. The parallel between the conservationists' vision and a steady-state directed by a Jeffersonian aristocracy on the basis of aristocratic principles cannot be ignored.

Gifford Pinchot offers that the following account of part of the inspiration that gave rise to the conservation movement:

> Here were no longer a lot of different, independent, and often antagonistic questions. . . . Here was one single question with many separate parts. Seen in this new light, all these separate questions fitted into and made up the one central problem of the use of the earth for the good of man [1947: 322-323].

Again the parallel between this vision and the steady-state characteristic of holism is clearly apparent. Finally, the conservation principles of wise use and sustained yield provide a parallel with the steady-state characteristic of stewardship.

Thus the conservation movement emerged as a response to a scarcity condition that in many important respects was not dissimilar to ecological scarcity. The nature of the response seen necessary by the conservationists was indeed similar to the prescriptions offered by Ophuls. From one perspective, these factors help reinforce the legitimacy of Ophuls's argument. From a different perspective, the same factors present a serious challenge to Ophuls's argument. The conservation movement succeeded in implanting many of the steady-state characteristics within our existing political and economic institutions.

An argument that might be raised here is that technological innovation was more important in averting the resource crisis at the beginning of this century than were the policy initiatives of the conservation movement. Granting that technology not only averted scarcity but increased abundance, however, avoids coming to grips with a more important consideration: Increased abundance did not lead to an abandonment of the basic conservation principles. The nation's resources are still owned publicly and regulated by federal managers who adhere to most of the basic conservation doctrines. In fact the primary change in natural resource policy over the last 80 years has been toward increased preservation of ecological values, a change precipitated by the rise of the environmental movement.

Although the origin of the environmental movement is often set at Earth Day 1970, philosophically, modern environmentalism can be traced from the work of Aldo Leopold in the 1930s. A basic tenet of Leopold's work was that human civilization followed a three-phase evolution. The first phase was accomplished when individuals learned to live in harmony with each other. The second phase came as mankind learned to live in harmony within a collective setting. Together, these phases provided mankind with a social ethic. The third, and future, phase of the evolutionary process is man learning to live in harmony with nature—what Leopold called the "land ethic" (1949: 201-226).

We need not search very far to discover that the underlying drive of the environmental movement is to develop a land ethic in this nation. Whether we direct our attention to specific policies—the National Environmental Policy Act, the Wilderness Act, the Wild and Scenic Rivers Act, or the Endangered Species Act—or consider instead the many tracts written by environmentalists, we cannot escape the basic message. Man's use of nature must be controlled so as to minimize damage to the fragile ecosystem called Earth.

By linking the values of the conservation movement with those of the environmental movement we arrive at an interesting conclusion. Over the past 80 years, the pragmatic public policy process has produced a significant shift in our collective attitudes regarding the use of nature. We have moved from a belief in the right of the individual to extract personal gain from nature regardless of the impact such actions might have on our social and natural communities, to the belief that the protection of our social/natural community must dictate the rights of the individual. Whether this change has gone too far, or not far enough, is a debatable point. The more important consideration is that this change has been effected through a Lockean mechanism of majority consent; it has not been imposed on us by a Hobbesian Leviathan.

REFERENCES

DALY, H. E. (1973) Toward a Steady-State Economy. San Francisco: Freeman.
HARDIN, G. (1968) "The tragedy of the commons." Science 162 (December): 1243-1248.
HOBBES, T. (1946) The Leviathan. Oxford: Basil Blackwell.
HOFSTADTER, R. (1945) Social Darwinism in American Thought: 1860-1915. Philadelphia: University of Pennsylvania Press.
LOCKE, J. (1980) Second Treatise of Government. Indianapolis: Hackett.
LEOPOLD, A. (1949) A Sand County Almanac and Sketches Here and There. New York: Oxford University Press.
NASH, R. (1976) The American Environment. Menlo Park, CA: Addison-Wesley.
OPHULS, W. (1977a) Ecology and the Politics of Scarcity. San Francisco: Freeman.
———(1977b) "The politics of the sustainable society," pp. 157-172 in D.C. Pirages (ed.) The Sustainable Society. New York: Praeger.
——— (1974) "The scarce society." Harper's Magazine (April): 47-52.
——— (1973a) "Leviathan or oblivion? pp. 215-229 in Herman Daly (ed.) Toward A Steady-State Economy. San Francisco: Freeman.
——— (1973b) "The return of the Leviathan." Science 29 (March): 50-52.
PINCHOT, G. (1947) Breaking New Ground. New York: Harcourt, Brace.
PIRAGES, D. C. (1977) The Sustainable Society. New York: Praeger.
ROOSEVELT, T. (1958) The Autobiography of Theodore Roosevelt. New York: Charles Scribner's.
SALE, K. (1980) Human Scale. New York: Coward, McCann, & Geoghegan.

4

RESOURCE POLICY IN
COMMUNIST STATES

SUSAN RIGDON

University of Illinois

Marxist theorists claim that environmental pollution and the misuse of natural resources are the inevitable and unique by-products of capitalist forms of modernization. Moreover, according to at least one official, "under socialism" it is possible to avoid the various problems that appear in the course of modernization, because economic development in a socialist society is conducted under the guidance of a unified plan" (Sun, 1979: 21).

It may be, however, that a growing number of party and state officials in Eastern Europe, the Soviet Union, the People's Republic of China, and Cuba would admit that such a statement, while ideologically pure, is factually inaccurate. The extent of ecological damage that has occurred both before and after the socialist transformations in these countries has only recently been acknowledged in their academic journals and official organs of communication. The severity of environmental pollution and resource scarcity is apparently so great that officials are coming to realize that nothing short of a massive public commitment can reverse its direction.

In the People's Republic of China, for example, it is estimated that deforestation is occuring at a rate of 2 percent a year in Heilongjiang Province, which supplies 50 percent of the nation's timber. Accelerating the process of deforestation are the estimated half billion people said to suffer from fuel shortages for three to five months out of the year and who meet their needs with any available vegetation. The associated soil erosion has contributed to China's loss of 30 percent of its arable land in the last two decades (Smil, 1982: 19). In 1979, China passed an environmental protection law to fight the chemical pollution that is destroying its rivers and that has reduced air quality so low that monitoring devices used by the U.S. government broke when trying to register the level of pollution in the industrial city of Wuhan (Butterfield, 1980b).

In the Soviet Union, the author of a recent article in a Siberian journal associated increasing infant deaths and genetic defects with environmental problems in the Kuznetsk Basin (New York Times, September 12, 1982). Official Western sources have confirmed the charge that the Soviet Union's rush to acquire atomic and thermonuclear weapons led to a disastrous explosion in a dumping site for radioactive materials that polluted many square miles of surrounding territory. And a new study confirms that the USSR has been transformed from a grain exporter in 1970, to an importer of 43 million metric tons in 1981, even though it has more arable land than does the United States (Brown, 1982: 6-7).

From Eastern Europe it is reported that only one-sixth of the total length of all of East Germany's rivers can be used to provide drinking water, that "the water in half of Poland's rivers [is] unfit even for industrial use," and that coal-mining regions of Bohemia in Czechoslovakia are now among the most polluted areas in all of Europe. The official press agency of Poland has written of "an approaching ecological disaster" in that country (New York Times, September 12, 1982).

It could be expected that in any industrialized, growth-oriented economy, whether capitalist or socialist, natural resources and the whole ecological status of the system would be heavily taxed. But from a superficial consideration of the differences in the political and economic organization of the various types of capitalist and socialists systems, one might expect that socialist systems would be better prepared to deal with environmental problems, and in particular, to manage problems of scarcity. Such an assumption is based on the notion that if waste is to be brought under control, and if rational, efficient use is to be made of finite resources, some limits must be set on the individual's right to consume. A prerequisite for this, some would argue, is to decrease the emphasis on the individual entrepreneur or consumer as the central actor in economic life and to increase the emphasis placed on group identity, social responsibility, and public forms of ownership (at least of the most vital resources).

In this respect Marxist systems have a considerable advantage over the capitalist democracies of the West. In addition, they place more severe limitations on the political rights of the individuals, so that they cannot use the political arena as effectively to pursue consumer interests as is done in the West.

Socialist countries may in fact be better prepared than are capitalist ones to manage, with policies such as rationing, problems of relative scarcity. These, however, are designed to deal only with the symptoms of larger problems that are as yet unsolved and perhaps even undiagnosed. Indeed, some would argue that such policies as rationing and central planning have caused or contributed to some or all of their current problems of short-term scarcity.

In the face of the evidence of environmental pollution, destruction or misuse of the land, deforestation, and extensive waste due in part to ineffective planning, it is difficult to argue that the record of socialist countries has not been at least as bad as that of the United States. With their ideological orientation toward subordinating individual interests to those of the community at large; their disposition toward, and relatively greater experience in, long-range planning; the variety of institutional mechanisms they have for regulation of most human and material resources; and their political ability to set uniform national standards for environmental protection, why have socialist countries not shown any greater ability to cope with environmental problems than have the consumer-oriented ones like the United States?

Part of the answer is very simple: Their leaders are no more disposed toward limited growth than are those of capitalist countries; all accept as one very important measure of political good the extent to which a system can satisfy human appetites through agricultural and industrial production. Moreover, any benefit to planned growth that might have resulted from restrictions placed on the political and economic rights of the individual have been largely, if not completely, offset by the unrestricted political and economic pursuits of the state. In addition, whatever tools scientific socialism offers for the analysis of economic conditions, they cannot overcome the political and intellectual limitations of those who use them.

RIGHTS AND LIMITS IN MARXIST
AND DEMOCRATIC THOUGHT

Within the broad political traditions of the Eastern and Western bloc countries there is a common attitude toward the relationship between nature and the polity, and of optimism about the ability of people to overcome all obstacles placed in their way by the forces of nature. It was John Locke (1947: 147) who wrote that "the earth and all that is therein is given to men for the support and comfort of their being," but it could have been written by Karl Marx. Neither Locke nor Marx viewed the evolution of political and economic organizations as a means for the successful adaptation of humans to their natural habitat in the sense that hunter/gatherer civilizations, for example, attempt to live in harmony with their environment. The Lockean and Marxian view of the polity was, by comparison, as a state apart from the nature, created as an alternative to a "natural" environment and from which nature could be harnessed to serve the polity and the needs of its inhabitants. Both Locke and Marx believed that generation after generation entered into social contracts as part of a long, upward struggle toward material prosperity.

Where Marx and Locke and their various political descendants have differed profoundly is on the question of how the state should function in regulating human appetites: Should it be an arbiter between competing individuals and interest groups, or should it claim for itself the function of determining the ways in which, and the levels at which, appetites can be satisfied? Marxists, of course, have chosen the latter alternative, and much of their legal and social structure is occupied with setting standards for, and limitations on, the individual's participation in political and economic life. Agencies of state divide resources between capital and consumption and act to limit the unbridled competition among individuals and private interest groups for the promotion of a common interest—the material welfare of the whole.

In capitalist democracies the rightful role of the state is more often viewed as one of protecting the individual's right to pursue economic and political self-interests, so long as this pursuit does not interfere with the rights of other individuals. In this view the state was created not to *grant* rights, but to *protect* the natural and inalienable rights of the individual. The main body of the U.S. Constitution, for example, is concerned largely with defining, for the purpose of limiting, the powers of the state, and with dispersing that power among the three branches of government. Individual rights are specified in the first ten amendments for the purpose of preventing government infringement on them, but clear limits on these rights are not set. In the First Amendment for example, it is written that "Congress shall make no law respecting an establishment of religion, or prohibiting the free exercise thereof; or abridging the freedom of speech, or of the press." This gives some kind of guideline to the legislature (it shall make *no* law), but it does not give a very exact indication of what is allowed to the individual.

The Cuban Constitution, in contrast, states: "Citizens have freedom of speech and of the press in keeping with objectives of socialist society. Material conditions for the exercise of that right . . . are state or social property and can never be private property" (Article 52). This article sets limits on the individual, not on the state, and as such provides an example of the fairly clear definition given by the constitution to the position of the individual in relation to the political system.

The Cuban government itself, to the extent and only to the extent that it is administering policies made by the Communist party, is by definition the institutional expression of the will of the people and therefore not something from which people are to be protected. The Cuban Constitution thus defines the economic rights and obligations of the individual, a subject not touched on (or even considered appropriate for inclusion) in the U.S. Constitution. The constitutions of all Communist states delineate a set of material *rights*—what many in the West would call "basic human needs"—using as a lower limit some subsistence standard, and as the upper limit, the basic socialist principle, "From each according to his ability, to each according to his *work*."(No contemporary Marxist system considers itself sufficiently advanced to employ the communist principle of "From each according to his ability, to each according to his *need.*")

In general, capitalists believe in the abstract principle that people are entitled to accumulate and to consume insofar as their abilities, inherited position, and the market allow. We in the West are more receptive perhaps to setting limits on liberties not associated with property rights and more ready to accept the idea that a public standard or the general welfare can be endangered by too much free speech, for example, than we are willing to admit to dangers associated with the accumulation of goods.

In the United States the right to accumulate and to consume has been given legitimacy in part by the unique phrasing of the Declaration of Independence, which lists the "pursuit of happiness" as an inalienable right. Of course, this must be selectively defined and can be used to refer to a range of nonmaterial goals such as artistic and literary expression and personal self-development, but it also surely encompasses the right to material prosperity. This whole conception of self-interest or self-fulfillment individually defined is absent from the mainstream of socialist philosophy. Whereas in capitalist societies the pursuit of self-fulfillment in theory benefits society, in socialist systems the subordination of selfish or narrow personal interest in favor of service to society in theory redounds to the benefit of the individual. There is no conception of true self-fulfillment apart from service to society or of individual interests placed above those of the community. In every important political and legal context within a Marxist society the individual is seen as part of a larger group.

In the constitutions of China, the Soviet Union, and Cuba, then, almost all rights specified for the individual are coupled with duties and obligations to society. All parties to these social contracts have obligations not only to one another and to the whole, but to their revolutionary ancestors and to posterity as well. The constitutions of socialist countries continue to place great emphasis on obligations to both past and future generations, but particularly to the immediately succeeding generations. In part this is a technique for justifying current material deprivations, as expressed in what is both truth and rationalization, "We must sacrifice now to make a better life for our children and grandchildren," or as expressed in the most common slogan of the Cuban revolution, "Children are the Revolution." Of course, Marxists are schooled in an ideology that analyzes any period or generation as a mere point in time along a political-economic continuum, so their constitutions make every effort to create an image of a united front of many generations allied in their commitment to one historical struggle.

While the constitutions of socialists and capitalist countries differ in their conceptions of limits and constraints, it can be said that all of these documents embody some concept of restraint: in democratic, capitalist systems these tend to be restraints on central authority for the benefit of individual liberty; in nondemocratic, socialist systems they tend to be restraints on the economic and political rights of the individual for the benefit of the collective good as that is defined by the party. In the United States there is also a general acceptance of the idea of limits on some aspects of political and economic life: For example, political rights are not absolute in the sense that they cannot overtly infringe on the public safety or on the exercise of these same rights by other individuals. We also have a general disposition toward limits on government spending and on the growth of state and federal bureaucracies, although for none of these are there any concrete cutoff points. Some, a very few perhaps, endorse the idea of a self-imposed limitations on the accumulation of wealth and material goods as a principle in itself. But rarely are people receptive to the state placing limits on the accumulation and consumption of personal wealth, save perhaps in case of national emergencies. Even then it must be a transparent crisis, as shown by public hostility to mere preparations for gas rationing during the energy "crisis" of the mid-1970s.

PLANNING AND ECONOMIC GROWTH

If it is true that limits are what give definition to a thing—that boundaries make it understandable—it is also probably true that people living in authoritarian, socialist systems have a far sharper definition than do we in the West of where they stand in relation to the state, as well as a clearer understanding of the share of national resources to which they are entitled. It is this that some argue should give their governments a clear advantage over capitalist societies in planning the development and use of their natural resources. However, the distinction between societies breaks down when one moves from a consideration of restrictions on individual appetites to a consideration of expenditures and consumption by the public sector. By looking even briefly at the long-range plans for economic growth and development of Marxist systems, one immediately sees that policies restricting individual consumption do not reflect fundamental values on conservation or even on the individual's right to consume. Rather, these policies are no more than temporary strategies for coping with what are perceived to be short-term deficiencies in production. While many individual Marxists may believe in "to each according to his need" as a fundamental value, no contemporary Marxist ruler is seriously offering this as an immediate consequence of greater productivity and relative abundance. This phrase belongs as much to the realm of myth as do Western conceptions of the free market principle. What Marxist leaders are in fact promising are increasingly higher standards of living, albeit guaranteed more by public spending than by earning and spending powers of the individual.

When Nikita Krushchev promised that the Soviet Union would "bury" the United States by 1970, he did not mean that the United States would be militarily defeated or that political freedoms in the Soviet Union would surpass those in the United States. He simply meant that Soviet agricultural and industrial production would surpass that of the United States. And what could be the point of this growth if not to increase individual living standards and/or the collective appetite of the state, as manifested in the growth of the military establishment, the expansion of state-owned industrial plants, and so forth?

Economic growth is an absolute good where it is essential to meeting the fundamental material needs of a growing population. But no political leader of a major country publicly accepts production rates that merely keep pace with population growth as anything other than a minimally adequate performance. None is committed to zero growth, nor even truly committed to limited growth.[1] Indeed, socialist leaders such as Mao Zedong, Joseph Stalin, and Leonid Brezhnev (as well as Fidel Castro before 1970) have tried to force quantum leaps in agricultural and industrial production, often causing instead a massive waste of resources.

One feature that distinguishes the conception of growth in capitalist and socialist systems is the notion that it can be centrally planned. It has been one of the mystiques of Marxism that it can be used to formulate policies that will produce rapid growth through judicious and equitable use of natural and human resources.

The political commitment to rapid but planned growth is evident in Article 11 of China's 1978 constitution:

> The state adheres to the general line of going all out, aiming high and achieving greater, faster, better and more economical results in building socialism, it undertakes the planned, proportionate and high-speed development of the national economy, and it continuously develops the productive forces so as to consolidate the country's independence and security and improve the people's material and cultural life step by step.

This article promises growth that is on the one hand, "greater, faster, better," and on the other hand, "economical, planned, and proportionate."

What is supposed to make such a goal possible is the central planning process, wherein the highest-level policymaking organs of the Communist party, in conjunction with the state planning offices, set production goals for most sectors of the economy and coordinate the distribution of raw materials accordingly. Marxist governments do not engage in any process comparable to the 30- to 50-year planning recommended by "steady-state" advocates; some have experimented with 20-year plans but most have difficulty sticking to 5-year guidelines. At any rate, these production schedules are not plans in the sense of providing for the long-term conservation of resources on the conviction that they are exhaustible, but rather, for the short-term distribution of raw materials for the purpose of maximizing the rate of growth of the national economy. It is planning in the sense of coordination to achieve maximum economic results.

This planning process has produced or contributed to some great leaps in production, such as industrial growth in the Soviet Union under Stalin, but it provides no guarantee that it can be used to provide limited growth proportionate to need and to the present and future availability of resources. And the evidence is all to the contrary that it has been used to produce environmentally sound or waste-free growth. Due to poor transportation and storage, and failure to compensate adequately for tremendous climatic problems, the Soviet Union reportedly loses 25 percent of its grain between harvesting and the processing plants. Brezhnev apparently admitted that the tremendous investment in agriculture during his years of leadership (an estimated 27 percent of total investment) was largely wasted (Goldman, 1982).

The mismanagement of agricultural investment inevitably affects the entire plan and makes difficult the prudent use of other resources. Due to four consecutive bad grain harvests, the USSR has had to import grain, beef, feed grain for livestock, and sugar at an estimated cost of from 12 to 14 billion dollars in 1981 alone (New York Times, March 14, 1982: 12). To earn the dollars to pay for these imports the government will have to step up the development for export of its huge energy reserves. This is, of course, part of the reason behind construction of the natural gas pipeline to Western Europe.

Planners in Marxist countries who are too thoroughly schooled in historical determinism and scientific socialism may have preset goals that are so inflexible that they interfere with a realistic assessment of current or future needs and the demands they will place on known resources.[2] In other words, planners may not be assessing resources for the purpose of determining what can be achieved over a set period of time, but rather, planning to use available resources to get where they know they want to go and where political demands may dictate they have to go. This tendency must be exacerbated by international competition between socialist and capitalist countries in which growth rates, GNP levels, military capacities, scientific and technical achievements, and standards of living are constantly being compared.

Further, the process of drawing up a central plan in a country like the Soviet Union or China must be subject to some of the same political forces as is, for example, our budgetary process. Of course, our government has no authority to formulate, let alone to implement, a central plan, but government officials are constantly assessing our resources, projecting growth rates, and providing economic information to assist the private sector and to help bureaucrats and politicians identify economic tendencies, plan for possible emergencies, and formulate economic and monetary policies as part of larger political strategies. The gathering, assessing, and reporting of this information is very much geared to election cycles in our country, and there may be some creative manipulation or reporting of statistics to fit one or another political need. Factory managers and administrators in the Soviet Union or China, operating under great political pressure to meet annual production goals, must certainly engage in some similar forms of statistical acrobatics.

The central planning process must also involve tremendous competition among various branches of the bureaucracy, the military establishment, and provincial administrations for a share of the national resources. For example, in Cuba, allocations mandated by central planning authorities (JUCEPLAN) were for years routinely overridden by the needs of Fidel Castro's Special Plans (experimental programs in agricultural and livestock production; Dumont, 1971: chaps. 2 and 6).[3] For China there is evidence to suggest that regional and departmental competition for the allocation of resources seriously affected the successful implementation of central planning.

China has tried a variety of organizational methods and combinations of methods to limit competition for scarce raw materials. It has had a regional bureau system, it has decentralized and given greater power to provincial governors and party commissars (often the same person), and it has tried a system in which principal authority for implementing the plan fell to the central ministries. All of these have at some time been subject to organizational reform under charges of "creation of fiefdoms," "commandism," and mismanagement (Chang, 1978: 47-64).

The central planning process, however, is not subject to the kinds of extragovernmental forces and private interests that play such a large role in the United States in identifying or publicizing short-and long-term economic problems and in establishing as political issues a wide range of environmental problems. Much of the attention now focused on ecological problems in the United States and Western Europe was attracted by the pressure of private interest and consumer groups. The lack of this input (except as it comes through the official established channels for the expression of opinion) in the planning processes of socialist countries can serve only to exacerbate the political and ideological constraints under which planning officials operate.

Consumer demands can put pressure on political leaders in socialist countries to deviate from the most judicious use of resources, however. The leaders of most of these countries have many consumer debts to pay, and they cannot simply say year after year that "this too will pass" or that next year will be better. There is recognition that after a certain point, too much stick and not enough carrot (the reverse of the West's consumer problems) will not only add to public dissatisfaction with national economic policies, but may also be a disincentive to productivity. In Cuba and China, for example, there is greater use of material incentives and evidence that patterns of investment have been slightly altered to deal with consumer dissatisfaction. (In the former respect, Hungary is, of course, in a class by itself among socialist countries.)

In 1979, China entered a three-year economic readjustment period, the theme of which was: "The aim of Socialist production is to satisfy the needs of the people." Increased investment in agriculture and light industry at the expense of heavy industry is evidence that these measures were intended to increase the availability of consumer goods. In a country in which it is estimated that 35 percent of the urban population live in inadequate housing, the production of television sets rose sixfold (from 200,000 to 1.2 million) in 1980 (Butterfield, 1980a). Material incentives have been increased, for example, by increasing the price peasants could recieve for grains produced in excess of state quotas and by allowing them to sell such grain in local farmers' markets. Of course, in increasing material incentives the state is not trying to satisfy consumer demands as an end in itself, but rather, it is attempting to spur higher and more efficient productivity. When these incentives do not have the effect of aiding economic growth, they are often withdrawn. For example, some of China's experiments in allowing enterprises to retain a percentage of profits on goods produced after fulfillment of the state quota were apparently short-lived, as some enterprises chose to use most of these profits for higher wages or fringe benefits instead of for expanding industrial plant.

Cuba's leaders, who manage an economy that is in worse shape than is China's, have also given a greater role to material incentives and to the private marketing of some produce. They have legalized much of the trading that used to take place in the black market, in part because this is an effective way of recycling scarce goods and providing for the exchange of services that the state cannot provide.

In risking and sometimes experiencing great waste of resources and damage to the environment, and in expending scarce resources to satisfy consumer demands, leaders of socialist countries exhibit the same kind of "gamble now, hope we don't have to pay later" optimism shown by many Western leaders. There is confidence in the ability to discover or develop new energy sources, to exploit successfully known energy and mineral reserves, and to develop technology to resolve what are thus seen as short-term scarcity problems.

MECHANISMS FOR REGULATING RESOURCE USE IN COMMUNIST NATIONS

It is often suggested that if projected shortages of vital resources prove real, and if drastic adjustments in lifestyles become necessary, socialist countries will be better prepared to make the adjustment because they already have in place, or have had experience with, agencies and institutions that regulate access to most goods and services. Most of these countries ration (in some or all regions) certain manufactured goods, most luxury items, and many food staples; the state controls the assignment of most jobs as well as access to educational institutions. (This means that they can and do set quotas in fields of specialization according to the needs of economic development.) In these countries all mineral and other natural resources are state owned, and while all land is not publicly held, its sale and inheritance, and the markets on which most of its produce is sold, are government regulated. In addition, as has already been mentioned, these societies officially embrace a set of norms that places a higher value on sacrifice for the good of the community than it does on individual achievement.

Three of the several mechanisms that have been adopted for the distribution of goods and services and the management of human resources include labor mobilization, mass campaigns, and rationing. A brief discussion can help highlight some of the obstacles to their efficient utilization.

LABOR MOBILIZATION

Socialist countries utilize labor mobilizations of various kinds to help meet production goals, to facilitate the harvesting of crops, and to undertake large construction projects, as well as for environmental control and conservation-oriented projects. The most common form of labor mobilization is that used to facilitate the planting and harvesting of crops; sometimes this involves, as it does in Cuba, crops such as sugar cane or coffee for which machinery does not exist or is not widely available. This kind of mobilization has several drawbacks—some harvesting requires special skills (e.g., knowing precisely how and where to cut a cane stalk), and inexperienced workers recruited just for the harvest can cause waste and perhaps even damage to future crops. There are also serious housing and transportation problems, difficulties in transporting a large number of people to and from the countryside and, in some cases, housing them for weeks and, as in Cuba, even months at a time. In the Cuban cane harvest, and apparently also for some of the Russian harvests, many of the people mobilized are recruited from full-time jobs in other sectors of the economy (many also continue to draw regular salaries that are much higher than are those of the agricultural workers, who are far more skilled). Such practices can, if not very prudently employed, damage the quality of services and the performance of the economy as a whole. In Cuba's largest mobilization, the 1970 effort to achieve what was supposed to the largest ever cane harvest, the siphoning off of labor and resources from other sectors of the economy produced a national economic disaster. The cane harvest, although large, fell considerably short of its goal, and probably would have had, even if fully realized, a greater political than economic significance.

MASS CAMPAIGNS

Mass campaigns are often launched to implement some new economic or social policy, to achieve some very specific goals, or to familiarize the public with a new political line. These campaigns sometimes take the form of emulations, group competitions to achieve or surpass agreed-upon goals, such as the collection of x number of tons of glass or metal for recycling. Because we do not yet know decisively the ultimate savings that might result from recycling certain materials, perhaps we can not say that all recycling campaigns save energy in the long run. But they do help establish an energy-conscious population.

Other kinds of mass campaigns are more obviously successful—for example, the use of intensive volunteer labor to accomplish tasks that otherwise might have to be done by machinery or entail large-scale public expenditures; this includes such activities as periodic street cleaning, neighborhood fix-up, painting campaigns, and public health and sanitation programs. A classic example of this use was the national fly-catching campaign in China in the 1950s. By setting up a nationwide emulation among school children for the catching of flies, China effectively eliminated a serious health hazard without resorting to widespread use of pesticides. This provided a double savings to the extent that materials that would have been used for production of pesticides were saved, and environmental hazards that might have been caused by their production and use were prevented. China has also recently made extensive use of mass campaigns to publicize its modernization and birth control policies. Clearly, these campaigns can produce results, but when they become too intense, as they often have in China, they leave participants physically and emotionally exhausted.

Socialist leaders (Castro is a leading example) have acquired the habit of endlessly quoting statistics on volunteer labor hours donated, tons of materials collected in recyling campaigns, metric tons of grains or cane harvested by "volunteer" workers, and so on (perhaps because they believe it helps to cultivate the image of scientific socialism). But the efforts represented by these figures are not necessarily conservationist in effect. Labor mobilizations and mass campaigns have great potential, however, if their efficiency with respect to achieving a given task is properly calculated before they are put into use.

Most Marxist governments have initiated these programs in part to create in their citizenry a certain sense of community responsibility and integration in the political system, and to emphasize the value of manual labor. Inculcating in people a general awareness of the need to conserve and to engage in cooperative efforts to achieve national goals can promote a sense of social responsibility, and the importance of this should not be underestimated.

RATIONING

Another scarcity-related practice that most socialist countries have considerable experience administering is the rationing of food and manufactured goods. These goods may or may not be scarce in terms of the country's ability to produce them, but they may be made scarce proportionate to need or demand by import/export policies. For example, Cuba grows a great deal of citrus fruit, but it is usually in scarce supply in domestic markets because it is used to earn dollars abroad. What countries gain from rationing is a relatively equitable distribution (below the highest levels of power and influence) of scarce goods and an opportunity to keep before the public the value of placing limits on personal consumption.

One of the most serious problems encountered in the administration of rationing programs has been in controlling the amount of time required of each household to purchase its rations. Where there is a labor surplus and many hands to keep occupied (as is now true in China and in Cuba), such labor-intensive activities as shopping for rationed goods will not be a great economic handicap, even though it is obviously trying on the patience and without doubt not the best use of most people's talents. But if energy problems cause cutbacks in mechanization and more labor-intensive practices become the rule, or if some systems have labor shortfalls as does the Soviet Union, the waste of labor-hours is going to be very difficult to absorb.

Rationing may provide an equitable distribution of food, but it does not always operate efficiently; like other forms of centralized allocation, it can result in considerable waste. In Cuba, for example, fixed amounts of rationed foods are transferred on set days to the individual markets according to the number of people registered to shop in them. If transportation is not available on a strict schedule, or if an error in the amount of shipment is made, waste through spoilage of the most perishable goods can very easily occur (especially in Cuba's climate). Futhermore, since people know they must go to a store on a particular day in order to purchase certain items (e.g., meat on Tuesday, rice on Friday), they miss the opportunity to purchase the many unrationed items that may come in unannounced and disappear very quickly. It behooves someone from each household to visit the market every day (thus producing the long queues, which really should not occur in grocery stores if the ration system operated as intended).

RESULTS

One difficulty with all of the various mechanisms for controlled use of resources in socialist countries is that they do not pay enough respect to the conservation of human resources; there is such a thing as their overuse and—putting aside the basic humanitarian issue—there is the possibility, and in some cases the reality, of declining worker productivity. Political loyalties and patience can also be overtaxed, especially through policies that produce scarcities that through better management might not occur. It might even produce the same effect as crying wolf once too often, so that when the need to combat the most serious problems of scarcity and resource depletion is at its height, people may respond with massive passive resistance or even open rebellion to all conservation measures. If true long-range planning is to be effective, it will be necessary to pace demands on human as well as natural resources; otherwise, the overall stability systems require for effective planning may be put in jeopardy.

CONCLUSIONS

Economic growth has become the most visible and the most intensely pursued, if not the ultimate, goal of all political systems that perceive themselves as competitors in the struggle to prove which form of economic and political organization can best utilize the world's resources to satisfy individual and collective appetites. Growth rates are now universally accepted by nation-states as one of the most important standards of measurement of the worthiness and effectiveness of any political system or its ideology. The centrality of this value can be seen in its triumph over ideological tenets of economic organization. Although there are many examples of this, the most prominent today are probably the economic policies of Deng Xiao-ping in the PRC. The first purge of Deng reportedly came in part as a response to his often-quoted remark that "it does not matter whether a cat is black or white as long as it catches mice." In other words, good economic performance is more important than are the means used to achieve it, so long as they are not overtly exploitative of human labor. An even franker version of this attitude was expressed to a U.S. diplomat by a Chinese official: "We are having trouble defining what our system is. We are trying out a number of experiments, and those that work we will call socialism. Those that don't, we will call capitalism" (Butterfield, 1980c: 32).

If China does achieve its monumental goal of quadrupling GNP by the turn of the century, it will have produced a total output that would be just slightly more than half (1.4 trillion dollars) the U.S. GNP today (2.6 trillion dollars). Still, its present GNP of approximately 364 billion dollars is remarkable considering that its average per capita product for the 1930s has been estimated as four times *less* than that of preindustrial England (Eckstein, 1977: 5). Although far ahead of China's, the GNP of the Soviet Union is only about 60 percent that of the United States compensate it has adopted what Roy Medvedev has called the "full-steam ahead" principle, in contrast to the Bukharin theory of gradual, balanced development (Topping, 1981: 17). There is little chance that these leaders, who see themselves locked in international political struggle with the capitalist West, will give up the race while they are so far behind their leading competitor.

In Marxist systems, where there are so few checks and balances against the political power of the state, an attitude of irresponsibility toward resource management is encouraged as least as much as it is in our own system, with its lack of constraints on the individual. In neither type of system are those who wield the greatest economic power—those who exercise greatest control over resource use—elected or held truly accountable. And there is no guarantee, given the individual's commitment to job security, growth, and consumption, that they will be held accountable as long as they meet those needs. Because of their preoccupation with material needs and with the creation of the means of distribution for meeting those needs, socialist systems sometimes get more credit than they deserve. The most fundamental question is not who gets what, but who gets what at what cost?

Edmund Burke wrote:

> Government is a contrivance of human wisdom to provide for human *wants.* Men have a right that these wants should be provided for by this wisdom. Among these wants is to be reckoned the want, out of civil society, of a sufficient restraint upon their passions. Society requires not only that the passions of individuals should be subjected, but that even in the mass and body, as well as in the individuals, the inclinations of men should frequently be thwarted, their will controlled, and their passions brought into subjection. This can only be done *by a power out of themselves,* and not, in the exercise of its function, subject to that will and to those passions which it is its office to bridle, and subdue. In this sense the restraints on men, as well as their liberties, are to be reckoned among their rights [1955: 68-69].

This is the fundamental dilemma for which neither socialist nor capitalist doctrine has found the solution.

NOTES

1. In Western democracies, the most vocal advocates of zero growth have been the Greens in West Germany. In September 1982, they drew 8 percent of the vote in the Hesse state elections, an increase from the 3.2 percent of the vote they received in the 1979 elections for European Parliament. But as yet they have not reached a working alliance with any major party.

2. This point is well made in Lester Brown's paper on Soviet agriculture. Because quotas have already been set (by the 1981-1985 Five Year Plan) for the production of nitrogen fertilizer and pesticides, for example, it is very difficult for farmers to make decisions on their use of these items based on immediate, local needs of any given growing season. See especially pp. 21-23.

3. The pressure on Cuba to make the most efficient use of its resources is greatly relieved by the USSR's meeting of Cuba's oil needs at one-third the world market price, while at the same time paying eight times the world market price for the sugar it imports from Cuba (1979 prices). A recent study states that "in past crises Soviet largesse has always been available to offset failures and diffuse pressures for any substantial change in the system" (Joint Economic Committee, 1982: 14). As the Soviet Union struggles to meet its own needs for hard currency it will probably have to cut back on its level of support for CMEA countries, and they may be forced to adopt more efficient levels of management.

According to the same report, Cuba has already implemented a new enterprise management system "to reduce inefficiency and misallocation of resources by measuring economic performance by 'realistic' standards of cost accounting and profitability" (p. 11).

REFERENCES

BROWN, L. (1982) U.S. and Soviet Agriculture: The Shifting Balance of Power. Paper 51. Washington, DC: Worldwatch Institute.

BURKE, E. (1955) Reflections on the Revolution in France (Thomas H.D. Mahoney, ed.). Indianapolis: Bobbs-Merrill.

BUTTERFIELD, F. (1980a) "China taking head of its consumers." New York Times International Economic Survey (February 3).

——— (1980b) "China wakes up to dangers of industrial pollution." New York Times (April 4).

——— (1980c) "The pragmatists take China's helm." New York Times Magazine (December 28).

CHANG, P. H. (1978) Power and Policy in China. State College: Pennsylvania State University Press.

DUMONT, R. (1974) Is Cuba Socialist (Stanley Hochman, trans.). New York: Viking.

ECKSTEIN, A. (1977) China's Economic Revolution. Cambridge: Cambridge University Press.

GOLDMAN, M. I. (1982) "Let's exploit Moscow's weakness." New York Times (April 4).

Joint Economic Committee, U.S. Congress (1982) Cuba faces the Economic Realities of the 1980s. Washington, DC: Government Printing Office.

LOCKE, J. (1947) Two Treatises on Government (Thomas I. Cook, ed.). London: Hafner.

SMIL, V. (1982) "Ecological mismanagement in China." The Bulletin of the Atomic Scientists. October.

SMIL, V. (1982) The Bulletin of the Atomic Scientists. October.

SUN, S. (1979) "Modernization: the Chinese way." Beijing Review (November 9).

TOPPING, S. (1981) "Why the Russians can't grow grain." New York Times (November 1).

5

SOCIAL RESPONSES TO PROTRACTED SCARCITY

ALAN BOOTH

University of Nebraska—Lincoln

The purpose of this chapter is to develop a model useful in predicting social responses to scarcity in industrialized societies, especially in North America. While there is considerable controversy over whether we are on the verge of a drastic decrease in resources, there is enough evidence for such a change (Meadows et al., 1972; Ophuls, 1977; Stobaugh and Yergin, 1979) to justify undertaking studies aimed at achieving an understanding of what might happen to the (1) quality of social relations, (2) orientation of the public toward community leaders, and (3) values people will embrace in response to scarcity.

We begin by reviewing briefly the contributions that various fields of study have made to our understanding of social responses to scarcity. A definition of scarcity suitable to our concerns is then suggested. This is followed by a description of two models that have made significant advances in our knowledge about responses to scarcity. These models are then integrated into a single framework. Some consequences of scarcity in industrialized societies are outlined and the problems of applying the model to such societies are reviewed. A discussion of the research needed to test and clarify the model concludes this chapter.

AUTHOR'S NOTE: *I am indebted to David R. Johnson and Lynn White, who provided valuable advice on earlier drafts of this chapter.*

CONTRIBUTIONS BY VARIOUS DISCIPLINES

The study of social responses to scarcity has largely been the activity of economists and historians. Economists have conducted hundreds of studies of reactions to scarcity. These studies detail the way in which scarcity of a commodity leads to price increases. Consumers adjust to the rising prices by avoiding the scarce resource and purchasing lower-priced substitutes. (Where substitutes do not exist, consumers influence lobbyists to pressure leaders to intervene so that the most efficient users gain access to the scarce resource.) A recent reformulation of this work by Hirschman (1970) has been the object of a good deal of attention. He suggests that people's initial response is to take economic action (stop consuming the scarce good and find another), which he terms "exit." In cases of more prolonged scarcity, people take political action (appeal to authority, lobby for a new law, and so on), which he terms "voice."

Economic models are limited in that they tell us little about the effect of scarcity on the quality of relations between members of society, the values they adopt, or their subordination to authority. Historians do deal with these issues in a limited way, having written extensively about famines and food shortages in recent history (see Tilly, 1971; Woodham-Smith, 1962). Their accounts tend to focus on the political responses of elites and on civil disorders. Political scientists, who have only recently begun to deal with scarcity, also tend to focus on the response of political leaders (see Ophuls, 1977). Other recent entrants to the field include sociologists, psychologists, and anthropologists. Sociologists Dunlap and Catton (1979) have identified scarcity as an important component of their field. Like political scientists, sociologists also tend to focus on public awareness and factors that differentiate between those who conserve and those who do not. Rudel's (1980) study of the 1973-1974 gasoline shortage is a notable exception. Psychologists, in addition to devoting attention to the characteristics of those who conserve, have been investigating the power of various appeals to conserve (see Hass et al., 1975) and methods that encourage conservation (see McClelland and Cook, 1980).

Perhaps anthropologists have made the greatest inroads into developing and testing models delineating general social responses at the micro level (see Dirks, 1980; Laughlin, 1978). Ethnographic material from preliterate societies is the primary source of the data supporting their models, which, of course, limits the application of their work to industrialized Western societies. Nevertheless, it is the work of anthropologists that we draw on here to try to understand possible responses to scarcity in North America.

PROTRACTED SCARCITY DEFINED

By the term "protracted scarcity" we mean a significant decline in the availability of resources (fuel, food, housing, water, or other commodities) that people deem essential. Declines that are viewed by the victims as temporary, occurring, for example, when a flood or tornado strikes a community, are excluded. Most residents in the disaster areas expect the deprivation (at least the acute phase) to last for a finite period, even though in practice it may extend far beyond original expectations. Also excluded is protracted or short-term scarcity that is essentially local in nature. Such declines in resources are almost always ameliorated by aid from other parts of the region or nation. Victims expect and receive aid within a short time. The social responses to short-term and local decrements in resources has been described in detail by those who study disasters (see Barton, 1969; Quarantelli and Dynes, 1977). Our concern is with declines in resource availability that are viewed as likely to continue for an indefinite period and that not subject to significant relief from other parts of the community, either because the resources are not available or because states are not capable of providing help or refuse to do so.[1]

TWO MODELS FROM ANTHROPOLOGY

The two models of social responses to scarcity we found helpful were developed by Laughlin and Brady (1978) and by Dirks (1980). They are cross-cultural models that reflect both the temporal and severity dimensions of scarcity. Both draw on ethnographic and experimental research to support their assertions. Dirks limits his analysis to prolonged food shortages, while Laughlin and Brady propose a more general model.

LAUGHLIN AND BRADY MODEL

The Laughlin and Brady model has roots in a study conducted by Laughlin (1972) on an East African people (the So) who experience severe crop failure every three or four years. Laughlin begins by noting

Turnbull's (1972) study of the Ik of Uganda, which shows that during severe scarcity the family no longer functions as an "economically corporate group." Small children and old people are expected to find their own food, and during extreme deprivation, are expected to die of starvation, leaving the breeding population relatively healthy, arrangements generally accepted by the Ik as normal. Laughlin carefully tracks the social behavior of the So from a period of little or no deprivation through a severe decrement in resource availability, and in doing so, is able to trace the process by which the Ik achieve their particular social order.

Laughlin and Brady draw on Shalins's (1965) formulation of three types of reciprocity: (1) *generalized*—characterized by long-term maximization of payoffs having little or no immediate return; (2) *balanced*—emphasis is on immediate exchanges of goods and services of equal value; and (3) *negative*—depicted by short-term maximization of payoffs yielding immediate returns. When resources are not scarce, generalized reciprocity characterizes relations with kin and people who live close by while the negative reciprocity is reserved for people who are residentially distant. When resources become scarce, after some initial increase in the generalized type, negative reciprocity occurs with increasing frequency among kin and those living in proximity. Generalized reciprocity is restricted to smaller and smaller groups. In extreme cases, generalized reciprocity, or at least balanced reciprocity, is restricted to people of reproductive age.[2]

In addition to an intensive search for new sources and considerable stockpiling, Laughlin and Brady suggest that the onset of scarcity is accompanied by a greater reliance on traditional beliefs and performance of rituals. These beliefs are used to interpret the scarcity and as a guide to behavior. The ideological shifts, according to Laughlin and Brady, maintain the solidarity that negative reciprocity tends to undermine. The shifts may also serve to get people through periods of high stress by providing a course of action when they might otherwise behave in destructive ways. Laughlin and Brady also note a cognitive shift from innovative and complex solutions to the resource problem, to simplified, concrete, short-term strategies.[3]

Finally, Laughlin and Brady observe that at the onset of a decrease in resources, the afflicted individuals increasingly look to traditional leaders for a definition of the situation and for redistributing, protecting, and expanding resources. Relinquishing control to authorities, the authors speculate, keeps the conflicts that characterize negative reciprocity from getting out of hand and leading to further disorganization. If, however, the leaders are ineffective, they are likely to be replaced.

The social response pattern proposed by Laughlin and Brady has two limitations. First, Laughlin and Brady confuse the *severity* of decline in resources with its *periodicity*. They conceive of unremitting scarcity as occurring in only those instances when it is acute. It is quite possible to have gradual, unremitting scarcity—similar, perhaps, to what may be facing North Americans today. I think the key element of unremitting scarcity is that people view resource availability as becoming progressively worse for an indefinite period, regardless of the severity of the decline, a point to which we will return.

Second, the ideological responses Laughlin and Brady propose are inconsistent with the cognitive responses. The return to traditional norms and beliefs is not compatible with complex and innovative intellectual approaches to dealing with scarcity. Traditional beliefs would limit the alternatives open to solving the decline in resources. The matter can be resolved by sequentially ordering the two responses so that the complex cognitive solutions precede the return to traditional beliefs.

DIRKS'S MODEL

Dirks's (1980) model relies on his studies of West Indian slave societies (see Dirks, 1978) as well as on extensive review of the literature. In reviewing the research of others, he noticed that some studies found that people became more generous in the face of scarcity, while others revealed opposite tendencies. He also found conflicting results with respect to the gregariousness of people and to the occurrence of civil disorder.

Dirks proposes that the resolution to the conflicting findings lies in viewing the social responses as an incremental process. He draws on Hans Selye's (1956) triparite response to stress, termed the "General Adaptation Syndrome," as the basis for understanding social responses to scarcity. Very simply, Seleye suggests that an organism's initial response to stress is an "alarm reaction" (*mobilization*) that activates a wide range of mechanisms to cope with the stress. If the stress persists, the mobilization itself becomes a stressor, and the "stage of resistance" (*conservation*) commences. Here, a number of bodily activities are reduced, and only those parts of the system needed to cope with the stress remain active. If the stress continues, "exhaustion" (*collapse*) sets in and the organism begins to deteriorate; without relief from stress, it will die.

In a comprehensive review of historical and anthropological accounts of social responses to food shortages, Dirks finds support for the tripartite model in social behavior as well as in physical elements. He also cites experimental studies of food deprivation (see Keys et al., 1950) that are consistent with his formulation.[4] For purposes of parsimony and clarity, the three stages will be termed mobilization, conservation, and collapse.

Mobilization. Hyperactivity characterized the initial response to a decline in resources in almost all of the studies reviewed. In some instances there were increases in sharing of resources, but this seemed to disappear quite quickly. An increase in the performance of ritual was observed in most studies. An increase in hoarding, which increases the severity of the crisis, was another common response to the onset of scarcity. A marked increase in irritability among victims of scarcity and a rise in interpersonal conflict, which may result from disputes over access to resources, were also noted.

Conservation. There is a marked decline in social activity as people conserve scarce resources. Distant kin, neighbors, and friends are dropped from social networks. Rituals are no longer performed as frequently. The individual's organizing unit becomes smaller and smaller. While part of the reduction in social activity during famines is due to a reduction in energy, diminished social relations also reduce the obligation to share the limited resources. The one activity that does not decrease is the search for scarce resources. Stealing increases markedly. When the search activity brings people into direct competition with others, agonistic behavior is observed. There are far fewer conflict incidents, however, than might be expected, and the incidence of civil disorder declines remarkably. As long as authorities have some control over resources, individuals increasingly behave in subordinate ways and act as if they wanted their lives to be controlled by leaders. When authorities no longer control resources, however, the reliance on authority diminishes.

Collapse. Most social networks collapse when the pressure of scarcity is not relieved. The family (with the possible exception of the reproductive pair) ceases to function as a resource distribution and protective entity. The elderly are pushed out first, and then the children may be sold or abandoned. In some studies, abandoned adolescents have been observed to form gangs that forage and steal the needed resource. But most social ties are dropped in favor of the individual quest for resources.

Dirks's model does seem to give order to many of the conflicting findings of prior research. Any generosity that does occur seems to be limited to the mobilization stage, as is any civil disorder resulting from scarcity. The erosion of social relations is most rapid at the conservation stage. Interpersonal agonistic behavior occurs in both the mobilization and conservation stages, as does increased subordination to authority. Presumably, the reliance on authority and interpersonal conflict drops off at the collapse stage, but Dirks does not make this clear.

There are two apparent contradictions in Dirks's model. First, conservation in the form of hoarding begins during the mobilization stage. Perhaps what differentiates such behavior in the first two stages is that conservation as manifested in a decline in social relations does not occur until the second stage. The other limitation is that there is an inherent inconsistency between both increasing subordination to authority and open defiance of authority in the form of civil disorder simultaneously occuring during the mobilization stage. Presumably, different people are involved in acts of relinquishing power and defying authority, but this is not made clear. The studies seem to suggest that those least affected by the decrement in resources who are not in positions of power (e.g., the middle class) are most likely to participate in civil disorders, an issue that needs to be studied further.

A GENERAL MODEL

The Laughlin-Brady and Dirks models lend themselves to a merger that more fully delineates the social responses we might expect from scarcity. Each offers some unique elements that clarify previously unresolved issues. The common elements of each lend credence to an integrated model because both draw on rigorously conducted ethnological and experimental studies to support their propositions.

We begin by examining awareness of scarcity as a crucial element in understanding social responses. We then turn to the three social responses (quality of social relations, return to tradition, and subordination to leaders), of primary concern in this chapter, and examine how they would vary throughout the course of a protracted scarcity.

AWARENESS OF SCARCITY

Laughlin and Brady draw our attention to the importance of being aware of a scarcity. Those who are unaware of the scarcity or do not believe that it is unremitting are probably going to respond differently than are those who feel there is a problem with resource availability. This is especially important in studies of industrialized societies, in which significant segments of the population are likely to believe that all shortages are temporary, especially at the beginning stages. The model we develop applies to those who recognize they are experiencing a significant decline in resources that will become progressively worse and continue for an indefinite period.

There are aspects of awareness deserving further comment. A decline in resources may be so gradual that it escapes detection, and the adjustment to it so slight that the decrement would not elicit the social responses stimulated by more severe shortages. This is especially apt to be true in affluent societies that have huge reserves. Thus, the decline in resources needs to be severe enough to gain some recognition among the general public before we expect the predicted responses to occur. Not only does the decline have to be steep enough to be recognized; it must also be threatening enough to cause some concern. The 1980 peanut butter shortage was not regarded as life threatening, but the petroleum shortages were because they had the potential for affecting production of food and medicine as well as transportation and home heating. Finally, once some sort of technological fix is generally accepted, or people change their lifestyles to get along without the scarce commodity, awareness of the decline would diminish as would the accompanying social responses we propose.

The perceived cause of the shortage may be another aspect of awareness relevant to the model. People who believe a shortage is inevitable and natural (for example, because of the finiteness of the earth's resources or because of God's will) may behave quite differently than would those who believe the shortage is manipulated by some group or individual. This attribution of cause may have consequences for the responses of individuals to the shortages, especially regarding relationships with leaders.

QUALITY OF SOCIAL RELATIONS

In examining the effect of scarcity, we follow Dirks's lead in the use of stages (mobilization, conservation, and collapse), recognizing at the same time that just as the progression from one stage to another is a matter of degree, so is the difference between the early and later phases of a particular stage. In our analysis little attention will be given to the collapse stage. Given the limited number of advanced societies near a collapse stage, detailed development of this aspect of the model would be purely speculation. Moreover, the likelihood of powerful industrialized societies reaching such a stage seems remote, severely limiting the utility of such an analysis.

We define social relations broadly at first, examining the effect of scarcity on the quality of relations in general, then turning to the negative aspect of social relations—attitudes toward individuals of lower status, agonistic relations, and stealing. Both Laughlin and Brady, and Dirks suggest that one of the initial responses to scarcity is the tendency to extend generalized reciprocity to genetically and socially distant peoples. The tendency to share resources, however, is not uniformly observed among the studies reviewed. We would propose that such responses would be found only in cases of local and short-term scarcity such as that brought about by an earthquake or storm. It is doubtful that people who believe they are facing unremitting scarcity will share resources that will soon be in short supply. This, however, remains a question needing further study.

Both Laughlin and Brady and Dirks agree that increases in agonistic behavior are an early social response to scarcity. We would propose that agonistic behavior begins when the resource is not available on demand. For example, during the 1973-1974 gasoline shortage, numerous incidents were reported in which people in gas lines would get into fights with other patrons.

The role of agonistic behavior as a response to scarcity is not suggested by Laughlin and Brady or by Dirks. It may have some physiological origins in the case of food shortages. But the fact that it has been observed where food is not an issue suggests that it may have other roots. For example, in nonhumans, when space becomes increasingly less abundant, aggression has been observed to increase remarkably (see Calhoun, 1962). This has been explained as a mechanism for establishing dominance. Those at the top are accorded a sufficient supply of space, which ensures the survival of the species. Crowding has not been observed to have similar effects among humans, except possibly children (Booth, 1976). This may be due to the fact that humans in Western society do not ordinarily experience sufficient crowding to produce aggression. In Rhesus monkeys, food deprivation does not result in agonistic behavior except when strangers are introduced to the community. On those occasions, the aggression is so violent as to be life threatening (Southwick, 1967). It would appear that where the dominance hierarchy is already established, agonistic behavior is not apt to play a significant role in resource deprivation. In cases in which status is undifferentiated (e.g., patrons waiting in a gas line), agonistic behavior is a more likely occurrence.[5] Perhaps that is why the amount of aggression observed in connection with resource deprivation is so much lower than is expected. Most of the systematic observations have been made in small preliterate societies in which status hierarchies have already been established. Even in Ireland during the potato famine (1846-1948), agonistic incidents were infrequent. While the population affected by scarcity was extensive, the people were not mobile. The lack of mobility allowed the dominant hierarchies established in each community to continue to determine access to scarce resources. In North America, where a greater number of relationships are undifferentiated because of the high mobility of a large population, agonistic behavior may be higher than that in preliterate societies and in states in which the population is less mobile.

One negative social reaction that is reported in most studies of scarcity is stealing. It probably begins in earnest when the commodity is no longer available on demand to significant numbers of people, that is, when its distribution is controlled in some way either by dealers or the government. When gasoline was available only from certain stations on some days or parts of days, theft increased considerably. In the proposed model stealing would continue to increase as scarcity becomes more acute.

I would propose that what is unique about the conservation stage is that it signals the beginning of major diminutions of social relationships as a means for coping with scarcity. Laughlin-Brady and Dirks found declines in social activity to be a uniform response to scarcity.[6] Distant social relations are characterized by negative reciprocity or may atrophy altogether. They may become atomized to the point at which the only social structure consists of small groups (two to six persons) that not only share resources but protect the collective supply of the scarce commodities.

Not only should people's behavior change, but their attitudes toward socially distant groups should also undergo modification, although this has not yet been documented in the studies cited by Laughlin and Brady and Dirks. We would expect individuals to be less tolerant of minorities and persons having lower status than themselves. Feelings of obligation to help individuals more deprived than themselves would most likely disappear. The feeling that such individuals should fend for themselves, and that they are responsible for their own dilemma, would be prominent attitudes among people facing unremitting scarcity.

As social relations diminish, the weaker will be the sentiments people have for one another, according to Homans (1950: 334-368). This leads to a breakdown of informal ties. To the extent that social contact is a reward and isolation is punishment, social control becomes weaker. People more willingly violate community norms because being isolated by other community members is not an important consideration. As a result, individuals in the conservation stage are even more apt to become involved in agonistic encounters, be victims of personal and property crimes, and engage in such activities themselves.

TRADITIONAL VALUES AND THE PERFORMANCE OF RITUAL

The tendency to return to traditional norms and beliefs and the practice of rituals that Laughlin and Brady note probably begin late in the mobilization stage, although this point needs to be documented by research. Increases in the performance of rituals would probably occur prior to a reduction in social activities, perhaps when the individual believes that a decline in the quality of social relations is about to occur. Reaffirming the values of society through ritual may forestall diminished social relations. We would propose that increases in ritual performance would decline once the conservation stage commences, as such acts often entail meals and the sharing of provisions.

The return to traditional beliefs may occur early in the mobilization stage, perhaps when resources are no longer available on demand. The agonistic behavior and stealing threaten the social order. Traditional beliefs imply the restoration of order. Traditional norms and values may also be used by elites to restore a social hierarchy that calls for distributing scarce resources in a way favorable to themselves. This may be especially widespread in industrialized societies in which those who would be hit first by scarcity constitute a minority of the population.

SUBORDINATION TO AUTHORITY

Dirks proposes that the increased reliance on authority begins in earnest during the mobilization stage. Perhaps people give up their independence of action and become more reliant on those in power to ensure that they will get more favorable shares of the scarce resource. People may do this as a way of currying favor with elites, or it may be seen as a way to prevent stealing and aggravated competition for resources—a disorder that is stressful. By being subordinate, those in authority have greater power to prevent such disorganization and thereby reduce individual stress. It appears that subordination to authority continues throughout the conservation state—at least as long as people believe their leaders have resources to allocate.

CONSEQUENCES FOR INDUSTRIALIZED SOCIETIES

It would be tempting to mark the recent swing to conservative politics and religion as a return to tradition and an increase in ritual, and the Reagan presidency as a sign of increasing subordination to authority on the part of a society in the early phase of mobilization. However, the proposed model is hardly strong enough to support a sustained explanation of contemporary political events, so we must limit ourselves to a few general speculations about the possible meaning of the model for industrialized societies. What could be expected to occur?

Taking the decline in social relations first, there would be differences in outcomes at the community, neighborhood, and family levels. At the community level, individuals would feel less inclined to help the poor, unemployed, and other classes of the dispossessed. This would make it difficult for policy makers to institute programs that benefit the more deprived part of the population. The resistance to such programs would be likely to continue until the number of beneficiaries included a significant part of the population. If a tipping point of 40 or 50 percent of the population were reached, resistance might diminish.

At the neighborhood level, the decline in social relations may lead to a breakdown of the informal system of control. Except in heterogenous, highly mobile areas, neighbors will ordinarily keep an eye on each other's property and call the police when they notice something suspicious. Or, they will come to the aid of a neighbor who is being threatened by an assailant. This informal system of control plays a central role in preventing crime and in apprehending offenders once a crime has been committed. A scarcity-related breakdown in the system would cause crime to increase, particularly burglary and perhaps robbery. Public demands for police protection would then increase accordingly. With the decline in neighborhood relations, programs such as crime stoppers, block mothers, and others that depend on volunteer support would decline and new ones would be hard to start.

When family relations deteriorate as a result of scarcity, mutual aid, now so ubiquitous that it goes largely unnoticed, may decline. Relatives loan each other money; give gifts of food, money and other commodities; provide transportation; and help out with babysitting, cleaning, repairs, cooking, and other tasks. Problems ordinarily solved by relatives will go unchecked and later show up in the form of demands on the public sector. Health care facilities, aid for the elderly, and income supplements would experience new demands for expanded services.

A scarcity-induced crisis may be predicted to strengthen traditional attitudes and beliefs, thus leading to the election to office of those candidates promising to preserve the old ways or to bringing back the past. Legislators and executives would be more likely to represent conservative norms, and citizens would be more responsive to conservative or reactionary legislation. This aspect of the model only partly fits Western experiences with scarcity. Probably the most severe instance of scarcity in recent Western history is the Great Depression. In the United States, the policies of, and support for, Franklin D.

Roosevelt do not conform at all to the prediction that conservative or reactionary programs would be adopted in response to scarcity. On the European continent, the rise of Hitler might be seen in some ways as fitting the predicted pattern, although material scarcity was only one factor in his successful drive for power. However, his policies, once in office, certainly could not be characterized as conservative or reactionary. And the experience of Germany was not representative of other major European powers in their reaction to the Great Depression, where the politics of the center continued.

More recent experiences with scarcity, such as the sporadic oil shortages in the 1970s, also present a mixed picture in light of this predicted behavior. While both Britain and the United States elected conservative leaders, it is difficult to imagine that those voters supporting these conservative leaders were either the ones most affected by scarcity (i.e., the poor) or the ones believing that a permanent resource shortfall was inevitable. It is more likely that support for these right-wing leaders came from the traditional sources of support for the right plus those generally dissatisfied with the Democrats and Labour governments. If scarcity played a role in the elections, it is possible that some support for Reagan, for example, came from those who believed that shortages were a product of government ineptitude or conspiracies on the part of government and business.

These brief reflections on a few recent cases raise the question of whether a conservative reaction in response to scarcity can be predicted to come from those affected by scarcity or who believe it inevitable, on the one hand, or from traditionally conservative elements in society who fear that widespread scarcity would threaten their privileged positions. Thus far the evidence seems to point toward the latter explanation. If this is true, then scarcity will exacerbate existing societal divisions rather than reorder them. Reactions to a much more severe instance of scarcity may, of course, be different.

Perhaps the most ominous of the social responses to scarcity is the predicted tendency for people to subordinate themselves to authority. Not only does this mean that members of the public are less likely to protest practices about which they are unhappy, but it may mean a general withdrawal from a wide variety of forms of political participation. Furthermore, the public may be more supportive of efforts by public officials to suppress demonstrations of opposition. Such tolerance for repression makes it easier for those in power to control the opposition and to prevent it from gaining strength. In addition, the public may be more tolerant of surveillance activities employed by authorities to control crime. This acquiescence, as we know from past experience, is easily extended to the harrassment of political opposition.

The other major effect of subordination to authority may be that people would be more receptive to direction from public officials. While a greater degree of compliance may be effective in implementing policy, the risk is that obedience to a poorly conceived policy may be counterproductive.

LIMITATIONS TO THE MODEL

It can be admitted that there are problems in applying a model based on studies on nonindustrialized societies to modern nation-states.[7] There are four differences between industrial and nonindustrial societies that are substantial and could influence all those social responses predicted by our model. People in industrialized societies more than those in nonindustrialized areas: (1) are less subject to direct influence by the environment, (2) have a greater sense of control over their environment, (3) enjoy a better standard of living, and (4) live in a society in which the parts are more interdependent. Consider each difference in turn.

Less subject to environmental influences. Through technological advances in housing, transportation, and agriculture people experience more consistency in their exposure to the elements, opportunities for mobility, and access to food. In short, they are less accustomed to change. Any change they do experience, then, may be very stressful. This could have the effect of bringing about the onset of the proposed responses sooner in industrialized than in less developed nations.

Greater feeling of control over the environment. On the other hand, the feeling of greater control could retard at least some of the proposed responses. Residents of industrialized societies may believe that a technological fix will emerge in the near future even though they are experiencing scarcity at the moment. While the quality of social relations may decline (as there are fewer goods to share), complacence may cause their subordination to authority, and their basic values may remain unchanged.

Higher standard of living. The better the standard of living, the longer it will take for scarcity to have life-threatening effects. With great abundance, only minor changes in lifestyle may be required to accommodate scarcity because there is a greater reserve (of both the scarce item and alternatives) to be used to counteract the shortfall. This would have the effect of delaying the proposed responses. On the other hand, the greater number of goods in an industrialized society may mean that more of them may grow in short supply. As a result, scarcity may be more noticable, and the onset of the proposed responses may occur sooner.

Interdependence of the parts of society. Industrial societies are tremendously complex, and few people who live in them are self-sufficient. When one aspect of society changes, it affects all others. This means that scarcity in any one area could have deep and pervasive effects in a short time. With respect to interdependence, then, the proposed responses may occur earlier in industrialized societies than they would in other states.

From our discussion of the application of the model to industrialized societies, there are reasons to argue that the proposed responses to society may be either impeded or enhanced. Only further study of scarcity in industrialized societies can give us sufficient information on which to base a prediction regarding the onset of changes in the quality of social relations, adherence to traditional values, and subordination to authority.

NEEDED RESEARCH

An issue that needs to be addressed in early studies is the relationship between people's perception of scarcity and changes in social behavior. Individuals who believe they face unremitting scarcity need to be compared with those who think it is periodic, and both of these groups should be compared with those who do not believe they face scarcity.

All of the social responses proposed need to be monitored simultaneously so that shifts can be detected relative to one another. We proposed, for example, that embracing traditional beliefs and ritual activities would precede the decline in social relations in the conservation stage as a way of preventing disorganization. But, as noted earlier, these two responses may accompany the increase in thefts or agonistic behavior that are hypothesized to occur in the mobilization stage. Such events may signal ominous levels of disorganization. The return to traditional beliefs and ritual may provide a way of relieving anxiety about these events. In any event, studies are needed to sort out the ordering of responses.

Civil disorders in response to scarcity are phenomena noted in a large number of the studies reviewed by Dirks (1980). They occur less frequently and involve smaller numbers of citizens than might be expected however. Moreover, the participants and organizers seem to be from those only mildly affected by the scarcity. As civil disorders involve such a small minority of the population and only an elite group is unaffected by the shortage, they are not of primary concern in a model dealing with general social responses to protracted scarcity. Because of the alarm with which people regard civil disorder, however, further study is needed, especially in North American urban areas, where high mobility and large concentration of deprived people may weaken the constraints that are part of the web of the social life that has been the focus of previous scarcity studies. Therefore, people's attitudes about the legitimacy of civil disobedience, as well as the incidents themselves, should be monitored.

Perhaps the most productive approach to the study of social responses to protracted scarcity would be a large social survey in which the same people are monitored over a period of years. The incidence with which they are interviewed would depend on changes in the availability of basic commodities. During a period of increasing scarcity, respondents should be contacted more often in order to gain information on the causal relationships proposed. In the meantime an initial survey is needed soon so that a response baseline can be established. The first survey would also permit one to derive effective ways to assess people's beliefs and social responses to scarcity. Since fuel shortages are likely to become more severe in the future, there will be ample opportunity to test the ideas presented above. Drought (at least on a regional level) is another occurrence that may present opportunities for study.

NOTES

1. A useful refinement in our concept of protracted scarcity may be found in Laughlin and Brady's (1978: 18) distinction between protracted, decremental shifts that are seen by the victims as cyclical or repetitive, and those that are perceived as unremitting. The former are occasioned by events such as droughts, international incidents creating an interruption in the fuel supply, and so on. While not all of the victims of the decline are fully aware of its causes or duration, they understand enough to make sense of the disruption and put it into a time frame around which they can make short-term plans. Others may view the repetitive decreases in resources as a signal of unremitting decline that is getting progressively worse for an indefinite period.

2. Generalized or balanced reciprocity (pooling and sharing resources) at some level is essential to survival. Maintaining the integrity of the social unit not only ensures the perpetuation of the gene pool, but facilitates individual survival. Starving prisoners during World War II who formed social alliances were in better health than were those who did not. By sharing, not only were their chances of gaining access to food improved; they also were better able to protect the resources they acquired from others (Helwig-Carson, 1952, cited in Dirks, 1980).

3. It is of interest to note that this response is identical to those found in learning studies that show that inability to learn from previous experience or new information, increase in error, decrease in speed of performance, and decline in perseverance are all linked to protracted stress (Hokanson, 1969: 124-125).

4. One might question whether the study of food shortages and famines can be applied to understanding other types of scarce resources (especially in North America, where food is abundant), since part of the response would be physiological. Granted, social responses to food shortages are influenced by biological factors; however, Dirks contends they are not totally so, especially in the early stages. People work without impairment until weight loss is at least 10 percent of body weight. This would indicate that the early phases of a food shortage would not necessarily entail physiological alterations that affect social responses. Moreover, Selye's general adaptive syndrome is just that: a response to all types of stress, whether physical or social in origin. Thus, while we need to be cautious in generalizing Dirks's model to decreases in all sorts of resources, some extrapolation seems to be in order.

5. For an excellent delineation of the theory and research on dominance encounters between humans, see Rosa and Mazur (1979).

6. The diminution of social activities has been noted in other species as well (see Southwick, 1967). In a study of free-ranging rhesus monkeys during a food shortage, Loy (1977) found that social grooming, play, fighting, and mating behavior declined by more than 50 percent. While the drop in energy due to the food shortage was an important factor, it is unclear whether all of the drop may be attributed to this source.

7. It should be noted that both Laughlin and Dirks have also drawn on experimental studies done in North America to supplement their findings. Most, however, were ethnographic studies of nonindustrialized areas.

REFERENCES

BARTON, A. (1969) Communities in Disaster: A Sociological Analysis of Collective Stress Situations. Garden City, NY: Doubleday.

BOOTH, A. (1976) Urban Crowding and Its Consequences. New York: Praeger.

CALHOUN, J. (1962) "Population density and social pathology." Scientific American 206: 139-146.

DIRKS, R. (1980) "Social responses during severe food shortages and famine." Current Anthropology 21: 21-44.

——— (1978) "Resource fluctuations and competitive transformations in West Irian slave societies," pp. 122-180 in C. Laughlin and I. Brady (eds.) Extinction and Survival in Human Populations. New York: Columbia University Press.

DUNLAP, R., and W. CATTON (1979) "Environmental sociology." Annual Review of Sociology 5: 243-273.

HASS, J., G. BAGLEY, and R. ROGERS (1975) "Effects of fear appeals upon attitudes toward energy consumption." Journal of Applied Psychology 60: 754-756.

HIRSCHMAN, A. (1970) Exit, Voice and Loyalty: Responses to Decline in Organizations, Firms, and States. Cambridge, MA: Harvard University Press.

HOKANSON, J. (1969) The Physiological Bases of Motivation. New York: John Wiley.

HOMANS, G. (1950) The Human Group. New York: Harcourt, Brace & World.

KEYS, A., J. BROZEK, A. HENSCHEL, O. MICKELSON, and H. TAYLOR (1950) The Biology of Human Starvation. Minneapolis: University of Minnesota Press.

LAUGHLIN, C. (1978) "Introduction: diaphasis and change in human populations," pp. 1-48 in C. Laughlin and I. Brady (eds.) Extinction and Survival in Human Populations. New York: Columbia University Press.

——— (1974) "Deprivation and Reciprocity." Man 9: 380-396.

——— (and I. Brady [eds.] (1978) Extinction and Survival in Human Populations. New York: Columbia University Press.

LOY, J. (1977) "Behavioral responses of free-ranging rhesus monkeys to food shortages." American Journal of Physical Anthropology 33: 263-271.

MALINOWSKI, B. (1954) Magic, Science and Religion and Other Essays. Garden City, NY: Apple.

McCLELLAND, L. and S. COOK (1980) "Promoting energy conservation in master metered apartments through group financial incentives." Journal of Applied Social Psychology 10: 20-31.

MEADOWS, D., D. MEADOWS, J. RANDERS, and W. BEHRENS III (1972) The Limits of Growth. New York: Universe.

MILLER, R. (1967) "Patterns and process in competition," p. 1-74 in J. Cragg (ed.) Advances in Ecological Research, Vol. IV. London: Academic.

OPHULS, W. (1977) Ecology and the Politics of Scarcity. San Francisco: Freeman.

QUARANTELLI, E. and R. DYNES (1977) "Response to social crisis and disaster." Annual Review of Sociology 3: 23-49.

ROSA, E. and A. MAZUR (1979) "Incipient status in small groups." Social Forces 58: 18-37.

RUDEL, T. (1980) "Social responses to commodity shortages: the 1973-1974 gasoline shortage." Human Ecology 8: 193-212.

SELYE, H. (1956) The Stress of Life. New York: McGraw-Hill.

SHALINS, M. (1965) "On the sociology of primitive exchange," p. 147-148 in M. Banton (ed.) The Relevance of Models for Social Anthropology. London: Tavistock.

STOBAUGH, R. and D. YERGIN (1979) Energy Future: Report of the Energy Project at the Harvard Business School. New York: Random House.

SOUTHWICK, C. (1967) "An experimental study of intragroup agnostic behavior in rhesus monkeys Macaca mulatta." Behavior 28: 182-209.

TILLY, L. (1971) "The food riot as a form of political conflict in 18th-century France." Journal of Interdisciplinary History 2: 23-57.

TURNBULL, C. (1972) The Mountain People. New York: Simon & Schuster.

WOODHAM-SMITH, C. (1962) The Great Hunger: Ireland 1845-1849. New York: E. P. Dutton.

6

IMAGES OF SCARCITY
IN FOUR NATIONS

LESTER W. MILBRATH
State University of New York at Buffalo

Humans have always been concerned about scarcity. The levels of concern for scarcity have differed from time to time and place to place reflecting variations in population density, climate, technological development, and per capita wealth. In the United States, concern with scarcity diminished in the 1950s and 1960s as the country showed the greatest gain in wealth for large masses of people in history. Gains in material prosperity were evident in Europe and much of the rest of the developed world as well, although most people in other parts of the world were never free from the pressing recognition of scarcity. Experience with wealth and scarcity in that exuberant era inevitably created beliefs and values that influence our perceptions of wealth and scarcity today. Despite this affluence, during the 1970s some people in developed countries began to perceive that resource limits would soon affect them once more and that they should anticipate and plan for material scarcity.

AUTHOR'S NOTE: *I am grateful to Barbara Fisher for help in all phases of production of this chapter, but particularly for her critical and constructive comments on the manuscript.*

What do people in developed countries think about scarcity in the 1980s? How are views about scarcity distributed across groups in these societies? Why do some people perceive greater levels of scarcity than other people? What meaning do these views have for policy and politics? Our study provides information on these questions for four countries: the United States, Germany, Britain, and Australia.[1]

DATA AND METHODS

The data for this study come from two sources. In 1979, the U.S. Soil Conservation Service contracted with Louis Harris Associates to conduct a large national survey of the beliefs and values people hold about soil and water resources. In this study, the Harris organization interviewed a random sample of 7000 persons in hour-long interviews, providing an exceptionally thorough look at this general subject. One section of the interview examined the perceptions that people held of possible scarcities by 1989 of a variety of resources, yielding a detailed look at perceptions of specific resource scarcities.

The additional data, resulting from a collaboration between researchers at the Environmental Studies Center at SUNY/Buffalo and scholars at the International Institute for Environment and Society (part of the Science Center) in Berlin, the Sociology Department of the University of Bath in England, and psychologists based at two universities in Sydney, Australia, are from a four-nation comparative study of environmental beliefs and values. We utilized a mail questionnaire that was distributed to a random sample of the general public in each of these countries. In addition, we sent questionnaires to samples of several different elite groups: business leaders, labor leaders, environmentalists, and elected and appointed officials.

The response rate to the questionaire varied from group to group but, on the average, was about 50 percent.[2] Although we had hoped for a greater than 50 percent response to our questionnaire, we have had sufficient experience with this data set to be reassured that the differences we have found reflect true differences in the respective populations. There are remarkable consistencies in these belief structures across the four nations.

TABLE 6.1   Perceptions of Scarcity by 1979[a]

Shortages 10 Years from Now in . . .	Very Likely	Somewhat Likely	Somewhat Unlikely	Very Unlikely	Not Sure
(1) Gasoline and oil	59	22	9	8	2
(2) Natural unspoiled places for fish and wildlife to live	34	34	19	11	3
(3) Wood, lumber, and paper	30	35	20	12	3
(4) Good land for producing food	27	35	21	14	2
(5) Electrical power for homes, offices, and factories	27	34	21	15	3
(6) Pleasant views of scenic landscapes	26	30	23	17	3
(7) Lakes and rivers suitable for recreation	25	32	24	16	3
(8) Food	24	31	23	20	2
(9) Irrigation water for growing food	18	35	26	15	6
(10) Water for household use	17	34	26	19	3
(11) Water for business and industry	16	34	27	19	5

SOURCE: "A Survey of the Public's Attitudes Towards Soil, Water, and Renewable Resources Conservation Policy." Study Number 792802 by Louis Harris and Associates, Inc., for the U.S. Department of Agriculture, March 1980.

a. Percentage of U.S. respondents answering in each category.

THE 1979 U.S. STUDY

Table 6.1 presents the results of the study conducted for the U.S. Soil and Conservation Service that are relevant to this inquiry. With each resource examined, 50 percent or more of those surveyed thought that it was somewhat likely or very likely there would be shortages within the next ten years. Gasoline and oil were most likely to be perceived as being scarce, with only 17 percent of the respondents believing that shortages would be unlikely within ten years. Natural habitat, forest products, farmland, electric power, scenic landscapes, and recreational water bodies also were perceived by a substantial majority as likely to be scarce. Views about the possible scarcity of food were spread widely across the categories, with 24 percent of the respondents believing that food shortages are very likely and another 20 percent believing that food shortages are very unlikely. The United States has been so blessed with plentiful food that many people find it difficult to think that the situation could change significantly.

Americans' perceptions about the availability of water also were interesting; fewer people were certain about the prospects for water scarcity than were certain about scarcity in other areas. Only a slight majority believed that a shortage was likely, leaving a substantial minority who believed that shortages were unlikely. About the same percentage foresaw shortages in water for irrigation as predicted shortages in water for household and business use. Because certain regions of the country are drier than others, one might suspect there would have been substantial differences in views about water scarcity by region. However, persons living in rural areas in the West and Midwest were only slightly more likely to recognize the possibility of a water shortage than were people living in other regions according to this study.

Are these variations in beliefs about scarcity related to demographic variables or to other beliefs? In this study, the similarities across various social and belief categories were more striking than were the differences. Some differences were detectable, but the reader should keep in mind throughout the following discussion that they were very slight. The most important finding was that beliefs about scarcities tended to be generalized across resources; if a person believed that one resource would be scarce, he or she tended to believe that other resources would be scarce as well. This suggests that people hold a generalized perception of resource scarcity. Factor analyses of data from the four-nation study confirmed this tendency; seven resource items loaded on the same factor in the German, British, and American data sets (see Appendix).

There was a slight but detectable tendency, across several resources, for females to be more likely to believe there would be scarcities than were males. The Harris study does not disclose why this is the case. It is known from other studies, however, that females are more likely to hold environmentalist beliefs and values than are males, and these studies also show that a belief in the scarcity of resources is a component of environmentalism.

The Harris data also show, for many resources, that persons of higher income and education are less likely to believe there will be shortages than are persons of low income and education. This difference is probably related to personal experience with shortages. For example, an exceptionally large percentage of poor, rural blacks believed that there will be shortages. The data also show that persons who are concerned with inflation and who are having difficulty making ends meet, were more likely to believe that there will be shortages than were the relatively affluent.

The Harris analysts developed a summary index of soil conservation knowledge and also an index of belief in a conservation ethic; high scores on each of these indices were positively associated with a perception that there is a greater likelihood of scarcity. Since both of these indices were also positively associated with higher education, it can be suggested that education tends to pull in opposite directions with respect to perceptions of scarcity; greater knowledge led to a recognition of the probability of scarcity but, at the same time, better-educated people had less direct experience with scarcity. This is a major reason why differences in perceptions of scarcity were so small across demographic groups and belief categories.

A summary index of perceived extent of scarcity across all eleven resources referred to in Table 6.1 was also developed. A multiple regression analysis explaining variance in that index and utilizing sex, soil conservation knowledge, education, belief in a conservation ethic, income, and race as explanatory variables disclosed that sex was the most prominent predictor. The relationships were so weak, however, that only 8 percent of the variance was explained by the multiple regression.

THE FOUR-NATION STUDY

Let us now turn to the four-nation study to sort out more thoroughly people's beliefs and values with respect to resource shortages and limits to growth. It was noted above that beliefs about scarcities are part of a general attitude dimension. Many people seem to have arrived at a general philosophy about scarcity. Either they were inclined to believe that there were not enough resources for everybody to have all they needed and wanted, or they believed that economic growth would continue indefinitely, eventually helping everyone to be better off.

Even though a belief that resources are scarce is likely to lead people to conclude that there are limits to growth (the two ideas are correlated), the connection is not necessary. Some people recognize that there are likely to be serious shortages but deny that there are limits to growth. In a less restrained factor analysis than that reported above, items relating to resource shortages (items 1, 3, and 4 in the Appendix) fell on a separate factor from items relating to limits to growth (items 2, 5, and 6 in the Appendix).[3] The two ideas are related but not tightly joined logically. This phenomenon can be clarified by looking in detail at three of the items.

Table 6.2 reports the distribution of responses when respondents were asked to indicate the extent of their agreement or disagreement with the statement that "there are likely to be serious and disruptive shortages of essential raw materials if things go on as they are." The findings are shown for public and leadership groups in each of the four countries (leader data were not yet available for Australia). The most important finding is that high percentages of respondents in all groups in all four countries agree that we are likely to experience serious and disruptive shortages of raw materials. As might be expected, in each country environmentalists most strongly agree to that statement; other groups agreed, but less strongly. In comparing the publics in the four countries; the German residents agreed somewhat more strongly and UK residents somewhat less strongly than did U.S. and Australian publics; still, there is a remarkable similarity in distributions across all four publics. German environmentalists most strongly agreed on the probability of shortages, while British and American environmentalists lagged somewhat behind their German counterparts. British public officials were far less likely to believe in the probability of shortages than were such officials in the United States, who in turn trailed German public officials in their perceptions. Finally, U.S. and German business leaders exceeded British business elites in their perceptions of probable shortage. Thus in both public and elite samples, the German respond-

TABLE 6.2 "There are likely to be serious and disruptive shortages of essential raw materials if things go on as they are."

	N	Strongly Disagree −3	−2	−1	0	1+	Strongly Agree 2+	3+	Mean
United States									
Environmentalists	225	0	2	1	0	8	23	65	6.43
General Public	1513	2	3	5	3	16	28	43	5.84
Labor Leaders	85	4	6	6	4	18	20	44	5.60
Appointed Officials	153	1	3	5	1	18	37	35	5.83
Elected Officials	78	5	1	4	5	23	30	32	5.56
Business Leaders	223	0	6	6	2	15	27	43	5.78
United Kingdom									
Conservation Society	176	0	1	1	2	10	22	63	6.44
Nature Conservationists	200	0	1	2	6	23	18	49	6.07
General Public	725	2	2	4	9	24	23	37	5.67
Labor Leaders	308	4	1	4	14	20	20	36	5.53
Public Officials	188	2	3	12	15	27	19	21	5.05
Business Leaders	261	1	6	11	15	31	19	17	4.94
Germany									
Environmentalists	98	0	0	1	1	6	17	75	6.63
General Public	1088	1	2	2	5	14	24	52	6.11
Public Officials	102	1	1	2	6	8	36	46	6.12
Business Leaders	130	3	4	2	8	21	26	35	5.60
Publics									
Australia	390	3	4	7	2	17	26	42	5.75
United States	1513	2	3	5	3	16	28	43	5.84
United Kingdom	725	2	2	4	9	24	23	37	5.67
Germany	1088	1	2	2	5	14	24	52	6.11

NOTE: The scale positions were coded 1 to 7 from left to right for data analysis. The mean score for each group is based on that numerical scale. Percentages of respondents are given in each category.

ents seemed consistently most aware of potential problems of scarcity and British least aware, with the American and Australian publics occupying intermediate positions. Within each nation, the public seems as aware, or more aware, than does either business leaders or public officials; this is particularly striking in Britain.

Despite the near-unanimous agreement that we are likely to suffer serious and disruptive resource shortages, there is very little agreement that we are likely to experience limits to the growth of our industrial

TABLE 6.3   "There are limits to growth beyond which our
             industrialized society cannot expand."

	N	Strongly Disagree −3	−2	−1	0	1+	2+	Strongly Agree 3+	Mean
United States									
Environmentalists	225	5	5	5	7	15	19	43	5.55
General Public	1513	11	11	12	17	18	15	16	4.29
Labor Leaders	85	23	13	12	10	14	13	14	3.77
Appointed Officials	153	10	12	18	12	21	16	10	4.09
Elected Officials	78	10	9	22	14	17	18	10	4.13
Business Leaders	223	22	19	14	9	14	11	10	3.47
United Kingdom									
Conservation Society	176	1	1	2	5	9	18	63	6.29
Nature Conservationists	200	3	2	6	15	21	22	32	5.44
General Public	725	7	5	9	15	21	18	24	4.90
Labor Leaders	308	11	8	13	14	18	13	23	4.50
Public Officials	188	8	7	8	13	26	19	18	4.71
Business Leaders	261	10	13	15	13	15	16	18	4.32
Germany									
Environmentalists	98	0	0	1	3	7	13	76	6.59
General Public	1088	2	3	4	10	14	20	47	5.78
Public Officials	102	0	4	3	10	15	21	47	5.88
Business Leaders	130	5	4	13	9	21	20	28	5.12
Publics									
Australia	390	7	7	7	18	15	18	28	4.93
United States	1513	11	11	12	17	18	15	16	4.29
United Kingdom	725	7	5	9	15	21	18	24	4.90
Germany	1088	2	3	4	10	14	20	47	5.78

NOTE: The scale positions were coded 1 to 7 from left to right for data analysis. The
mean score for each group is based on that numerical scale. Percentages of respondents are given in each category.

society (Table 6.3). Responses to the limits to growth item ranged widely
across the scale and varied considerably from group to group and from
country to country. In each country, environmentalists were most likely
to believe that there are limits to growth, and business leaders were least
likely to believe it. Responses from the general public in the United
States were spread almost evenly across the scale, but in Germany,
England, and Australia, the public was more likely to agree than disagree with the item.

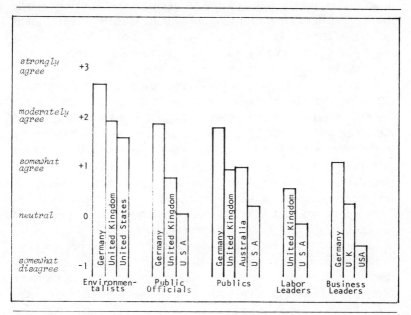

Figure 1   Extent of Agreement to "There are limits to growth beyond
which our industrialized society cannot expand." (mean score
by group)

The national differences are profound, much more pronounced than
are those in Table 6.2. Germans were much more likely than were
Americans, in all groups, to believe that there are limits to growth; the
public and leaders in the United Kingdom fell somewhere between those
two countries. The distinctions just discussed are summarized graphi-
cally in Figure 6.1, which reports the mean score on this item for each
group for each country. These data suggest that there is reluctance in the
United States to accept the idea of limits to growth, whereas in Germany
this idea is fairly readily accepted. Even environmentalists in the United
States seem less ready to accept this idea than does the general public in
Germany. It can be speculated that the comparatively low population
density in the United States, with its richness of agriculture, forests and
minerals, makes it difficult for Americans to believe that the time will
come when they cannot grow further. German and British citizens, on
the other hand, have had much more experience with high population

density and resource shortages that are likely to lead them to recognize that there are limits to growth. It is not clear, however, why the Germans seem to believe this more strongly than do the British, whose base for many resources is quite limited, or why the Australians are more likely to believe this than are the Americans.

It can be seen in Table 6.4 that most people believed that depletion of natural resources is an urgent problem. This belief is related to the perception that there are likely to be disruptive shortages and also to the perception that there are limits to growth but, curiously, the relationship to the belief about limits to growth was stronger than it was to the perception that there will be shortages. People can believe that there will be disruptive shortages and yet not agree that this is an urgent problem for public attention. (It is also possible that they may believe that depletion of natural resources is urgent and still not believe that there are limits to growth.) The data pattern shows, however, that the belief about urgency of resource depletion and the belief about limits to growth are part of a general "environmentalism" belief structure. The belief that there will be serious and disruptive shortages seems to be accepted by nearly everyone, whether or not they hold environmentalism beliefs and values.

Table 6.4 shows that the national differences in beliefs about the urgency of resource depletion are less than the national differences in beliefs about limits to growth. People in the United States seemed a little bit less concerned about resource depletion than did people in the other three countries; again, this could relate to the general U.S. experience of having a wealth of resources. In Table 6.4 we note also the general pattern for environmentalists to be most likely to believe that this problem is urgent and business leaders and public officials to be least likely to believe it, although a majority of the latter two groups do believe that resource depletion is urgent.

It is interesting to compare the two fairly different environmental groups sampled in the United Kingdom on these questions. Conservation Society members tended to have a comprehensive ideological environmental belief structure that emphasizes social change as the best way to solve environmental problems. The members of the Somerset Trust for Nature Conservation, on the other hand, believed strongly in the conservation of nature but tended to accept the current social structure as appropriate and to resist efforts at major social change

TABLE 6.4   "How urgent is the depletion of natural resources
in this country?

		Not Urgent						Very Urgent	
	N	*1*	*2*	*3*	*4*	*5*	*6*	*7*	*Mean*
United States									
Environmentalists	225	2	1	2	4	14	25	50	6.09
General Public	1513	3	2	5	10	17	18	42	5.64
Labor Leaders	85	5	5	4	12	14	20	38	5.45
Appointed Officials	153	2	4	8	12	22	28	22	5.25
Elected Officials	78	4	6	9	13	24	27	15	4.92
Business Leaders	223	6	4	13	19	23	16	17	4.67
United Kingdom									
Conservation Society	176	0	0	1	2	7	23	66	6.53
Nature Conservationists	200	0	0	1	0	6	19	74	6.67
General Public	725	2	1	3	4	10	19	62	6.22
Labor Leaders	308	1	1	2	7	13	22	55	6.17
Public Officials	188	2	2	4	11	19	27	36	5.67
Business Leaders	261	1	2	3	8	21	30	35	5.76
Germany									
Environmentalists	98	0	2	0	3	7	15	70	6.50
General Public	1088	5	2	2	6	9	16	58	6.00
Public Officials	102	2	2	3	7	20	26	40	5.80
Business Leaders	130	2	1	7	17	19	23	30	5.45
Publics									
Australia	390	2	3	3	9	13	13	58	6.02
United States	1513	3	2	5	10	17	18	42	5.64
United Kingdom	725	2	1	3	4	10	19	62	6.22
Germany	1088	5	2	2	6	9	16	58	6.00

(Cotgrove, 1982). Note that on the shortages and the limits-to-growth items, members of the Conservation Society scored significantly higher than did members of the Somerset Trust for Nature Conservation but, on the question of the urgency of natural resource depletion, the Nature Conservationists scored higher than did members of the Conservation Society. Conservationists were more likely to believe that environmental problems can be resolved by technical fixes and less likely to believe that resource depletion problems will get worse in the future than were members of the Conservation Society.

CORRELATES OF BELIEFS ABOUT RESOURCE
SCARCITY AND LIMITS TO GROWTH

The following analysis is based on the U.S. data alone; it incorporates leadership groups as well as the public in the analysis sample. The correlates on which this analysis is based are reported in Table 6.5; generally, they will not be repeated in the text. The Harris study (reported above) showed that females were more likely than were males to perceive resource scarcity in the future. In this study, also, females were more likely than were males to believe that depletion of natural resources was urgent; however, sex was only weakly related to beliefs about limits to growth or to beliefs about serious and disruptive shortages.

Even though it has generally been found that young people are more environmentally oriented than are older people, age showed no significant relationship to any of the items dealing with scarcity or limits in this study. As in the Harris study, higher-income persons were somewhat less likely to perceive limits to growth or to perceive resource depletion as an urgent problem than were lower-income people; income showed no relationship to beliefs about serious and disruptive shortages. Persons of higher education were slightly more likely to believe that there would be shortages than were the less educated, but education did not relate significantly either to limits or to a sense of urgency about resource depletion. By and large, demographic variables are ineffective in explaining beliefs about scarcity.

The correlation analysis showed that a belief that there are limits to growth was part of an environmentalism belief structure; the sense of urgency about resource depletion also seems to be part of that structure, but the belief that there will be serious and disruptive shortages is only weakly related to that structure. The components of an environmentalism structure can now be delineated more thoroughly. It will be discussed in the context of a set of variables that show significant correlations with the belief that there are limits to growth. Most of these variables also show a significant but weaker relationship to a belief in serious and disruptive shortages; when a variable does not fit this pattern, it will be noted as the discussion proceeds. Most of the variables that correlate significantly with a perception of limits also correlate similarly (often more strongly) to a perception of urgency of resource depletion.

TABLE 6.5 Pearson Correlations of a Variety of Variables with Resources Scarcity Variables[a]

	Disruptive Shortages of Raw Materials Likely	Urgency about Depletion of Natural Resources	Recognition of Limits to Growth
Sex (females more concerned)	−.07	−.13	−.05
Age	.01	−.07	−.02
Income	−.02	−.17	−.13
Education	.07	−.04	.03
Environmental protection over economic growth	.15	.36	.26
Mankind severely abusing environment	.29	.44	.32
Pollution rising to dangerous levels	.28	.40	.31
Nuclear power dangerous	.26	.31	.30
Environmentalism scale	.24	.39	.22
Belong to environmental groups	.12	.15	.20
Cherish nature	.20	.39	.22
Enjoy wilderness experience	.16	.28	.20
Adapt to vs. remake nature	.18	.31	.19
Preserve nature for its own sake	.12	.28	.21
Save resources for future generations	.15	.25	.17
Resource conservation to meet energy needs	.17	.26	.21
Average urgency about environmental problems	.21	.49	.20
Urgency of over population	.19	.41	.29
Urgency of energy (1980)	.25	.42	.11
Urgency of energy (1982)	.34	.53	.18
Lifestyle change vs. better technology	.19	.27	.32
Basic change in society vs. technical development	.17	.24	.27
Trust in environmental groups	.17	.35	.20
Trust in industry	−.09	−.16	−.15
Trust in scientists and technologists	−.004	−.01	−.16
Attitude toward direct action	.12	.30	.23
Changed parties because of environmental stance	.16	.22	.25
Liberal vs. conservative leaning	.07	.18	.15
Emphasis on cooperation vs. competition	.10	.26	.23
Economic rewards for initiative and achievement vs. minimum standard for all	.06	.12	.16

a. These correlations are based on approximately 2350 cases. With that size sample, a correlation of .05 is statistically significant. A correlation of .10 is significant at the .001 level.

One of the items asked respondents if they would prefer to live in a society emphasizing environmental protection over economic growth or in a society emphasizing economic growth over environmental protection (a seven-point scale separated these extremes in a semantic-differential-type format). As might be expected, persons who believed that there are limits to growth were much more likely to select environmental protection over economic growth than were persons disagreeing that there are limits.

Persons who believed that there are limits to growth were much more likely to agree with an item that said, "Mankind is severely abusing the environment." They also were more likely to believe that pollution is rising to dangerous levels and that nuclear power is dangerous. People who believed that there are limits also scored significantly higher on an envrionmentalism scale and were much more likely to belong to environmental groups.

Persons who believed in limits to growth tended to cherish nature and to enjoy wilderness experiences. They also preferred to live in a society that adapts to, instead of emphasizes remaking, nature to suit humans' needs. Similarly, they preferred to live in a society that emphasizes preserving nature for its own sake instead of in a society that emphasizes using nature to produce the goods we use. In addition, these people preferred to live in a country that saves its resources to benefit future generations instead of using them up to benefit the present generation; they also would prefer to live in a country that emphasizes resource conservation to meet its energy needs instead of emphasizing greater production of energy.

Persons who believed that there are limits to growth had a general sense of urgency about seeking solutions to environmental problems. A high percentage of them believed that overpopulation is an urgent environmental problem. Believers in limits to growth were not, however, distinctively more likely to have a sense of urgency about energy. This is because the urgency of the energy problem was recognized by most people, environmentalists and nonenvironmentalists alike (the resource shortages item showed a stronger relationship to a sense of energy urgency).

After this chapter was written, but before it was dispatched to the printer, the findings from a second (1982) wave of the comparative international study were received. The data were inspected for changes from 1980 to 1982. By and large, there were hardly any changes; what has been said here about 1980 also applies to 1982. One exception was people's perception of the energy shortage. There was a clear decline in sense of urgency about energy in England, Germany, and the United States (Australia did not join this round). This decline was modest (most people still saw energy as urgent but now at about the same level as other environmental problems) and was found in elites as well as among the public, even environmentalists. The energy urgency item in 1982 behaved more like the other environmental variables; correlations with the three main items in Table 6.5 were clearly higher in 1982 than they were in 1980. There also was a perceptible decline in 1982 in strength of agreement as to the likelihood of disruptive shortages of raw materials, but the decline was less than that for energy. The items measuring limits to growth and sense of urgency about depletion of natural resources showed no change, however.

Believers in limits to growth were distinctive in their perceptions of the need for social and political change. There were much more likely to believe that a long-range solution to environmental problems would require changes in lifestyle and basic changes in society, whereas disbelievers in limits to growth were more likely to believe that environmental problems could be solved by technological development. Most people trusted environmental groups to solve environmental problems, but an unusually high percentage of believers in limits to growth had that trust while distrusting industry. They also expressed lower levels of trust for science and technology to solve these problems than did disbelievers in limits.

Believers in limits to growth were more likely to support direct action, such as marches and demonstrations, in order to influence governmental decisions on environmental issues. Believers in limits also were more likely to say that their vote in the next election would be influenced by the stand of a political party on environmental issues. There also was a slight tendency for believers in limits to growth to be politically liberal rather than conservative.

Believers in limits to growth were more likely to prefer to live in a society that emphasizes cooperation, while disbelievers were more likely to favor a society that emphasizes competition. Disbelievers in limits to growth preferred a society that emphasizes economic rewards for initiative and achievement, whereas believers in limits to growth preferred a society that plays down differential rewards, helping to ensure a minimum standard of living for everyone.

THE MEANING OF BELIEFS ABOUT SCARCITY AND "LIMITS" FOR CONTEMPORARY POLICYMAKING

The evidence is clear that, in these four developed countries, most of the public and the leaders recognize that there likely will be disruptive shortages of essential raw materials. Most of them believe that resource depletion is an urgent problem that is likely to get worse rather than better. Many people infer from the factual acceptance of resource scarcities that there are limits to population growth and also to economic growth. Many others, however, believe that scarcities do not necessarily mean that there are limits to growth. They generally argue that technological development and resource substitution within a market system will enable the economy to continue to grow.

The limits-to-growth debate that occurs in all countries, but is particularly vigorous in developed countries, is the most basic and profound issue in contemporary domestic policymaking. It goes to the heart of our social structures and ways of life. As with most basic and profound questions, people tend to approach it from an ideological perspective. Each side in the debate builds its argument on a factual base, but the theory that is used to interpret the facts leads the proponents to quite different policy positions. The argument is really about what will happen in the future, and there are few facts, as yet, to settle that argument. Each side believes that its theory is superior to their opponents', but adherence to the theory is based largely on emotion rather than on facts. In other words, people believe what they want to believe.

Thorough review of the arguments and facts on the limits-to-growth debate discloses that most people approach this debate from a philosophical perspective as to the best way to organize the economy and society. People who believe that we should limit growth in population and in economic activity place a higher value on the welfare of future generations, of people in other countries, of other species living in our biosphere than do the progrowth advocates. They have a deep love for nature and resist the idea that humans in their exuberance to maximize the quality of their own lives, should continue to crowd other species out of their niches. Proponents of continued growth in population and economic activity are more likely than are those favoring limits to growth to believe that quality of life is enhanced by increased material wealth; believing that this is their destiny, they see no reason to limit the scope of human activity on this planet.[4]

Thus policymakers in these developed countries confront a public that, on the one hand, widely recognizes that there are resource scarcities, that the problem is serious, and that public action must be taken to try to deal with the problem. On the other hand, substantial proportions of the public in all four countries, but particularly in the United States, resist the idea that there are limits to growth. They will resist efforts at long-range planning to slow down economic activity and stretch out resource supplies. If that slowdown occurs as a result of market forces, the outcome will be considered inevitable and acceptable, whereas a planned approach is likely to be perceived as contrary to their theory as to how the world works best.

The evidence is quite clear that the environmental-sociopolitical perspective is acquiring a significant number of adherents. This movement seems to be most advanced in Germany but is already quite significant in the United States as well. A large proportion of the population has accepted substantial belief and value components of the environmental-sociopolitical perspective even though they have barely begun to connect these beliefs to their votes and other political action.

Since this debate (the limits-to-growth question is at the heart of it) goes to the very root of our socioeconomic-political structure, it is increasingly likely that policy debates relating to resources will wind up in stalemates. We are coming into an era when no group of leaders will be successful in governing modern democratic society (Milbrath, 1982).

If resource scarcity turns out to be as serious and as permanent as the proponents of limits to growth believe, it will produce profound socioeconomic-political changes that progrowth proponents will be helpless to prevent. The public seems to be at least partially prepared for that eventuality. While the public at large probably does not appreciate the depth and extent of the change that it is likely to face, people at least recognize that times will be hard and that the era of growth and affluence that we experienced in the 1960s is unlikely to reappear in the forseeable future. This is a viable foundation for social relearning. Humans have proven over the centuries to be an enormously adaptive species. The change we face will not be easy; we can expect a tense, exciting, and frustrating political future, but somehow we will survive.

APPENDIX A: Seven Items That Fell on the Same Factor in the Four-Nation Study

	Strongly Disagree					Strongly Agree	
(1) There are likely to be serious and disruptive shortages of essential raw materials if things go on as they are.	−3	−2	−1	0	1+	2+	3+
(2) We are approaching the limit of the number of people the earth can support.	−3	−2	−1	0	1+	2+	3+
(3) We are fast using up the world's oil resources.	−3	−2	−1	0	1+	2+	3+
(4) Economically disruptive energy shortages are likely to become more frequent if we go on as we are.	−3	−2	−1	0	1+	2+	3+
(5) There are limits to growth beyond which our industrialized society cannot expand.	−3	−2	−1	0	1+	2+	3+

How urgent are the following environmental problems in this country?	not urgent						very urgent
(6) Overpopulation	1	2	3	4	5	6	7
(7) Depletion of natural resources (trees, minerals, wildlife)	1	2	3	4	5	6	7

NOTES

1. We would have liked to have had comparable information from other countries, particularly from those of the Third World, but we could not locate scholars interested in this subject in other countries who had the time and resources to do similar studies.

2. Persons desiring further information on the methodology and return rate for the study should contact the author for details.

3. By "less restrained" we mean a factor analysis that used a lower eigenvalue as a cutoff point for determining major factors.

4. The observations just made of the characteristics of the opposing sides in the limits-to-growth debate are largely based on findings from the four-nation study of environmental beliefs and values. Full presentation of the evidence is not central to the thrust of the chapter and would unduly lengthen it.

REFERENCES

COTGROVE, S. (1982) Catastrophe or Cornucopia. New York: John Wiley.

MILBRATH, L. (1982) "Can anyone successfully govern modern democratic society?" Presented at the 12th World Congress of the International Politica Science Association, Rio de Janeiro, Brazil, August 9-14.

7

POLITICAL RESPONSES TO ENVIRONMENTAL SCARCITY

HELEN M. INGRAM
University of Arizona

DEAN E. MANN
University of California—Santa Barbara

Scarcity of environmental resources is the result of a relatively new set of demands imposed on the environment. The environment historically has been a free good and therefore neither priced nor considered the object of public policymaking. The quantity of environmental resources was sufficiently large and the quality sufficiently high that little thought was given to conservation or protection. Land, air, and water as receptacles for pollution, resources such as wilderness areas and wild rivers, animal and vegetable species, and to some extent, even space were considered sufficient to meet human needs without allocation by various mechanisms, such as the market or government regulation.

All this is past. The new condition of environmental scarcity is expressed in various ways: the spaceship earth concept, lifeboat imagery, ecological consciousness. These images and concepts suggest the absolute limits to the earth's capacity to satisfy the biological demands imposed on it; they also imply the moral dilemmas imposed on decision makers in allocating resources among those asking for a share of the limited supply and the awareness that the conception of scarcity must encompass not only obvious scarcities of immediately useful resources such as air and water, but also genetic strains and complex relationships that provide both biological diversity and strength in ecological communities and the food chain.

THE CONCEPT OF SCARCITY

Scarcity can be considered in several different contexts: technical, economic, and political. In the technical sense, there are absolute physical limits, as in droughts or in air sheds having to accept quantities of effluent that make the air unhealthful and unsightly. Even in this sense, however, the scarcity is measured by human expectations and public regulatory standards that reflect those expectations. In the long-term sense, scarcity is an economic concept, i.e., a relationship between supply and demand reflected in prices paid in the marketplace or costs assumed by government and paid for by taxes. In the economic sense, scarcity is seldom absolute but only a statement of comparative circumstances—a declining supply with constant demand, or increasing demand with constant supply.

In the political sense, scarcity also has several dimensions. For problem solvers, there is the substantive problem of scarcity itself: whether and how to grapple with it. Those groups that fear increasing scarcity are likely to seek political solutions, especially if the scarce goods are perceived to be "vital" or a common good. Politicians have to decide whether these pressures should elicit a favorable response in terms of the scarce resources they must deal with, namely, tax money and governmental authority. What political risks are they willing to run in not reducing the risk of higher costs or absolute shortages? What methods and standards will be used to avoid shortages, with options ranging from rationing (as in water shortages), to governmental sponsorship or production of the commodity (in providing additional stored water) or to the use of government authority to allocate costs (as in preempting private decisions with respect to nuclear or toxic waste disposal sites).

Political capital is itself scarce, not only for dealing with environmental scarcity but in undertaking most governmental programs. Political capital expended on environmental protection has both negative and positive elements. Programs to protect air and water quality or for toxic or nuclear waste management can be attacked as wasteful and burdensome, costing jobs and providing minimal perceived benefits, or as too intrusive behaviorally (e.g., exclusive bus or multipassenger car lanes, limitations on downtown parking, rationing of access to national parks). Scarce political capital is also expended in research programs in recognition of the complexity of environmental issues; such programs may be vulnerable precisely because they are expensive, long term, and frequently inconclusive.

SCARCITY AND FUTURE GENERATIONS

Concern for scarcity of environmental resources is a clear expression of an obligation to avoid imposing scarcities unnecessarily on future generations. Like military nuclear policy, but unlike most other public policies, environmental policy (at least in some of its manifestations) deals with the maintenance of the earth as a habitat for human beings. Policies dealing with persistent pesticides, nuclear wastes, agricultural monocultures, and endangered species are all reflections of the objective of ensuring the productivity and habitability of the earth in the long term. Policies designed to arrest both natural and human-induced soil erosion and permanent impairment of land and water supplies through increased salinity are similarly designed to ensure both the productive capacity and the aesthetic enjoyment of those resources.

The obligation one feels toward future generations is, to a considerable extent, an ethical or moral question. It can be justified as an extension of one's feelings toward one's own children and grandchildren, as an obligation one has to a moral community that extends both backward and forward in time, or as a moral contract one has with future generations comparable to the contract past generations had with this one (Partridge, 1981). While some will debate the ethical issues, we will not do so here. Rather, we will be more concerned with two other derivative considerations: (1) the extent of the obligation (i.e., what sort of environment are we obliged to provide) and (2) the appropriate mechanisms for ensuring environmental qualities in the future.

The first question is whether the current generation has an obligation to reproduce the environment they presently enjoy (some would immediately respond, "God forbid"), an environment with an enhanced quality, however defined (and perhaps at some considerable sacrifice to the current generation), or some basic resource capacity that allows future generations to decide these kinds of issues for themselves. Questions of this sort raise judgmental issues regarding rates of technological change, improvement, and control, and with respect to rates and kinds of change in social and cultural values. There appears to be no calculus that will resolve these issues conceptually, and it is particularly difficult to argue that existing generations should endure sacrifices in conserving resources that they might use to provide for basic needs. Moreover, it would be extreme arrogance on the part of current generations to assume that future generations should prefer existing resource and environmental conditions over those that they devise. Thus it would seem appropriately humble to aim for sustaining the basic resource capacity and environmental or ecological relationships that would ensure the productivity and the aesthetic qualities of the earth in order to fulfill both lower and higher needs into the dimly seen future.

POLITICAL APPROACHES TO SCARCITY

The question of how to deal with scarcity is at least as tricky and controversial: For the neoclassical economist, the market contains within it the constraints on current use to ensure that future generations will be protected. Entrepreneurs, it is argued, respond to price signals, and the markets respond to interest rates, which together reflect the scarcity value of given commodities (Stiglitz, 1979). Both are predictions of levels of scarcity in the future in which canny investors may withhold commodities from the market in the expectation that future generations will have greater need and therefore be willing to pay a higher price.

The neoclassical economists have almost unlimited faith in the economy and research institutions to provide adequate substitutes for that which becomes excessively scarce as measured by price. Indeed, they find the notion of limits to resources and therefore to growth nonsensical because of this substitution capacity. Steady-state economists simply deny the universal application of the principle of substitution, particularly with respect to energy. For the steady-state economist, scarcity that reflects continued population growth will rapidly overcome society's capacity to produce substitutes and will force society to expend its scarce resources in profligate fashion without reckoning on the absolute limits to the earth's resources (Daly, 1979).

But environmental resources, as defined here are largely common property resources in which government intervention may be required to prevent too-rapid exploitation of the resource as in a ground water basin or a common oil pool. Individuals have an incentive to extract at a rate that may be detrimental to their neighbors, thus creating competition to get their fair share before economic exhaustion, and at the same time to engage in practices that may be inefficient both technically and economically. Government action is therefore required to establish rules for exploitation of the resource and to ensure some measure of equity among competing users.

One of the critical factors in this determination of appropriate institutional arrangements is the generation and utilization of information. Market prices and interest rates are estimates not only of current values but also of current values in relationship to potential future values. Perfect information is seldom available; indeed, it may be very faulty, leading to over- or undervaluation of future demand and need. Thus the market may be incapable of estimating the value to the food chain of bird populations as they feel the impact of uncontrolled use of DDT (Dunlap, 1981). Similarly, the market may place excessive importance on current values in energy resource exploitation, leading to too-rapid depletion of the resource and the permanent transformation of highly useful, low-entropy materials to virtually useless high-entropy ones. The market may not provide useful signals about the appropriate rate of exploitation of the atmosphere as a waste sink, given the difficulty of sorting out the conflicting and sometimes incommensurable values of economic development, human health, and aesthetics (Georgescu-Roegen, 1979).

Reliance on bureaucratic arrangements to make socially appropriate decisions is also no guarantee that decisions will be based on adequate information or that efficient long-term exploitation of the resource will result. Responding to preferences of voters and elected officials, competing pressures of other public programs, their own values, and technical information, bureaucrats are forced to make decisions that may be socially efficient or may over- or undervalue a resource either now or in the future. Decision makers may not be able to predict environmental effects or economic costs (National Academy of Sciences, 1975). Equity considerations may play a prominent role in such calculations. To the extent that their decisions are based on public preferences, it may be argued that their decisions do reflect at least majority sentiment and therefore have legitimacy, if not necessarily prescience, in a democratic political system.

Each system, therefore, has potential for "failure." Where public preferences approach consensus, where public feeling is intense, where there is a perceived need to err on the side of caution in exploiting a resource, and where a common property resource is involved, public intervention may be entirely appropriate. The hard fact is that in some situations in which markets might have developed, they have not, and only public intervention could alter the situation. The disposition of toxic chemical wastes is an example; manufacturers took little care in the disposition of such wastes, treating dumps as virtually free repositories with no agency, public or private, making an effort to impose the true social costs on the producers for marketing their chemicals.

On the other hand, it is possible as a matter of public policy to utilize marketlike arrangements to ensure that resources are allocated to their highest valued uses within the framework of public preferences. The task for decision makers is to establish the appropriate arrangements, including a system of public and private incentives that will cause individuals and groups to seek the desired goals.

It should be noted that public intervention is often conceived solely in terms of public decision making regarding actual allocations of resources. At least as important and perhaps as pervasive an influence is the public's capacity, indeed obligation, to define property rights in such a way as to determine the protection of public values while allowing maximum opportunity for market forces to allocate values. Thus with coastal resources—beachfront, marshes, visually aesthetic sites— the public has taken steps in many states to redefine property rights in order that individual decisions with respect to this scarce land are made within a system of public priorities (Zile, 1974; Douglas, 1973). Similarly, new forms of property rights may be created to facilitate the establishment of a market as in rights to pollute the air in a metropolitan area. Such "rights" or permits may be bought and sold under limitations established by an air quality agency acting under legal authority (Kneese and Schultze, 1975).

Abandoning the market system is not even a remote consequence of political process changes. Nothing as radical as abandoning the market system is implicit in contemporary political interactions to preserve scarce environmental resources. While Ophuls believes market forces and individual initiative produce the tragedy of the commons (1977: 227), private business has come to be an important actor in the politics of environmental scarcity. Unwanted regulations are challenged, and business argues that environmental goals can be more efficiently reached by allowing business leeway and incentives to innovate. The pollution control industry has itself begun to exercise influence in favor of certain types of technological requirements. Rather than placing more decisions under government, the current trend appears to be toward returning more decision-making authority and even some public lands to private owners. The argument that these "privatizers" make is that individuals have a greater incentive to protect their property than do agency stewards (Baden and Fort, 1980: 69-82).

POLICIES TO DEAL WITH SCARCITY

There are essentially two interrelated approaches for dealing with scarcity: expand supply and/or reduce demand. Economic theory and empirical evidence demonstrate that demand varies with supply in terms of a scarcity signal: price. The unfortunate problem for environmental resources has been the difficulty of generating a price for such resources: They have largely been priced at zero. Thus there was no economic cost to the producer associated with emissions into water supplies and the atmosphere. The individual who killed an eagle or a condor paid no price that reflected the scarcity value of those creatures; the cattle grower came nowhere near paying the cost borne by society of erosion caused by overgrazing the public land.

In a market economy, it is expected that the market will generate the information necessary to elicit the price signals that reflect the demand-and-supply relationship. With respect to mineral resources, the market appears to have prevailed for the most part, although various restrictions, subsidies, and stockpiling arrangements have made mineral resources an imperfect example of market economics. In most other situations involving scarce resources, approaches that emphasize governmental roles and responsibilities have been used. We now turn our attention to these.

ISOLATION AND PROTECTION

At one end of the policy options spectrum is isolation and protection (Nash, 1967), an approach most clearly represented by policies on wilderness, parks, and some aspects of endangered species. In the eyes of most policymakers, the values associated with these resources are essentially infinite or beyond price. The realization of other values that are producible through exploitation of those resources are either deferred or rejected permanently. Justification of such a policy of isolation and absolute protection is found in the alleged uniqueness of the resource. National parks and monuments are established to preserve unique geological and historical sites and to enhance public understanding of natural and historical processes and events and appreciation of natural beauty. Wilderness is designed to provide a unique experience with nature, untrammeled by human beings. Endangered species are valued for their uniqueness and for their contribution to the overall genetic strength of the biosphere (Harrington, 1981). In preserving and isolating public land, the public is not denied access to the resource but permitted access under conditions designed to ensure the preservation of the resource in its pristine condition. In some instances, this policy utilizes rationing. When traffic becomes so heavy that the natural condition of the site is impaired, as on the John Muir Trail in California, only those who have met certain conditions (such as priority in time) are allowed to have the experience.

The costs of protection are opportunities forgone, such as mining or power production in or adjacent to protected sites. It is difficult to estimate the costs because even exploration is often precluded by such a policy. Protectionists argue that opportunities for economic exploitation abound in other locations, and that a more conservative use of existing and known resources makes development of resources within or near protected sites both unnecessary and unwise.

REGULATION

A second form of environmental scarcity—the finite capacity of the natural environment or the social structure to receive pollutant materials—is dealt with largely through regulation. In some instances regulation takes the form of prohibition of the polluting material itself, as in the case of DDT. But in most cases, regulation concerns quantity, distribution, concentration, rates of emission, threshold levels, and economic and health benefits and costs. Bureaucratic controls, whether supplemented or not with economic or marketlike incentives, establish limitations on both public and private polluters based on standards that purport to protect some balance of societal interests (Martin, 1982). Regulation of pollution entering the atmosphere and rivers and lakes is the most obvious example, but regulation is also used for oceans, groundwater, and land fill.

Regulation is also a rationing approach to environmental scarcity, although it differs markedly from the isolation and preservationist approaches. Statutes and administrative regulations establish air and water quality standards, and the costs of meeting those standards are then apportioned among those who pollute, in some cases in proportion to their contribution and in others through flat administrative fiat that has little or nothing to do with the extent to which they are sources of pollution. Rationing is often criticized by economists as grossly ineffi- cient; they argue instead for marketlike incentives, which permit pollut- ing firms and public agencies to respond to overall goals established by legislative and administrative standards in ways that are most efficient (and therefore most profitable) in terms of their own operations and, presumably, in terms of social benefits. Despite these arguments, regu- lation remains the fundamental approach to most pollution problems in the United States.

DAMPENING OF DEMAND

The approach to scarcity taken in a growth-oriented society tends to emphasize the expansion of the supply as an antidote. If there are water supply and water quality problems, the traditional answer is to import additional fresh water to meet the demand, even if the cost to society of the additional water far outweighs the benefits provided or the benfits foregone. The dampening of demand is clearly an alternative approach, one that has a long history in other areas of public policy but is just now achieving serious consideration with respect to pollution problems.

Taxes on tobacco and alcohol—so-called sin taxes—are justified in terms of both the capacity to raise revenue and their tendency to reduce demand because of added cost.

Effluent charges are the most widely known examples of demand-reducing strategies. The charges are imposed on the basis of the quantity of effluent emitted by a given plant. The logic is that the firm will adapt its productive processes so as to reduce the quantity of its effluent and hence minimize the charge. The result is less pollution and greater quantities of unpolluted water or air. Such charges can also be applied to other forms of pollution, such as noise.

The method of imposing charges may have a distinctive effect on demand. The rates of municipal water users are often low because some of the true cost is hidden in property taxes. Large users, who sometimes impose the highest marginal cost because of the size and timing of their demands, are given reduced block rates. Putting all of the cost in the rate charge and imposing higher rates for large block users can induce a willingness to conserve the scarce supply of water.

Policymakers often must consider competing goals in using demand-reducing strategies (Majone, 1976; Russell, 1979). For example, low water charges in reclamation projects are designated to enhance the survival of the family farm but work against water conservation. As another example, steel manufacturers, arguing that charges for pollution reduction reduce the competitiveness of American industry in world markets have resisted pressures to adopt pollution control technologies. Small firms argue that they are less able than are larger firms to bear the cost of pollution control thus are disadvantaged in the marketplace.

INCREASES IN SUPPLY

Scarcity of environmental resources is in many cases relative rather than absolute and thus subject to expansion or supplementation through technology and substitution. These concepts are most readily appreciated when dealing with minerals and food supply. Increased demand and higher prices have led to increased exploration and augmentation of the known reserves of numerous minerals. Shortages in food, as reflected in higher costs and absolute deprivation in some areas of the world, have led to expanded food sources from improved seeds and new methods, such as mariculture. Reclamation has added to the storehouse of land available for production.

It may appear that there is little elasticity of substitution with respect to environmental resources because they are bounded by the biosphere and the energy resources of the sun. Yet substitution can provide for even these seemingly finite resources. It is possible to substitute labor and capital for some limited environmental resources. Capital or labor may substitute for water, for example, in both agriculture and industry. As water becomes more scarce, and presumably more expensive, water-saving technology or additional labor can ensure more conservative use. In such instances, public policy may facilitate substitution by permitting market adjustments rather than by intruding to displace economic incentives by bureaucratic judgments. Public policy can also facilitate the expansion of potentially scarce supplies through research and development that may not occur without public investment. Research has produced technology that reduces crankcase pollution of the atmosphere and seeds that have permitted vast expansion of agriculture production; it has improved the efficiency of water use in agriculture, increased the probability of extracting large quantities of water from clouds, and reduced the toxicity of some substances that threaten the lives and health of human populations.

Of course, confidence in technology and the infinite substitutability for environmental resources is an act of faith, based on rather limited experience. Those who lack that faith counsel policies based on assumptions of absolute limits.

CREATION OF RESERVES

Creating reserves to protect against scarcity is a device familiar to those concerned with resource management. The construction of storage reservoirs to meet fluctuating demands and seasonable variations in flow supplies of water is standard practice for all sorts of water uses. Judgment about the size of such reserves depends on estimates of risk, which in turn reflect experience and potential threats. Estimates of reserves of oil in the face of an OPEC embargo reflect the uncertainties of demand and the international political situation.

The policy of creating reserves applies also to such subjects as endangered species and gene pools. Public policy may ensure that the populations of species do not decline to the point that they are endangered, i.e., so scarce that the species is likely to become extinct. Reserves may be established of biological and botanical species that may be driven out because of the adoption of monocultures that concentrate on certain simple strains that are marvelously productive but have less certain survival properties. The reserves, whose purpose may be the maintenance of diversity, are also insurance against the risk that the more productive strains may prove to be less hardy and therefore incapable of sustaining their productivity against diseases and pests.

ADAPTATION TO SCARCITY

All of the above policies are essentially adaptations to scarcity, but some policies are specifically designed to live with the existing level of scarcity. There are costs associated with such policies, but they are by nature societal tradeoffs that reflect multiple sets of values.

Water supplies are scarce in most nations, as are depositories for various other forms of waste. Before the passage of the Clean Water Act of 1972, public policy permitted the use of river water as a dilutant and as an agent for assimilating sewage and other wastes dumped into it. Some would argue that a policy aimed at returning rivers to a pristine state is an unrealistic and quite inefficient adaptation for a highly industrialized nation.

Agricultural land is scarce also, in some areas partially because of its increasing salinity. One form of adaptation may be the substitution of more salt-tolerant crops rather than endeavoring either to remove the salts or simply to allow the land to return to its formerly unproductive state.

The problem with a policy of adaptation is the uncertainty regarding the thresholds between adaptation and permanent destruction of a species, an ecosystem, or a resource. Human beings obviously have tolerated, if not adapted to, large quantities of particulate and toxic matter in the atmosphere, albeit with heightened (but apparently acceptable) levels of morbidity and mortality. Marine life can apparently adapt to and even prosper with heightened ocean water temperatures around nuclear generating plants and oil extraction installations. On the other hand, DDT clearly constituted a serious threat to some bird species. Cessation of the usage of that pesticide was crucial factor in the protection of those species.

CHANGES OF ETHICS AND
INCREASED ENVIRONMENTAL AWARENESS

Underlying changed practices and public policies in democratic political systems (and probably in most nondemocratic systems as well) must be value systems that at least tolerate and in most cases actively support those practices and policies. To some extent those values reflect public experience—the smells and sights of garbage dumps and auto-mobile graveyards, the ugliness of a fouled metropolitan atmosphere, the inability to swim in a formerly clean body of water. But in some degree these values may be taught in the formal sense and inculcated through opportunities for personal experience.

There has been a measure of support for increasing the public's awareness of environmental scarcity through federal appropriations for environmental education programs in the schools. There was public and private support for Earth Day celebrations, and these in turn have emphasized scarcity. University curricula provide offerings in environmental economics, law, politics, planning and conservation, and numerous more specialized courses in the natural sciences have included environmental topics in their courses.

Education in conservation in the face of shortages of energy or other resources has become an important element in public policymaking. Water-purveying agencies have exhorted their clients to conserve water with at least important short-run effects on usage. Public utility commissions have required that their licensees—gas and electrical utilities—undertake conservation programs in which subscribers are offered incentives to conserve energy through low-interest loans or advisory services. Public campaigns have been launched to encourage motorists to conserve fuel by limiting their driving speeds to the national speed limit of 55 miles per hour.

These, then, are policies designed to deal with scarcity as it is perceived in the United States. They are varied in their approaches utilizing different mixes of institutions and incentives involving both the public and private sectors. All involve to some extent and in varying ways the basic institutions and structures of the political process. We have looked at them without considering the manner in which the institutional structure has or might be changed to deal with scarcity. We now turn our attention to that question.

SYSTEMIC CHANGES:
PROCEDURAL AND STRUCTURAL

In a world of increasing scarcity, some argue that the holistic environment rather than its dissected constituent parts is the appropriate focus of government (Ophuls, 1977: 231; Caldwell, 1964: 1-16). Concern with interrelationships in the whole environmental system motivated the adoption of new procedures and structures during the 1970s. Yet these modifications have themselves proven to be resource intensive and have led to scarcities. Moreover, the fragmented, disjunctive procedures and structures for environmental decision making show few signs of becoming more integrated.

The National Environmental Policy Act of 1969 (NEPA) was formulated within the context of widely shared criticism of administrative fragmentation. The Hoover Commission had long since identified and deplored conflicting and overlapping missions of various agencies, and the remedy proposed then and seriously reconsidered in many succeeding administrations since the 1950s was a department of natural resources. The environmental movement of the late 1960s added ecological irrationality to the indictment of executive branch fragmentation. They noted that the impact of government on the environment was comprehensive, but government's response was piecemeal. Knowledge about potential impacts of governmental actions on the holistic environment had to be made to affect the most remote recesses of federal administrative machinery in order to influence the multitude of decisions affecting the environment (Dreyfus and Ingram, 1976: 245).

The environmental impact statement requirement in section 102c of the NEPA was designed to generate and transmit information about all the adverse environmental effects and the irretrievable commitments of resources that would predictably result from proposed governmental action. This holistic knowledge was supposed to "force" more environmentally sensitive decisions on the agencies whenever they proposed to take actions substantially affecting the environment. The agencies were to prepare and send these statements to other agencies and the public to review. Without question, the environmental impact statement (EIS) requirement has prevented a number of actions that would have squandered scarce environmental resources (Liroff, 1976). Nonetheless, preparing impact statements requires large investments of agency resources and biases decision-making processes toward interests "rich" in environmental expertise.

Reviewing agency compliance with NEPA in 1976, Wichelman found that excess organizational capacity (i.e., uncommitted technical expertise, staffing, and monetary resources) explained differential agency implementation more than did the degree of environmental orientation (Wichelman, 1976: 264). In fact, powerful agencies like the

Corps of Engineers have gained even more power by exploiting the NEPA to build a new image and constituency (Mazmanian and Nienaber, 1979). In contrast, weak agencies like the Bureau of Land Management lost power to the central management of the Department of Interior, which took over the task of writing EISs, ostensibly to exercise more quality control (Fairfax and Ingram, 1980). The EIS process created new information channels that were clearly biased toward those outside interests with ample resources of expertise. Utility companies that could pay millions of dollars for environmental assessments by engineering consulting firms could dominate the information going into government EISs. Impact statements have become useful means by which such powerful interests can justify and rationalize their actions (Ingram and Ullery, 1977). On the other hand, many locally based interests and environmental groups have lacked the data base, time, and skills to participate effectively even though the procedure is supposed to open up decision making. Partly because EISs became a tool for serving established interests, the documents themselves failed to become the holistic, comprehensive appraisal the authors of the NEPA envisioned. Instead, impact statements grew to be bulky, disjointed catalogues that were mainly descriptive and not useful to decision making. Material was included, not because it was necessary to a holistic, systematic overview, but to prevent court challenges against agencies on grounds that some impacts were unspecified (Bardach and Puglearesi, 1977). Further, environmental assessment grew to be a costly enterprise in the federal establishment. A former head of the Bureau of Land Management, the underfunded and understaffed steward of millions of acres of public land, estimated that over 30 percent of the budget went to inventories, data management, and environmental assessment (Gregg, 1982).

In recognition of the serious deficiencies in the environmental impact analysis, a serious effort was made toward the end of the Carter administration to streamline the process. This effort resulted in an agreement that was supported by most elements of business and the environmental movement and promised to provide documents that were less bulky, more focused, and better designed to give decision makers the kinds of information needed in order to take rational action (Yost, 1980).

A holistic approach to the environment has also been pursued through reorganization. The result has been to fragment even further the loose structure about which the Hoover Commission complained. For instance, the Environmental Protection Agency (EPA), reorganized in 1970, took control of water quality while water quantity jurisdiction remained in a half-dozen other agencies. Even within the EPA, an agency established to regulate pollution comprehensively, regulation of each disposal media, air, water, and land remained in separate, only loosely coordinated, units (Davies and Davies, 1975: 109). Meanwhile, a department of energy with broad jurisdiction came into being, and a department of natural resources reorganization that might have consolidated federal land and water agencies failed. The federal government now faces the impending shortages in resources and the environment without holistic procedures or structures and little discernible trend in that direction.

CHANGES IN THE POLITICAL PROCESS

The environmental movement has continued to fare well in public opinion despite the negative implications pollution controls have for jobs and the tax base. One poll found that 73 percent of the public said that the term "environmentalist" applies to them "definitely" or "somewhat" (CEQ, 1980: 4). Pollster Lou Harris (1981) told Congress, "this message on the deep desire on the part of the American people to battle pollution is one of the most overwhelming and clearest we have ever recorded in our twenty-five years of surveying public opinion." Lopsided majorities of all the key groups (urban/rural, East/West, young/old, rich/poor, union member/white-collar workers, and so on) have said they want environmental laws to remain as or more strict. While still strongly favorable, public opinion has changed since Earth Day, 1970, marked the emergence of environment as a major national issue. The public is more aware of costs and trade offs and is willing to make some sacrifices to maintain environmental quality. Clearly, though, there are limits. According to a recent survey, only 27 percent of the public believes we should slow economic growth to protect the environment (CEQ, 1980: 17).

It may well be that the public is aware that the costs of controlling pollution and ensuring protection of scarce environmental resources are not as burdensome as some critics of environmental policy would suggest. Clearly there are heavy costs to some industries that have refused to respond to new policy demands, perhaps because their technology developed many years ago (e.g., the steel industry). But overall costs to the economy are modest and presumably will decrease as new industrial plants with improved technology are built. Recent studies at Resources for the Future conclude that in neither the short nor long run are the costs of environmental policy likely to be a significant factor in the economic health of the country, especially if one counts not only the costs but also the benefits of such policy (Ridker and Watson, 1981; Portney, 1981).

Voters' opinions in favor of the environment, strong as they are, have done little to modify established political processes in response to emerging scarcities. Environment is a cross-cutting issue that attracts liberals and Democrats as well as conservatives and Republicans. Nor do the usual demographic characteristics of age, education, or income explain much of the variance in environmental concern (Dunlap and Van Liere, 1977). As a result, environmentalism does not provide the basis of a new governing majority that could take command of and reorient either political party. Note that Harris found that among those voting for Ronald Reagan in 1980, 76 percent were against relaxing the Clean Air Act despite the president's clear wish to modify the legislation (Harris, 1981). Further, the environment is not one of the "single issues" that can elect or defeat candidates on the basis of their stand on it alone. Single issues tend to be ones in which relatively small numbers of people feel intensely on opposite sides of a question. Protecting scarce environmental resources, in contrast, is a consensual issue that most people espouse; citizens want a clean environment along with numbers of other goals like energy, jobs, and a healthy economy (Goodwin and Ingram, 1980).

PORTENT FOR THE POLITICAL SYSTEM

"Politicking," in Ophuls's view, characterizes the incremental, structural, and process modifications that have so far been made in response to environmental scarcity (1977: 223). True politics is the art of creating new possibilities for human progress, and Ophuls envisions sweeping changes in the political system to correspond with the steady-state society. He may well be correct in believing that the systematic impacts of scarcity will be profound, yet attempts at prediction must be highly speculative. Analysts may differ, as we do, with Ophuls's prognostications.

Ophuls sees increased communalism with the underlying political consensus achieved through coercive regimentation (1977: 226). We admit that conflicts that erode community consensus may develop, yet there are countervailing forces short of coercion that may also operate.

The great differences among groups in our pluralistic society have been masked historically by shared interest in a growing economy, an ever-expanding pie. Scarcity implies a halt to expansion that may cause groups to look more jealously at the positions and possessions of competing groups. Differences between the haves and have-nots are likely to be exacerbated even if there is no cleavage between groups over the desirability of environmental quality. How to distribute scarcity is bound to be more contentious than is the distribution of positive benefits. Exacerbated conflict may reduce support for the overall political system that is seen by each group as favoring other groups while it suffers deprivation.

At the same time, citizens may be convinced to cut back collectively on the use of some resources if they believe the sacrifice being asked of them is necessary and equitable. The lesson of the California drought is that people will reduce their use of vital resources if they perceive that a real crisis exists and everyone is cutting back equally. Whether or not the husbanding of resources outlasts the short-term shock of crisis among consumers is open to question. Frugality may become a habit, or people may slip back into their profligate ways. Response in the long term is likely to depend on the resource, the extent to which new habits can be institutionalized, the extent to which people's positive behavior can be reinforced, and whether individuals feel they are being treated equitably. Nevertheless, it is possible to imagine that a voluntary community commitment to respond to shortages could strengthen political system support.

Along with voluntary individual action, we expect most traditional values and practices to persist, but with modifications. Rather than the disappearance of the market system that Ophuls (1977: 227) envisions, we see markets, constrained by government, being employed to allocate scarcity. Economists argue that raising prices most efficiently allocates resources to their highest economic purpose. Resource allocation decisons on the basis of price also avoid implementation of cutbacks in resource use by cumbersome, corruptable bureaucracies. However, the equity of the basic distribution of financial resources is widely perceived as unjust, and distribution of environmental amenities on the basis of ability to pay will not be politically acceptable. In many cases economic rationality and political feasibility are at odds. It seems most likely that while market-type incentives will be embodied in policies to address scarcity, the market will continue to be constrained by deliberate governmental policy.

Just as we expect the mixed economic structure of private enterprise with governmental intervention to persist, we also expect most traditional forms of decision making, individual rights, and protection of private property to remain strong. Environmental externalities of development such as dirty air and water and the production of toxic substances are most heavily felt in the geographical area surrounding the site of development or disposal. Whatever favorable consequences accrue from economic growth are most likely to be felt there, too. Consequently, the region of project impact is likely to have the most intense interest in the disposition of scarce environmental resources. Further, the residents of the region who bear the benefits and costs have a strong claim to participate in decisions affecting them directly. Past federal predominance in natural resources decision making has often been based on federal financial superiority and amassed experience and expertise in federal agencies. In an age of increasing scarcity of federal financial and bureaucratic power, the ability of the federal government to buy local cooperation by funding and constructing projects is likely to be attenuated. States and localities will be more apt to insist on an important role in decisions that affect them when the federal government has few positive rewards to distribute for deferring to federal objectives.

Despite the strong sentiment currently against government regulation of private property, we expect most of the regulatory structure to continue. The scarcity of unpolluted air, water, and land is such that individuals will not be able to use their property as they please, no matter how strong our free enterprise values. At the same time, we would expect the private owners' motivations in favor of self-interest will be exploited in public policies aiming to limit the uses of environmental resources. For instance, Congress and the Environmental Protection Agency are currently experimenting with imaginative quasi-market mechanisms to control efficiently air pollution. The emissions offset program allows new, cleaner factories to move into areas that have not attained air pollution standards and, therefore, should not, under ordinary interpretations of the law, be given additional permits for new sources of emissions. New sources simply buy out an older factory's right to pollute and dirtier industries are replaced or are offset by incoming cleaner industries. The "bubble concept" as it applies to a company allows all emissions from all smokestacks, leaky doors, dirt roads and open tanks at a number of plants to be calculated together as if they were caught in a bubble to see if clean air standards are met. Polluters can concentrate clean-up where it is least costly. Further, companies that clean up more than necessary can trade or sell pollution allotments to another firm. Emission "banks" may eventually be set up to facilitate trading in pollution. Under the quasi-market systems that may eventually evolve, industry will see pollution controls not just as a bothersome government regulation, but as a source of revenue. We expect other similar innovations that will reduce heavy costs of implementing regulations.

Ophuls (1977: 163) believes that the Leviathan can be mitigated but not avoided. He asserts:

> Ecological scarcity in particular seems to engender overwhelming pressures toward political systems that are frankly authoritarian by current standards, for there seems to be no other way to check competitive overexploitation of resources and to assure competent direction of a complex society's affairs in accord with steady-state imperatives.

Further, because Ophuls believes it is easier to bear, this totalitarian guidance will emanate from a remote, centralized government. We disagree that scarcity makes the Leviathan inevitable and expect decentralized policy will be equally likely. We expect the burdens of government will vary with goals and preferred solutions. For instance, it is far from clear how acceptable environmental risks will be defined. Modern science has made it possible to calculate, often statistically, the probability of morbidity and moribundity resulting from pollutants and toxic substances. The process of sorting out public preferences on the basis of this information has only begun. Already it is clear that factors other than probability of death or illness, such as the element of individual choice involved and the extent to which risks are catastrophic, are important. In any case, society's decision to accept only very improbable risks will mean more government than if we were less risk averse.

Centralized industrial and economic solutions in response to other types of scarcity will prompt centralized governmental action to protect and allocate scarce environmental resources. For instance, large-scale adoption of nuclear power or mammoth increases in pesticide production would likely prompt a centralized bureaucratic regulatory response. On the other hand, medium- or low-technology means of generating energy or more localized marketing of agricultural produce would prompt more decentralized political decision-making structures. The scarcity of some environmental resources may be more amenable to decentralized handling than is the scarcity of others. Toxic substances that are lethal in very small amounts and are quickly dispersed through physical and biological systems may need to be universally and centrally banned. Less dangerous solid wastes dispersed in landfills are likely to be treated variously in a decentralized fashion, depending on particular physical conditions, such as depth to groundwater and competing claims for particular land.

It is probably useful to observe here that it is far from clear that centralized decision-making systems are more innovative in pursuing environmental policies than are decentralized systems. Decentralized structures allow for policy entrepreneurship by individuals who could not otherwise enter a policy system, the costs of innovations are lowered because subunits can make changes without comprehensive alterations of entire systems, competition fosters change as each competing unit seeks to outdo the others, and the legitimacy of results is enhanced by the accomodation of diverse interests (Ingram and Ullery, 1980: 664-682). For all the fragmentation in the American political system, the environmental record of the United States is better than are those of other, more centralized democratic or authoritarian polities.

Barring a return to a subsistence economy, the role of "experts" in the political system will probably expand. There is a distinct, antitechnological strain in environmentalist thought that suggests that technology is more apt to be the cause than the solution to pollution. It is argued that humankind is very much out of balance with the natural world, and that technology is destroying resources such as genetic diversity that humans are not yet wise enough to value. Human technological advances are destroying the laboratory that holds answers to questions we have not yet learned to ask (McPhee, 1971). Further, distrust of expertise is one of the legacies of the participatory democracy embraced in the 1960s (Beer, 1979: 25-28). Yet it is largely through advances in technology that we have learned of the perilous state of the environment and ecological structures on which life depends, and technology is crucial to finding solutions. Successful regulation of toxic substances, for instance, is highly dependent on certain scientific advances in in vitro tests for assessing carcinogenicity, evolution of knowledge about the relationship of chemical structure and predicting carcinogenicity and toxicity, and methods for extrapolating animal data to humans.

The continued and perhaps expanded role of expertise in dealing with scarce environmental resources leads to several conflicting considerations. One is the issue of bureaucratic overload and scarcity of experts within government. Already, federal regulatory agencies such as the EPA are under severe budgetary constraints. Relatively new programs like toxic substances control have never been fully staffed. State agencies are in no better condition. A National Governor's Association Survey of state environmental agencies in 1982 found that most states would not be able to fund environmental programs being slated for transfer to the states by the Reagan administration. For instance, at least eleven states indicated that they would be forced to drop their programs to prevent the deterioration of air quality in areas cleaner than the national average (Washington Post, 1982). For some time in the future it appears that demands on governmental agencies will outstrip their personnel resources.

At the same time, the crucial role of expertise will perpetuate a longstanding problem of governance: democratic control of administrative agencies. Ophuls writes of the priesthood of responsible technologists on whom our survival and well-being must depend in the era of coming scarcity (1977: 159). Environmental and occupational health agencies amassed enormous rule making and regulatory powers in the 1970s, and the legislative branch was not very effective in controlling their exercise. Clean air and water laws written by Congress were long and complex, and policymakers tried to anticipate implementation problems and constrain agencies with specific language. Yet experience has proven that legislative language was not very precise, and the interpretations of such criteria as "air clean enough to protect the public health" and "best practicable technology" are subject to various meanings. The courts, more than Congress, have come to play a critical role in holding administrative rule making accountable. Courts have insisted upon well-documented accounts of the considerations and participants in administrative decisions and have acted to ensure open and equitable access (Stewart, 1978: 68-138). The expanded role of experts will require the reinforcement of judicial and other political controls over experts.

REFERENCES

ANDERSON, F. et al. (1977) Environmental Improvement Through Economic Incentives. Baltimore: Johns Hopkins University Press.

BADEN, J. and R. FORT (1980) "Natural resources and bureaucratic predators." Policy Review 11: 69-82.

BARDACH, E. and L. PUGLEARESI (1977) "The environmental impact statement vs. the real world." Public Interest 49 (November).

BEER, S. (1979) "In search of a new public philosophy," in A. King (ed.) The New American Political System. Washington, DC: American Enterprise Institute.

CALDWELL, L. (1964) "Biopolitics: science, ethics, and public policy." Yale Review 54 (October): 1-16.

CATTON, W. Jr. and R. DUNLAP (1980) "New ecological paradigm for postexuberant society." American Behavioral Scientist 24, 1: 15-47.

COHEN, B. (1981) "High level radioactive waste." Natural Resources Journal 21 (October): 703-721.

Council on Environmental Quality [CEQ] Environmental Protection Agency. Department of Energy, and U.S. Department of Agriculture (1980) Public Opinion on Environmental Issues. Washington, DC: Government Printing Office.

DALY, H. (1979) "Entropy, growth and the political economy of scarcity," in V. Kerry Smith (ed.) Scarcity and Growth Reconsidered. Baltimore: Johns Hopkins University Press.

DAVIES, J. and B. DAVIES (1975) The Politics of Pollution. Indianapolis: Pegasus.

DONIGER, D. (1978) The Laws and Policy of Toxic Substances Control: A Case Study of Vinyl Chloride. Baltimore: Johns Hopkins University Press.

DOUGLAS, P. (1973) "Coastal zone management— a new approach in California." Coastal Zone Management Journal 1, 3: 1-25.

DREYFUS, D. and H. INGRAM (1976) "The national environmental policy act: a view

DUNLAP, R. and K. VAN LIERE (1977) "Further evidence of declining public concern with environmental problems: a research note." Western Sociological Review 8: 109-112.

DUNLAP, T. (1981) Scientists, Citizens and Public Policy. Princeton, NJ: Princeton University Press.

FAIRFAX, S. and H. INGRAM (1980) "The U.S. experience," in T. O'Riordan and W. Sewell (eds.) Environmental Review and Project Appraisal. New York: John Wiley.

GEORGESCU-ROEGEN, N. (1979) "Comments on papers by Daly and Stiglitz," in Kerry Smith (ed.) Scarcity and Growth Reconsidered. Baltimore: Johns Hopkins University Press.

GODWIN, R. R. and H. INGRAM (1980) "Single issues: their impact on politics," pp. 279-298 in H. Ingram and D. Mann (eds.) Why Policies Succeed or Fail. Beverly Hills, CA: Sage.

GREGG, F. (1982) Interview. Tucson, Arizona, June 19.

HARRINGTON, W. (1981) "The Endangered Species Act and the search for balance." Natural Resources Journal 21 (January): 71-92.

HARRIS, L. (1981) Testimony before the Subcommittee on Health and the Environment, Energy and Commerce Committee, U.S. House of Representatives, Washington, D.C. (October 15).

INGRAM, H. and S. ULLERY (1980) "Policy innovation and institutional fragmentation." Policy Studies Journal 8, 5.

———(1977) "Public participation in environmental decision-making: substance or illusion," in J. Coppick and W. Sewell (eds.) Public Participation in Planning. New York: John Wiley.

KNEESE, A. and C. SCHULTZE (1975) Pollution, Prices and Public Policy. Washington, DC: Brookings Institution.

LIROFF, R. (1976) EPA and Its Aftermath: A National Policy for the Environment. Bloomington: University of Indiana Press.

MAJONE, G. (1976) "Choice among policy instruments for pollution control." Policy Analysis 4 (Fall): 589-614.

MARTIN, J. (1982) "The interrelationship of the Mineral Lands Leasing Act, the Wilderness Act and the Endangered Species Act: a conflict in search of a resolution." Environmental Law 12 (Winter).

MAZMANIAN, D. and J. NIENABER (1979) Can Organizations Change? Washington: DC: Brookings Institution.

McPHEE, J. (1971) Encounters with the archdruid. New York: Farrar, Strauss & Giroux.

NASH, R. (1976) Wilderness and the American Mind. Cambridge, MA: Harvard University Press.

National Academy of Sciences (1975) Decision-Making for Regulating Chemicals in the Environment. Washington, DC: National Academy of Science.

OPHULS, W. (1977) Ecology and the Politics of Scarcity. San Francisco: Freeman.

PARTRIDGE, E. (1981) Responsibilities to Future Generations: Environmental Ethics. Buffalo, NY: Prometheus.

RUSSELL, C. (1979) "What can we get from effluent charges?" Policy Analysis 5 (Spring): 155-180.

SCHULTZE, W., D. BROOKSHIRE, and T. SANDLER (1981) "The social rate of discount for nuclear waste storage: economics or ethics." Natural Resources Journal 21 (October: 811-832.

STEWART, R. (1978) "Judging the imponderables in environmental policy: judicial review under the Clean Air Act," in A. Friedlander (ed.) Approaches to Controlling Air Pollution. Cambridge, MA: MIT Press.

STIGLITZ, J. E. (1979) "A neoclassical analysis of the economics of natural resources," in V. Kerry Smith (ed.) Scarcity and Growth Reconsidered. Baltimore: Johns Hopkins University Press.

Washington Post (1982) "Another by-product of the recession: states can't shoulder EPA's cleanup load." (May 20): A29.

WICHELMAN, A. (1976) "Administrative agency implementation of the National Environmental Policy Act of 1969: a conceptual framework for explaining differential response." Natural Resources Journal 16 (April): 264.

YOST, N. (1980) "Streamlining NEPA—an environmental success story." Boston College Environmental Affairs Law Review 9, 3: 507-512.

ZILE, Z. (1974) "A legislative political history of the Coastal Zone Management Act of 1972." Coastal Zone Management Journal 1, 3: 236.

8

TWO FACES OF SCARCITY:
BUREAUCRATIC CREATIVITY
AND CONSTRAINTS

JEANNE NIENABER

University of Arizona

It is the thesis of this study that most of the time we have things backwards when we think about scarcity and scarce resources. For instance, for those of us who believed that the energy crisis of the 1970s was real (that it had only to do with the physical, objective condition of worldwide oil supplies), imagine the chagrin caused by reading this recent newspaper item:

> **The U.S. Geological Survey has recently revised its estimates of the amount of oil remaining to be discovered in the United States—upward.**
>
> According to the USGS, 82.6 billion barrels of oil are sitting unearthed somewhere. . . . In 1975 the estimate was 82 billion barrels. Meanwhile, estimates of undiscovered natural gas have risen 23 percent over the 1975 figure to 598 trillion cubic feet (Shearer and Glenn, 1982: 4).

AUTHOR'S NOTE: *The research presented here is part of a larger study on which the author, together with Daniel McCool of the University of Arizona, is presently working. The author acknowledges the important contributions made by Dan McCool in the preparation of this chapter, and appreciates the flawless manuscript typing of Mary Sue McQuown.*

What the evolution of the energy crisis during the decade of the 1970s indicates for policy analysis is that we need to turn our common-sense notions of scarcity on their heads. That is, scarce resources—money, oil, trees, open space, and so on—do not exist apart from a social perception of them as goods in short supply. To put it another way, the sudden discovery (Eureka!) of a condition of scarcity in the United States is more the product of the pendulumlike swing between liberal and conservative political regimes than it is the natural reaction to a physical fact that has been documented and "scientifically" proven. This is simply to say that the public was on the right track in suspecting that the roots of the energy crisis were to be found as much in politics as in subsurface oil reserves. But this is not to say that one needs to subscribe, therefore, to a conspiratorial view of politics. Rather, it means that policy analysts and energy experts need to rediscover the importance of political beliefs and their role in defining resource-based and other crises.[1]

The present study utilizes such an approach. In this research, the linkages among society's resource base, its political orientation at given points in time, and the effects each of these has on bureaucratic behavior are examined. How are federal agencies affected by either perceived or real shortages, and how do they respond? Through an examination of seven resource-managing agencies over roughly a 100-year timespan, the data support the proposition that political/social factors are at least on an equal footing with measurable indicators of our collective wealth when it comes to accounting for changes in agency behavior and thus changes in governmental allocation of resources. The seven-agency sample consists of: the Army Corps of Engineers, the U.S. Forest Service, the Bureau of Reclamation, the National Park Service, the Bureau of Land Management, the Soil Conservation Service, and the U.S. Fish and Wildlife Service.

RESOURCE SCARCITY IN THE UNITED STATES: AN OVERVIEW

Putting the issue of resource depletion in a historical context is a useful undertaking, particularly if one tends toward an apocalyptic view of the future. It shows that our latest concern over energy shortages is nothing new; this society has lived with the fear of running out of something at least since the end of the Civil War. Leo Marx (1964) argues that even before 1865, writers like Hawthorne, Thoreau, Emerson, and Melville were eloquently expressing concern over the impending loss of the distinctive wilderness character of the American continent. This romantic reaction against the industrial revolution reached its apex in 1844, a full generation before the conservation movement, which expressed a generalized concern over resource depletion, began to affect governmental policy directly.

After the Civil War several concerns coalesced to produce the first of three periods during which resource issues dominated the public agenda. Beginning in about 1870, Americans began bumping up against limits. The result was that several significant actions were taken to ensure the wise use of the country's resources. Of this era Samuel Dana has written:

> Conservation as an organized movement, although not under that label, started in 1873, when the American Association for the Advancement of Science appointed a committee "to memorialize Congress and the several State legislatures upon the importance of promoting the cultivation of timber and the preservation of forests, and to recommend proper legislation for securing these objects." This action was motivated by fear of a future timber famine and by the conviction that such a famine could be averted only by governmental action [1958: 25].

America was concerned not only about timber, of course; the regulation and prudent use of water, land, fish, and wildlife also became objects of governmental policy during the progressive conservation era. For example, in 1871 Congress established the position of commissioner of fish and fisheries, whose duties would include "ascertaining whether any and what diminution in the number of food fishes of the coasts and lakes of the United States has taken place" (U.S. Congress, 1871: 594). In 1903 Congress enlarged the scope of the fish commissioner and created the Bureau of Fisheries with the responsibilities of conserving, protecting, and promoting the fishery resource. After several permutations along the way, the federal agencies now in existence and performing these functions are the U.S. Fish and Wildlife Service in the

Department of the Interior, and the Bureau of Commercial Fisheries in the Commerce Department.

Just one year after Congress acted to protect fish, it set aside the nation's first park in Yellowstone Valley. It was a 2.2-million-acre preserve, to be "withdrawn from settlement occupancy or sale" (U.S. Congress, 1872: 32-33). Several other national parks were created in the succeeding 25 years, and in 1906 Congress passed the Antiquities Act, which empowered the president to establish national monuments by proclamation and without explicit approval of Congress. By 1916, as the Progressive era drew to a close, there were 16 national parks and 21 national monuments in existence; in that same year Congress created the National Park Service to manage the park system. As of 1980, the agency was responsible for administering 323 separate park areas totaling some 72 million acres.

Altogether, four of the seven resource-managing agencies discussed in this research had their genesis during this era of scarcity: the Bureau of Reclamation in 1902, the Bureau of Fisheries in 1903, the U.S. Forest Service in 1905, and the National Park Service in 1916. Of the other three agencies, one was created long before this era (the Army Corps of Engineers, which boasts that it is able to trace its roots back to 1802 legislation), and two were the products of the second era of concern over scarce resources (the Soil Conservation Service, organized in 1935, and the Grazing Service in 1934, which became the Bureau of Land Management in 1946).

If we ask the question, "What resulted from a generation's concern with scarcity, with the closing of the American frontier and all that this implied?" the answer is clear: Concern about the possible overexploitation of our vast natural resource base led to government efforts to regulate and manage a portion of these resources. Inevitably, federal agencies were created to execute these broadly defined conservation policies.

Fears of dwindling supplies of trees, fish, wildlife, and water produced remarkable examples of resourcefulness. The conservation era was a creative and innovative period in which a permanent change in the balance of power between the public and private sectors was effected: What John Kenneth Galbraith would later call "the countervailing power" of the federal government had its genesis in this era. Some of the best minds of the country—people like Theodore Roosevelt, Stephen Mather, John Wesley Powell, John Muir, and Gifford Pinchot—were dedicated to the task of fashioning a national resource management program. One has only to read the chief forester's autobiography, *Breaking New Ground* (Pinchot, 1947), to appreciate both the native intelligence and the political understanding of these men.

One ought not assume from this discussion, however, that these conservation policies as a means of dealing with perceived shortages in essential goods were unanimously approved of by the American public. As will become clearer, scarcity can be used to justify both programs of governmental regulation and those that promote private enterprise. The historian Samuel Hays underscores this important point when he writes:

> Preservationists, for example, have cast the struggle to preserve areas from commercial development as a contest between private and public interest. But commercial development is just as much a public value as is preservation for recreation and wilderness areas. As a prominent irrigation leader complained during the fight over the dam in Dinosaur National Monument, "We are conservationists, too." Admittedly, one can choose between these values only with great difficulty, but to simplify the choice by invoking the mythology of the moral battle between public and private interest is to distort the issue. No such juggling of symbols can obliterate the fundamental conflict between preservation and development as perennial and competing public values [1958: 44-45].

The public outcry was great, for example, when President Grover Cleveland used his statutory powers in 1897 to more than double the existing national forest system. With just ten days left in office, Cleveland signed an executive order to set aside some 21 million acres of forests, an act that was praised by conservationists but which enraged many westerners, including a number of members of Congress. No one could have persuaded western timber interests that such an act was the only logical response to a perceived nationwide timber shortage, and few would have dared. The act, perhaps, looks less political today only because of the superior vision of hindsight. But surely the conflict over the proper response to scarcity was as heated at the turn of the century as it is in our own day.

America encountered scarcity a second time during the era of the Great Depression and the ensuing decade of the 1930s. Viewed from this perspective, Franklin D. Roosevelt's New Deal was in large part an attempt to deal with the various shortages and dislocations produced by an industrialized national economy that had virtually collapsed. What was most obviously in short supply from 1929 on was money and jobs; consequently, it appeared to be the economic system that was generating the most acute shortages throughout society. But underlying and certainly adding to the deterioration of the industrialized and urban sectors of the economy was the sad condition of much of the country's agricultural lands. The historian Ray Robbins summarizes the post-World War I situation and the 1920s like this:

> Even more tragic was the fact that the land was not used intelligently; it was exploited. Grazing lands were overgrazed and, in certain regions, actually plowed up in the hope that a crop of wheat might be obtained. With the end of the war came the agricultural depression. The submarginal wheat frontier came to an end. In the 'twenties, the High Plains of America presented a gloomy spectacle: abandoned homesteads everywhere, grazing lands in very poor condition, some beyond rehabilitation, and more significant still, the big stockmen gradually extending their influence as well as their fences over the public domain [1962: 411].

The drought years of the 1930s and the resultant dust bowl that characterized a large part of the west and midwest added more misery to an already dire situation. During this period, natural shortages of water and fertile land combined with shortages of jobs and money to create the worst depression yet experienced in this country.

The government's response to the various shortages was similar to that which occurred during the Progressive era. As everyone knows, with Roosevelt's landslide victory in 1932 the federal government stepped in to regulate the economy with a depth and breadth that far exceeded what was attempted during the progressive years. A number of new programs were enacted and dozens of new agencies created to stimulate and regulate the country's economic life.

The departments of both agriculture and the interior were central to the New Deal effort. If anyone besides Franklin Roosevelt epitomized a progressive and liberal way of thinking it was his secretary of the interior, Harold Ickes. Henry Wallace of the Department of Agriculture was not far behind. The creation of two new agencies, one housed in the Department of Agriculture and the other in the Department of the Interior, illustrate the manner in which the Roosevelt administration addressed deteriorating land conditions. In 1934 Congress passed the Taylor Grazing Act and with it created a new agency, the Grazing Service. The new political regime in Washington repudiated Hoover's Garfield Commission recommendations—to cede the remaining public domain lands to the states in which they lay—and instead allowed the Interior Department for the first time since 1897 to upgrade its grazing policies and to collect fees on the public domain. The act also established a permanent federal interest in these lands. The bill was introduced in Congress by Edward T. Taylor, who "had come to the House from Colorado in 1909 as an avowed enemy of Pinchotism" (Smith, 1966: 250), but who ended up supporting increased regulation of the livestock industry. In 1946, the Grazing Service was merged with the General Land Office to become the Bureau of Land Management.

The federal government had been involved in research on soil erosion since the 1920s. Most of the work was being conducted by a Department of Agriculture geologist named Hugh Bennett, who, with a $160,000 appropriation given him in 1928, set up a national program of erosion research (Smith, 1966: 248-249). When Harold Ickes became secretary of the interior he discovered Bennett's work and proceeded to set him up in the Interior Department as head of a new bureau, the Soil Erosion Service. Bennett's bureau was to function as part of the National Industrial Recovery Act; it would provide assistance to farmers for soil erosion control projects and create jobs for the unemployed through the Civilian Conservation Corps. In 1935 Congress passed the Soil Conservation Act, which formally created the Soil Conservation Service. With Bennett still as its director, the service was placed where Bennett preferred it to be—in the Agriculture Department. The philosophy underlying the new agency was that not so much through direct regulation or through federal ownership, but rather through technical assistance, education, and financial aid would the federal government make its impact felt on the conditions of the nation's rural economy.

Like the Progressive era, the New Deal was characterized by considerable experimentation and innovation. Public power projects were fashionable at the time, and so already existing agencies like the Corps of Engineers and the Bureau of Reclamation benefited from the prevailing liberal public philosophy. The Bureau of Reclamation, for instance, came back from an organizational slump in the 1920s so that by 1939 it was recharged with energy. FDR's New Deal, combined with some spectacular engineering feats, such as Hoover Dam, gave the agency a new lease on life.

Both the Bureau of Land Management and the Corps of Engineers were able to capitalize on the power-generating aspects of their activities. By 1939 hydroelectric power had become an important component of water resource development, and the budgets of the two agencies reflected this interest. Also, the corps was the prime beneficiary of the 1936 Flood Control Act, which established a national flood control policy and gave the Army engineers great authority to act in this new area of "national concern." By the end of the New Deal era, the corps was well on its way to becoming what Arthur Maass (1951) described in his classic study of the agency—the engineer consultants to and contractors for the U.S. Congress.

One of the clearest instances of organizational innovation occurred within the Forest Service during these years. In the early 1930s the agency turned its attention to the critical problem of soil erosion in the Great Plains states. Following another year of severe drought in 1934, the agency launched its Great Plains Shelterbelt Project. What this program envisioned was a huge windbreak of trees to be planted in a strip 100 miles wide and extending from Kansas to the Canadian border. By 1938 the chief of the Forest Service reported that "since 1935, and despite drought, grasshopper plagues, and dust storms, nearly 7,000 miles of new shelterbelts have been established" (U.S. Congress, House, 1938: 21). In 1942, after the service had planted over 18,000 miles of shelterbelts, the program was turned over to the Soil Conservation Service to administer.

World War II ended much of the experimentation with new domestic programs undertaken by the federal government by directing resources away from civilian/domestic policies and toward military expenditures.[2] However, the historical record prior to the outbreak of the war shows similar patterns with respect to these two eras of scarcity; under the two Roosevelts concern over scarce resources led to the expansion of the public sector. Liberals and progressives utilized widespread public concern to transfer hitherto privately controlled activities to the public domain and to create either a government-business partnership or a more strict regulatory relationship regarding resources in short supply. And, two world wars brought to a close both cycles of scarcity and public sector development.

TURNING THE TABLES: SCARCITY AND THE ADMINISTRATIVE STATE

The contemporary era of resource use, from the end of World War II to the present, differs significantly from the previous period. The factors impinging on our natural resource base changed markedly after the war; what remained constant was a generalized though episodic concern with resource depletion. The changed circumstances within which resource policies were debated were these: First, World War II, the ensuing Cold War, and the Korean conflict that began in 1950 were all great drains on the nation's resources. Unlike previous wars, the formal end to World War II did not mean an end to high military expenditures; there was little return to normalcy, and so our political economy had somehow to provide for both guns and butter. The 1952 report issued by the President's Materials Policy Commission, *Resources for Freedom*, addressed this issue.

Second among the changed circumstances was America's pattern of consumption. After the war the United States developed a "gargantuan and growing appetite" for materials of all kinds. In a 1958 article, the economist J. K. Galbraith pointed out that "our consumption of raw materials comes to about half that of the non-Communist lands, although we have but 10 percent of the population, and that since World

War I our consumption of most materials has exceeded that of all
mankind through all history before that conflict" (1958: 89-90). His
conclusion was that all discussions of resource use had to consider this
appetite as their point of departure.

A third changed circumstance had to do with the recognition that the
public sector—i.e., government—grew enormously during the first half
of the twentieth century. By 1950 there was firmly in place what has been
variously described as the administrative state, the organizational
society, the new industrial state, the welfare state, and so on. All these
labels were used to describe essentially the same phenomenon: that in
both the private and public sectors large, bureaucratic organizations
came to dominate the country's political, economic, and perhaps even
social life. The bureaucracy began to take on a little life of its own, and
so questions of resource use, after World War II, had to consider the
influential and frequently independent power center of the federal
bureaucracy.

The changed postwar conditions generally resulted in a change in the
nature of the dialogue over resource use and depletion: The issue
became less one of whether the government should regulate this or that
activity (although the rhetoric of the proper role of government lingers
on), and more the question of *degree*—i.e., how large or how constricted
a role should government have in determining resource allocation. This
is another way of pointing out that after the war entrenched interests
became even more entrenched.

This change became apparent when the more conservative Eisenhower administration followed the more liberal Truman regime into the
White House in 1953 and a Republican Congress returned to Washington. Republicans traditionally have favored a more circumscribed role
for government. According to Hugh Heclo, for instance, the Harding,
Coolidge, and Hoover administrations did much to dismantle the "big
government" that had developed as a result of the Progressive era and
the first World War. He writes:

Each of the two World Wars had a noticeable ratchet effect (a sharp
increase and then a decline to a higher than original level) on the trend of
government spending and employment. But whereas after World War I

Republican administrations did much to dismantle the instruments of
national government power accumulated during the war, the ratchet
effect was much larger after 1945 [1977: 15].

One reason for this was that a New Deal liberal, Harry Truman, managed to remain in the presidency until 1953, some eight years beyond the
end of the war. For another, it simply became politically impossible to
dismantle, wholesale, the executive establishment as it had developed
over the previous 50 years. Though the Republican victory in 1952 was a
"mandate for change" (Richardson, 1973: 81), the nature of the changes
proved to be much more selective, much more subtle, and much more
marginal than many Republicans would have liked.

Richardson documents the changes that occurred between the Truman and Eisenhower years in his book, *Dams, Parks, and Politics*
(1973). The Eisenhower victory promised several things: modification of
twenty years of federal domination of water and power development,
reduction in government spending in all areas, foreign and domestic,
dismantling of a significant portion of the federal government and
restoration of reliance on local and private initiative. (The promises
made in 1952 were remarkably similar to those voiced by Ronald
Reagan in the 1980 presidential election.) The Eisenhower policymakers
began their task in the natural resources area by making substantial
across-the-board cuts in agency budgets; even powerful bureaus like the
Bureau of Reclamation and the Corps of Engineers saw their budgets
cut substantially below the 1953 level. But "Western Republicans were
shocked" (Richardson 1973: 115). So it proved to be not long before a
good measure of selectivity entered the new administration's policymaking: "By 1955 the president called attention to the fact that Reclamation's and the Corps' projects had increased from thirty-nine to fifty"
(Richardson, 1973: 115).

The scarcity issue was defined in the 1950s as a "big government"
issue. That is, the policymakers in Washington wanted to see greater
economy, efficiency, and frugality on the part of the federal government. Many felt that the country was "on the road to socialism" with so
much federal intervention. What impact, then, did this new public
philosophy have on the federal bureaucracy, on the agencies administer-

ing natural resources programs? Richardson concludes that in the final
analysis the impact turned out to be very small:

> The intersection of the issues of preservation and development of resour-
> ces during that decade offered striking evidence against the American
> belief in the effectiveness of party turnover. In that time, there occurred
> on of the most impressive instances of partisan changeover in the nation's
> history. Yet an examination of federal resource policy in 1956 reveals no
> substantial alteration in procedure or substance from 1946 [1973: 201].

If one looks at the fortunes of the seven agencies whose origins are
discussed above, one finds support for Richardson's conclusions. Taking agency budget appropriations and permanent positions as indicators of agency size and vitality, Figures 8.1, 8.2, and 8.3 trace the size of
the seven organizations over a thirty-year timespan. The assumption is
that transformations in public policy and public philosophy, such as
those that occurred during the Truman-Eisenhower changing of the
guard, will be reflected in the fortunes of federal agencies. If the intent is
to cut down the size and scope of the federal bureaucracy, then agency
budgets and personnel numbers should drop, and vice versa. What the
figures show is that a significant decline in the budgets of the two largest
water resource agencies—the Army Corps of Engineers and the Bureau
of Reclamation—did occur between 1950 and 1954). (The budgets of the
other five agencies remained about the same, though the Forest Service
and the National Park Service show increases in 1954). According to
Richardson (1973: 115), the decline in the budgets of the Army Corps of
Engineers and the Bureau of Reclamation was caused by military spending for the Korean conflict under Truman and by the Republican
commitment, in 1953, to whittle down the size of the federal government. However, after 1955 agency budgets again began creeping
upward. Six of the seven agencies with the exception being the Bureau of
Reclamation were larger in 1960 than they were in 1950.[3] The data thus
support the thesis that the executive branch establishment developed
during this century into a virtually independent fourth branch of
government. More will be said about this important point as we look, in
the next section, at responses to the third cycle of scarcity in our history.

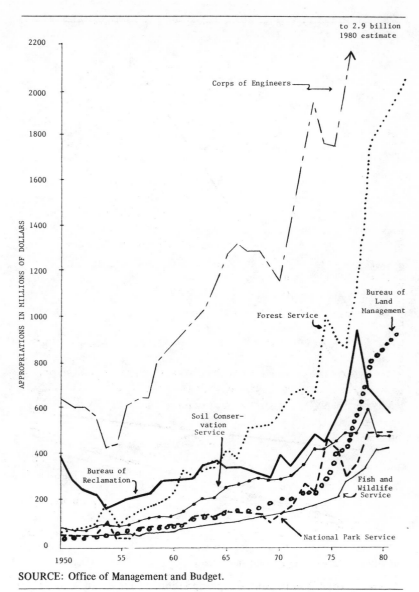

SOURCE: Office of Management and Budget.

Figure 1   Total Annual Budget Appropriations of Seven Agencies for the Years 1950-1980

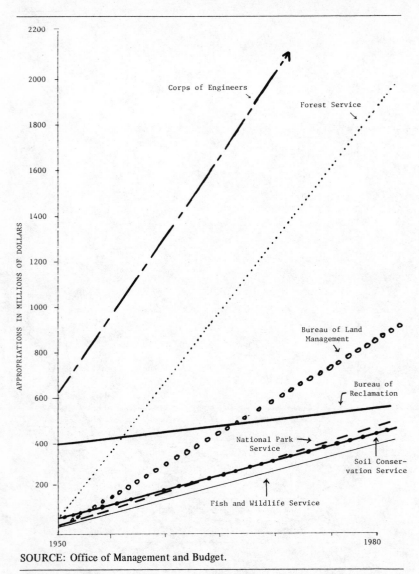

SOURCE: Office of Management and Budget.

Figure 2   Total Annual Budget Appropriations of the Seven Agencies for 1950 and 1980

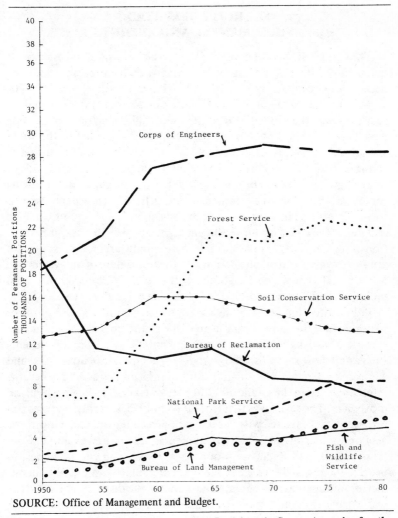

SOURCE: Office of Management and Budget.

Figure 3   Total Number of Permanent Positions in Seven Agencies for the Years 1950-1980 (in 5-year intervals)

SCARCITY REVISITED:
THE ENVIRONMENTAL AND ENERGY CRISES

The first great wave of concern with scarcity was national in scope: It had to do with the closing of the American frontier and with the necessity of recognizing certain spatial limits to our expansion. The second era can be described as Atlantic, or perhaps international, in scope: as was the United States, the industrialized nations of Europe were experiencing a collapse in their economies that led to the widespread unavailability of essentials and hence to certain fundamental changes in the political economies of these countries. The third cycle of scarcity is characterized by nothing less than a global vision: Worldwide ecological and economic interdependencies have been widely assumed to be the root causes for our present-day supply/demand imbalances and hence the cause of our recent energy shortages. But as our perception of the scope of the problem gets increasingly larger, the less able we are as a society to do much about it. A little fine tuning of the system this way or that appears to be about all that can be done about global pollution problems and declining worldwide energy reserves.

Public attention focused once again on environmental and resource issues during the latter years of the 1960s, and concern was directed toward what was labeled an "environmental crisis." Singular events such as offshore oil spills, smog-producing temperature inversions, and a presumed decline in the quality of life in this country suddenly became interconnected in the public mind. A pattern emerged. So did a political movement. The result was that from 1965 to 1975, several governmental programs were enacted with the intent of protecting or enhancing in one way or another the nation's environmental health. For example, Congress passed laws to clean up our lakes, rivers, and coastal zones; to protect endangered species; to maintain and improve air quality in our metropolitan areas; to regulate and monitor the disposal of hazardous wastes; and to create a national wilderness system. Many believed that the environmental movement's crowning achievement was the passage of the National Environmental Policy Act of 1969 (NEPA). NEPA primarily did two things; it set up the Environmental Protection Agency, and it required, for the first time, federal resource managers to consider environmental effects when contemplating particular actions. For obvious reasons, NEPA has been a controversial and widely studied piece of legislation.

We saw that public attention to any given issue is relatively short lived (Downs, 1972). As interest began to wane over environmental issues, a new, albeit related, problem came to the forefront of national attention. Uncertainty over the adequacy of energy supplies was dramatically felt by many Americans during the winter of 1973-1974, as motorists waited in long lines at local gasoline stations. Familiar themes were reiterated during this latest of crises: Were we running out of oil and other valuable energy resources? Had our natural resources been grossly mismanaged, possibly squandered away by short-sighted entrepreneurs now making policy in both the private and public sectors? Was it necessary to devise more rational policies for the coming worldwide era of frugality? One presidential ship of state was largely wrecked on the shoals of the energy crisis, and another was swept into office by the tide of popular sentiment favoring a political economy of conservatism—particularly as it pertained to the federal government. Scarcity and frugality became the key political concepts of the decade of the 1970s, although they were much more important at the symbolic (electoral) than at the substantive (operational) level of government.

What happened during the 1952-1953 changing of the guard was, by and large, repeated with the electorate's repudiation of the Carter administration in 1980 and its substitution of the avowedly more conservative Reagan administration. Both presidents (Carter and Reagan) grappled with the scarcity issue, but how each defined the issue, as well as how each translated these broad concerns into programmatic budget increases/decreases, differed considerably. Each, however, found himself operating at the margins.

Carter's approach to the energy crisis was to follow the lead of environmentalists and to take it at face value. The series of shortfalls in the supply of oil beginning around 1973 signified declining underground oil reserves. Like liberals before him he felt that the government should do something about the shortages, especially if they were indicative of a larger problem. Thus the energy issue became a high priority one for at least the first two years of his term. He sent several energy-related measures to Congress, but few were passed. Frustrated by congressional inaction (a result in part of the mishandling of Congress by the Carter staff), the president went on national television about halfway through his term to inform the public about the gravity of the crisis. The columnist Nicholas von Hoffman has summed up Carter's predicament:

> About energy Carter did the supposedly potent thing that presidents are supposed to do: he went over the head of Congress to tell America the present situation was "the moral equivalent of war." The response may have taught him that the only two real and enduring parties in American politics are the presidential versus the congressional. It's not an even contest at the moment, with Carter looking like Hapless Hanoverian George being dismembered by the House of Commons. Again, without patronage or party, a president must deal with Congress by showing he is president of all the people, as Lyndon Johnson used to say, but all of the people are none of the people. While Congress, with its allies in the bureaucracy and its close association with every known interest group, represents something more potent that all the people: it represents the organized people [1979: 4].

Nevertheless, certain changes were eked out in resource/energy policy during the Carter years. The Department of Energy came into being (though its future under Reagan at this point is uncertain), an informal moratorium on promoting nuclear power plant construction was put into effect, legislation decontrolling natural gas prices was passed, and federal expenditures for research and development into synfuels and so-called soft energy alternatives were signficantly increased. The administration was also publicly supportive of efforts at conserving scarce resources by cutting back on demand. Though most of these efforts were of a voluntary—some would say moralistic—nature (drive at 55 mph, turn down/up your thermostats, wear more sweaters, carpool, insulate the home), America's consumption of energy in fact went down dramatically during this period and the society has been more energy-conscious ever since.

How did federal resource managers fare between 1977 and 1981? In general, the government response to the scarcity issue this time around shows some interesting differences, and some similarities, compared to the two previous eras. There was not an enlargement of the public sector due to the creation of new federal agencies during these years, as happened in the past. One supposes that this was because the federal bureaucracy was already in place and presumably equipped to respond to a crisis of this nature. Carter did ask for, and get, a reorganization that resulted in the Department of Energy, and it is telling that the Reagan people are presently trying to dismantle even this relatively modest reshuffling of programs. But beyond that, little proliferation in the flora and fauna of the federal bureaucracy took place.

In terms of similarities, Carter did not mind spending federal money to search for solutions to resource-based problems. However, he differed from his Democratic predecessors (and Reagan differs from all of them) in his spending priorities. This is only to restate the point that, by 1975, a Roosevelt-like response had been largely ruled out as a feasible or appropriate policy. It has been replaced by a greater degree of selectivity on the part of our top policymakers. The Carter record on water resources development is illustrative of this. Breaking with liberal Democratic tradition, Carter entered the White House in 1977 committed to cutting out a good portion of the notorious water project "boondoggles." His objective was a major overhaul of federal water resources policy, so his staff began the task by compiling a list of some 19 public works projects, totaling $289 million, to be cut from the 1978 budget. An additional 320 projects were thought to be in need of further executive review. The action, labeled Carter's "hit list," immediately raised a storm of protest from western governors and powerful southern and western members of Congress. The Congress and the influential public works lobby geared up for battle. A month or so later, the president announced that fourteen additional projects would be reviewed, but also announced that he decided to reinstate funding for three Army Corps of Engineers projects that were on the original cut list. A month later the Carter staff created a revised list of 29 projects: full funding was restored for 8 projects, 5 were to be partially funded, and 14 projects were slated for termination.

By early May, 1977, the battle over water politics intensified. The Congress—traditionally a stronghold of support for water development projects in both boom time and bust—vehemently resisted the proposed cuts in its projects. For instance, the House Appropriations Subcommittee on Public Works voted to fund 17 of the original 18 projects targeted for abandonment. A month later the Senate compromised with Carter's policy by voting to cut out half of the original 18 projects. The struggle continued throughout the summer and fall of Carter's first year in office. By the fall the president's "redirected public works program" was in disarray. It was widely recognized that the president did not emerge from the confrontation a victor, so in an effort to salvage at least a portion of his original goal he signed a compromise public works bill amounting to $10.9 billion (which was nearly $80 million over his budget request). In a classic illustration of the triumph of politics over reason, Carter agreed to meet the Congress halfway by funding exactly half of the projects that were on the original hit list. The president called the bill a "precedent-setting first step." His former allies, the environmentalists, called it a sellout. And Congress stabbed the president in the back by promising to renew the fight during the next budget cycle to fund the projects, a mere nine of them, that went unfunded in 1978. Subsequent skirmishes between the Carter administration and Congress over public works showed little variation from what transpired in 1977.

Ronald Reagan's election to the presidency in 1980 promised yet another kind of response to the scarcity issue. As in 1952, many Americans believed that the federal government had gotten out of control, that inflation was eroding real income, and that Democrats had been on a spending spree for too long. It was thought that scarce resources were scarce because of excessive governmental meddling in the economy. The Reagan campaign thus promised the electorate that it would effect three major changes in governmental policy: It would increase spending for national defense, cut income taxes, and balance the budget for the first time in twelve years (Greider, 1981: 29). The theory that undergirded these programmatic objectives was supply-side economics—a theory espoused by conservative economists like Milton Friedman and Arthur Laffer and which challenged the New Deal, Keynesian orthodoxy.

Aided substantially by a Republican majority in the Senate, the new administration achieved some dramatic victories in its first year in office. It set out to reduce the entire federal budget by some $40 billion, and this was to be achieved without cutting defense spending. In the words of David Stockman, Reagan's director of the Office of Management and Budget, it was an enormous task:

"Do you have any idea what $40 billion means?" he said. "It means I've got to cut the highway program. It means I've got to cut milk-price supports. And Social Security benefits. And education and student loans. And manpower training and housing. It means I've got to shut down the synfuels programs and a lot of other programs" [Greider, 1981: 32].

Nevertheless, after several exhausting months in which the administration wrestled with Congress over the 1981 budget, the final reconciliation measure authorized $35 billion in budget reductions. No one denied that in political terms it was a major victory for Reagan and his administration. Yet for the OMB director it was merely the tip of the iceberg:

"It [the budget cuts] has really slowed down the momentum, but it hasn't stopped what you would call the excessive growth of the budget. Because the budget is not something you reconstruct each year. The budget is a sort of rolling history of decisions. All kinds of decisions, made five, ten, fifteen years ago, are coming back to bite us unexpectedly. Therefore, in my judgment, it will take three or four or five years to subdue it. Whether anyone can maintain the political momentum for that long, I don't know" [Greider, 1981: 51].

In the natural resources area, the Reagan administration is sympathetic to the interests that have coalesced around what has been labeled the "Sagebrush Rebellion." This primarily western-based movement seeks to reduce the federal presence in the policy areas of land-use, water, and energy development. Its principal bureaucratic target is the Bureau of Land Management (BLM), whose responsibilities and authority were significantly strengthened during the Carter years, but the other resource-managing agencies have also been affected by the change in priorities that the 1980 election signaled.

How has Reaganomics been translated into resource policy? Increases and decreases in the Bureau of Land Management's budget reflect the new conservative sentiment. As mentioned above, the BLM was given an organic act in 1976 that mandated that it pursue a multiple-use philosophy similar to that of the Forest Service. That is, the 417 million acres under bureau management (which makes it the federal government's largest land manager) are to be used for various purposes: livestock grazing, energy development, wilderness preservation, wildlife management, recreational use, and so on. Throughout the latter half of the 1970s the agency placed increasing emphasis on wilderness and recreation use; its wilderness inventory surveyed some 174 million acres for possible inclusion in the National Wilderness System. Of necessity, this emphasis meant reducing the traditional hegemony that ranchers have had over the bureau. Their reduced control has been the main impetus behind the rebellion.

Under the Reagan administration, particularly under Secretary of the Interior James Watt, a different set of values has been applied to BLM and other federal lands. There has been a shift away from wilderness and recreation and toward the increased development and production of energy resources. For instance, the largest line-item in the Bureau's proposed 1982 budget, Management of Lands and Resources, calls for an increase of $16.6 million to be used for an accelerated lease program of oil, gas, oil shale, and tar sands, and leases for the outer continental shelf lands (which are also under BLM administration). The total appropriation for these activities is estimated at $117.2 million (U.S. Congress, House, 1981, Part 9: 268-269). And while budget increases have been allowed in order to expedite the private development of energy resources on bureau lands, decreases have been authorized in its planning and environmental impact assessment programs. The 1982 budget, for example, calls for a $10 million reduction in outer continental shelf environmental studies (U.S. Congress, 1981, Pt. 8: 2, 13).

The deemphasis on agency planning, data collection, inventories, and environmental impact studies is part of a program designed to reduce what Secretary Watt has called "paralysis by analysis." Conversely, the increases in the agency's leasing programs are intended to facilitate that process with a minimum of bureacratic red tape. Watt explains: "We have studied too many things too long. We need to make America move" (U.S. Congress, 1981, Pt. 3: 10). Virtually every area that the Carter regime emphasized the present administration has cut.

This is the case for the other resource managing agencies as well. The budget for the Forest Service rose dramatically throughout the 1970s (see Figure 8.1). The 1982 budget maintains this high level of spending but alters program priorities: Funds for recreation and planning have been cut while timber production programs are either held at existing levels or increased. The agency's total proposed budget for 1982 amounts to $2.236 billion, and while this represents a 10 percent reduction from the previous year, it compares favorably with the proposed 14 percent reduction slated for the Department of Agriculture as a whole. Most of the 10 percent comes from the elimination of the Land and Water Conservation Fund, and from cuts in the Youth Conservation Corps and the Young Adult Conservation Corps—programs that aid the Forest Service in its reforestation and recreation projects (U.S. Congress, 1981, Pt. 10: 248).

The U.S. Fish and Wildlife Service may have been the hardest hit of the seven agencies discussed in this study. In discussing the 1982 budget before Congress, Secretary Watt made no bones about his intention to revamp the agency's priorities:

> There will be major—and I want to underline the word "major"—there will be major changes in the management of the Fish and Wildlife Service. . . . It [the Service] need not stop economic activity, economic growth, and job opportunities . In too many instances I believe that it has. . . . With the changes in budgetary requirements that I am requesting, we will get the attention of the management of the Fish and Wildlife System and new ways and techniques will be installed throughout that Service.
>
> I mean throughout, not just in Washington [U.S. Congress, 1981, Pt. 3: 7-9].

The administration's proposed budget called for reductions in resource management, habitat preservation, construction, and the endangered species program. Perhaps with the specter of the snail darter in mind, this latter program was particularly hard hit, losing a third of its total funding. The agency was not even able to convince the departmental budget-cutters that many of its programs contributed to economic growth and resources development, and so should not be cut. Clearly, the Reagan administration views the agency, as has many of its past critics, as not much more than an organizational nuisance, contributing only to the red tape in which the federal government is presently mired (U.S. Congress, 1981, Pt. 8: 100-111).

CONCLUSION

Two conclusions emerge from this research. First, as I mentioned at the outset, scarcity is as much a political issue as it is a physical fact of life. Its history strongly attests to this observation. Eras of scarcity appear, then gradually disappear, and appear again in an almost rhythmic fashion. There may be differences in terms of which resources are perceived to be in short supply at any given time, but beyond that the rhetoric and the governmental responses to these perceived shortages are strikingly similar from era to era. When liberals are at the helm of government they respond by enlarging the public sector, by imposing greater regulations on the economy, and by increasing governmental expenditures. Then it is the turn of the conservatives, who react to the perceived excesses and extravagances of their counterparts by reining in government, by "freeing" the private sector, and by loosening up supply by encouraging development. Society then discovers that it had more of X than it originally thought, estimates are revised upwards, and the cycle repeats itself after an appropriate amount of time has passed.

The second conclusion is that increased consumption and the short-term shortages that this (as well as other factors) produces have significantly contributed to the creation and the perpetuation of the administrative state. The bureaucratization of political life is, as many have observed, a characteristic of industrialized, urbanized nations. The development of the bureaucracy has not always been associated with the scarcity issue, but I think that the history of the issue, at least in this country, supports the argument that there is a causal relationship between public sector development and perceptions of a scarce or diminishing resource base. The establishment of federal agencies to manage natural resources during the Progressive and New Deal eras clearly points in this direction.

Furthermore, as every student of organizations since Weber has observed, once bureaucracies are in place they do not just wither away.

Herbert Kaufman's recent study of agency longevity finds that most agencies "continue indefinitely, whether or not they are needed or useful or even wanted" (1976: 1). Federal agencies, such as the seven analyzed in this study, tend to take on a life of their own; they become relatively impervious to the *Sturm und Drang* that may be raging in the political world outside their organizational boundaries. Richardson concluded his comparison of resource politics during the Truman-Eisenhower years by noting that resource policy was pretty much the same in both 1946 and 1956. The same conclusions could be drawn for the Carter-Reagan changeover. As the figures on agency budgets and personnel levels show, since 1950 the ups and downs have had little to do with electoral politics. With the interesting exception of the Bureau of Reclamation, the other six agencies show steady growth. Two agencies, the Army Corps of Engineers and the Forest Service, display startling growth, especially over the last 20 years. As a result, many liberals have joined with conservatives in a mutual search for ways and means to control further growth of the bureaucracy. Working through the budgetary process, the present administration has been more successful at this than have most. Yet even here, as Stockman and others see, the changes are in the margins.

The real question in any discussion of the interplay between politics and scarce resources has to do with whether we as a society are prudently managing our resources. It is hoped that the analysis presented here provides some illumination on this complex question. Of course, it would make the task of finding an answer to this question infinitely easier if we could say, with any confidence, what our resource base looked like and whether we were using it up at an excessive rate. The problem is that we do not know this. Estimates of resources—whether of underground oil and gas reserves, water, timber, uranium, or whatever—are notoriously unreliable.[4] Even the estimates are modified by political factors.

I think an honest answer to the question of whether or not we are heading for a resource-based catastrophe, as some scholars have prophesied, is that we do not know. Whether one likes it or not, there is evidence to support both a positive and a negative response to this question. it is like asking whether a glass is half-full or half-empty. The answer depends primarily on whether one is an optimist or a pessimist, and on whether or not one believes that scientific and technological discoveries will provide us with solutions to our current problems. As has been the case in the past, data can be supplied to support either scenario. And it is likely that in subsequent debates over resource use and its proper management projections of supply and demand will have the same marginal utility as they have had up until now.

NOTES

1. Resource policy is not the only issue area that is characterized by these fluctuations in public concern and attention. A recent newspaper article by Don Anderson, executive director of the National Association for the Southern Poor, is titled "Poverty as a fad: Society's mood governs attitude and awareness of nation's poor." It makes the same point that I do in this essay.

2. An extreme example of this shift in priorities is found in the transfer of the headquarters of the National Park Service form Washington, D.C., to Chicago literally to make more room in the nation's capitol for the war effort.

3. The Bureau of Reclamation has a pattern of development different from the other six agencies analyzed in this study. For several reasons, the bureau began a cycle of organizational decline, starting about 1950, from which it has never quite recovered. For an examination of the Bureau's history, see Stratton and Sirotkin (1959).

4. For a discussion of this issue, see Wildavsky and Tenenbaum (1981).

REFERENCES

DANA, S. T. (1958) "Pioneers and principles," pp. 24-33 in H. Jarrett (ed.) Perspectives on Conservation: Essays on America's Natural Resources. Baltimore: Johns Hopkins University Press.

DOWNS, A. (1972) "Up and down with ecology: the issue-attention cycle." The Public Interest 28 (Summer): 38-50.

GALBRAITH, J. K. (1967) The New Industrial State. New York: Signet.

——— (1958) "How much should a country consume?" pp. 89-99 in H. Jarrett (ed.) Perspectives on Conservation: Essays on America's Natural Resources. Baltimore: Johns Hopkins University Press.

GREIDER, W. (1981) "The education of David Stockman." The Atlantic 248, 6: 27-54.

HAYS, S. P. (1958) "The mythology of conservation," pp. 40-45 in H. Jarrett (ed.) Perspectives on Conservation: Essays on America's Natural Resources. Baltimore: Johns Hopkins University Press.

HECLO, H. (1977) A Government of Strangers: Executive Politics in Washington. Washington, DC: Brookings Institution.

KAUFMAN, H. (1976) Are Government Organizations Immortal? Washington, DC: Brookings Institution.

MAASS, A. (1951) Muddy Waters: The Army Engineers and the Nation's Rivers. Cambridge, MA: Harvard University Press.

MARX, L. (1964) The Machine in the Garden: Technology and the Pastoral Ideal in America. New York: Oxford University Press.

PINCHOT, G. (1947) Breaking New Ground. New York: Harcourt, Brace.

RICHARDSON, E. (1973) Dams, Parks and Politics: Resource Development in the Truman-Eisenhower Era. Lexington: University Press of Kentucky.

ROBBINS, R. (1962) Our Landed Heritage: The Public Domain, 1776-1936. Lincoln: University of Nebraska Press.

SHEARER, C. and M. GLENN (1982) "Here and now." Arizona Daily Wildcat (April 30): 4.

SMITH, F. E. (1966) The Politics of Conservation. New York: Harper Colophon.

STRATTON, O. and P. SIROTKIN (1959) The Echo Peak Controversy. University: University of Alabama Press.

U.S. Congress (1872) 42d Cong., 2d sess. Ch. 24: 32-33.

——— (1871) 41st Cong., 3d sess. Res. 22, 23: 594.

U.S. Congress, House, Committee on Appropriations (1981) Hearings before the Subcommittee on the Interior Department and Related Agencies, Appropriations for 1982. 97th Cong., 1st sess., Pts. 3, 8, 9, 10.

———(1938) Hearings before the Subcommittee on Agriculture, 75th Cong., 3d sess.

von HOFFMAN, N. (1979) "Winner take nothing." New York Review of Books 13 (August 4): 3-4.

WILDAVSKY, A. and E. TENENBAUM (1981) The Politics of Mistrust. Estimating American Oil and Gas Reserves. Beverly Hills, CA: Sage.

PART II
CASES IN RESOURCE POLICYMAKING

9

WATER SCARCITY AND
THE FRUGAL SUSTAINABLE STATE

MICHAEL W. BOWERS

DOROTHA M. BRADLEY

University of Arizona

The publication of William Ophuls's *Ecology and the Politics of Scarcity* (1977a) came on the heels of the oil embargo of 1973-1974 and the first popular realization in America that there were limits, both real and political, to the earth's resources. The work proved to be primarily a critique of the inadequacy of the American political system in functioning effectively in an era of ecological scarcity. According to Ophuls, the political system provides at best a series of distributive or "pork-barrel" policies by means of which political conflict is reduced by giving everyone a little more of the economic and resource pie. Continuing down this path requires ever-increasing resources and cannot be an acceptable solution to the problem of scarcity.

Ophuls proposes two possibilities for avoiding the social and economic collapse inherent in policies that ignore scarcity. The first of these is the *maximum feasible sustainable state*. This type of society "aims to exist in equilibrium with its environment, but . . . is still based on such fundamental 'modern' values as the dominance of man over nature, the primacy of material and other hedonistic wants, and so on." In this state man could continue, and even increase, his current demans on resources. The solution to ecological scarcity would be that the society would have to "squeeze" technologically all that it could from nature. But he warns that mankind would have to make a "Faustian bargain" by turning the direction of society over to a "priesthood of responsible technologists" and by rationalizing our social lives to accord with the imperatives of ecology and technology (Ophuls, 1977b: 162).

Given that all men are fallible, it is inconceivable to Ophuls that we should turn our fate over to a group of technical experts. Besides, even with the maximum feasible sustainable state in place, at some point in the future resources will once again become scarce. Therefore, any attempt to create such a society would prove self-defeating for it would only defer and greatly exacerbate the ultimate ecological crisis.

The second alternative available to society is the *frugal sustainable state*. Unlike the first alternative, this society would not set goals of maximizing the amounts of resources that will be used. Instead, it would seek the goal of "neither poverty nor abundance, but rather an ample sufficiency" (Ophuls, 1977a: 242). This system, a Jeffersonian polity with small autonomous units, would not have to be a threat to civil liberties of its members.

For Ophuls, the frugal sustainable state is far superior to the maximum feasible sustainable state in dealing with ecological scarcity. A frugal state, by definition ecologically viable, would provide greater individual freedom since there would be no need for a system that would "control all areas of life in order to make the system work"; it would also "demote the economic side of life to its proper place" by providing people with enough to allow them to promote their "individual self-development" (Ophuls, 1977b: 168).

Ophuls, of course, recognizes that "the frugal alternative is alien to our way of thinking and threatens many of the material and psychological vested interests we all have in the current order." Yet to wait for ecological duress is to invite disaster. Instead, he argues, we need to develop a social vision—"some kind of awareness of where we do and do not wish to go" in order to prevent the political system from inexorably grinding out outcomes nobody really wants (Ophuls, 1977b: 170). It is in this spirit that we have chosen to explore the question of water scarcity in the Southwest and to analyze two legislative attempts to ameliorate it within the state of Arizona.

WATER SCARCITY IN THE SOUTHWEST

It would be difficult to overstate the importance of water in the American Southwest. In this desert water is a life-giving property, and there is rarely too much of it. Concern about water scarcity in this area has a long history. Even pre-Columbian cultures of the area, no matter how well adapted to the desert environment, suffered greatly from the prolonged dry spells of the late thirteenth century.

The association of the availability of water with survival occurs at a nearly elemental level of feeling. Along with famine and pestilence, drought is "an age-old threat against which it is inconceivable to have too much security" (Ingram et al., 1982: 1). A Durango, Colorado, city councilman probably spoke for many Westerners when he said, "If you don't believe in the importance of water for this region, then there's nothing you can believe" (Pasztor, 1982: 27).

Where it is scarce, as in the arid Southwest, water takes on almost mystical qualities. It is the key to prosperity—water can make the deserts bloom or transform a dusty crossroads into a thriving metropolis (Ingram et al., 1982: I-3). Where having water can make so much difference, deciding who gets it and who does not assumes special importance. Yet despite, or more likely because of, its crucial and varied roles, water is often treated in very contradictory ways. Frequently it is seen as priceless—something "so precious it cannot be given a price [but] instead is expected to be made available to everyone practically free in whatever quantities a person can use" (Ingram et al., 1982: I-3). Access to water is regarded as a moral right and resistance to having to do with less is very strong (Ingram et al., 1982: III-1). That this is true even in arid areas where one might have expected that scarcity would be anticipated sometimes seems puzzling or even irrational. As Ingram et al. (1982: I-3) have observed, Arizona has historically treated its water as if water had some magical property so that "the more you gulp the more you get."

We will argue, however, that this apparent contradiction is not really irrational. Instead, it is a product of the different social visions inherent in the state's legal water doctrine, its economic history, the nature of the water resource itself, and people's perceptions of it. Ultimately, it must be recognized that the real conflict underlying the apparent contradictions is between different social visions. One encourages growth and development; the other is concerned about finite resource limits.

Water law in Arizona has frequently been described as fostering a "use it or lose it" approach to water. While this may be true in some ways, a closer look reveals the complexity of water rights in Arizona. For surface water prior appropriation doctrine essentially applies. "The law of prior appropriation, while maintaining the public character of all water, bases the right to use of the water upon the application of that water to some beneficial purpose" rather than upon the relation of water to the land which it borders or upon which it will be used (Mann, 1963: 30). A water right is also affected by time. "He who diverts water for beneficial use earliest has the better right and other rights of subsequent appropriators are subject to his." This is the familiar "first in time, first in right" aphorism (Mann, 1963: 30).

Prior to the passage of the Arizona Groundwater Management Act of 1980, the legal approach to groundwater was two-pronged. Water in underground channels is appropriable. Groundwater that oozes, seeps, or percolates through the ground has traditionally belonged to the overlying land owner and has been allocated for reasonable uses. Since groundwater physically oozes, seeps or percolates through the ground, it has been treated by the courts as a property right and allocated under the doctrine of "reasonable use." This protection of property rights has in turn served to encourage landowners to make the expenditures necessary for development.

To some economists, Arizona's actions regarding water "appear irrational because they are poorly related to the economic value of water in alternative uses" (Ingram et al., 1982: I-4). Water, as we have seen, is believed to be too special to allow it to be divided simply on the basis of money. Because water is viewed as a basic human right, it is considered practically immoral to charge much at all for it. Consequently, to economists using free-market models, water is priced too low and for this reason it is overused. There are no incentives to conserve when something is dirt cheap.

Historically, economic development, not conservation, has been the goal; water policy has consisted largely of providing subsidies, particularly for irrigation. These subsidies were believed necessary to encourage the development of the west and to aid in fulfilling the Jeffersonian agrarian ideal. As Dean Mann (1963: 36) reports:

> In the considered judgment of many observers, the state had virtually reached the limit of its agricultural development under the conditions existing at the beginning of the twentieth century. . . . The only possibility for increasing the water supply was to improve storage facilities. . . . Major structures required more capital than the local water-users could amass. The answer to their needs was supplied by the National Reclamation Act of 1902 [which provided] an unmitigated boon to the West.

Traditional water development within cities has followed a similar pattern. "The prevailing objective of water managers has been to supply constant, dependable, and cheap service to everyone without error or controversy" (Ingram et al., 1982: I-5)

Reflecting on these policies, one must conclude that they are not irrational. Rather, they represent conscious choices made to achieve certain aims and to meet the needs of certain beneficiaries. The inconsistency appears when a new generation of economists applies powerful free-market models to subsidy situations and concludes that water rights, water utility management practices, and the history of subsidies are irrational.

Public perceptions about water issues are mixed. Saarinen and Cooke (1971) found that residents of Tucson ranked "falling water table" seventh in a list of 16 environmental problems; less than half felt it was a serious problem. In a regional survey, two-thirds of the Arizonans surveyed said water shortages in Arizona were a serious problem, 22 percent said they were not very serious, and 6 percent said there was no problem (Dettloff and Laney, 1978). In a Tucson survey in which Buckley (1981) asked whether Tucson has a water shortage, half of the respondents said "some shortage" and 11 percent said "serious shortage." Another 11 percent felt that while there is presently no shortage there could be one eventually. Asked when the city's water supply might run out, 57 percent had no idea, 22 percent said within the next 25 years, 3 percent said within the next 10 years and 5 percent said within 1 year.

These contradictory responses are made more understandable by contrasting newspaper headlines—"Southern Arizona Running Dry"

(Meissner, 1981)— with a report on water resources in the Tucson Basin by the U.S. Geological Survey (Davidson, 1973). The *Arizona Daily Star* article begins: "Most people don't know it yet, but Southern Arizona has already started to run out of water. That's the grim news." The Geological Survey (Davidson, 1973: E1-E2), on the other hand, reports that the aquifer units underlying the Tucson basin "are more than 2,000 feet thick.... In most of the basin, the depth to water in 1966 was 50-100 feet below the land surface along the major streams to about 500 feet below the land surface in the eastern part of the basin." The amount of groundwater in storage "to a depth of 1,000 feet below the water table was about 52 million acre-feet."[1]

Clearly this is a lot of water. The problem comes when one asks how long it will last. Based on the 1965 consumptive use rates (85,000 acre-feet), the aquifer could provide water for 500 to 700 more years. Encouraging growth and increasing rates of use would, of course, shorten the period of water availability.

Traditionally, water scarcity has been viewed as a problem of timing or distribution (Pereira, 1973). Defining the problem this way has commonly led to engineering solutions such as building reservoirs and transbasin diversion projects. We find the two cases discussed below— the Tucson City Council's water rate increases and the passage of the Arizona Groundwater Management Act of 1980—particularly interesting because they break with this tradition.

THE TUCSON RATE HIKE CASE

With a population of approximately 500,000, the Tucson area is entirely dependent on groundwater. Although the Rillito and Santa Cruz Rivers transverse the area, they are generally dry during more than 300 days each year, and the flows generally last no more than 3 days. Because of the erratic occurrence and quantity of flow, streamflow is not suitable as a dependable source of water. Prior to 1940, however, the relatively small city (population 60,000) actually consumed less water than was recharged into the aquifers by drainage from the surrounding mountains and "infiltration through the riverbeds when the rivers [were] flowing" (Ingram et al., 1982: I-14).

With the unprecedented increases in population after that time, the residents of the Tucson basin began overdrafting or pumping more water than was naturally recharged in order to meet the needs of the moment. With an average per capita use of 204.6 gallons per day in 1973-1974, the area faced the prospect of drawing down its aquifers and eventually causing land subsidence in those areas where the land would sink into the depleted aquifer (Ingram et al., 1982: I-11). To avoid this, major pumpage was shifted from the aquifer directly underlying the city of Tucson to the Santa Cruz and Avra Valley subbasins.

As we have seen, the Tucson water department has historically tried to provide customers with as much water as they want at reasonable prices. It has not, conversely, been in the position of penalizing the most profligate users of that resource. As we would have expected, prior to 1976 the city responded to water demand by attempting to increase supplies even though that meant overdraft. In 1976, however, a newly elected city council proposed to alter radically this increased-supply philosophy to one of allocation based on market incentives.

By 1976, four of the city council's seven members were aligned with the "new politics Democrats." These individuals were primarily environmentalists who wanted to control growth in the beautiful desert surroundings and to open up the decision-making process at city hall to the public. In January of that year, the council was informed of serious problems in the city's future ability to provide water services. A consulting firm reported to the council that the costs of delivering water had begun to exceed revenues and that there would be a shortfall for 1976-1977 and 1977-1978. Furthermore, "serious capital improvement problems were forecast by 1981," and the city's chief hydrologist reported that the aquifers were falling at alarming rates (Ingram et al., 1982: I-22).

With very little discussion in the local press or with their constituents, the council forged ahead with plans to ameliorate the problem. The council adopted a plan that would create a voluntary program, known as "Waterless Wednesdays," that would ask residents not to use water on swimming pools or outside landscaping on Wednesdays during the summer months. The plan also contained a new rate structure that would raise the price of water to the consumer. These rates would be based on the amount of water used and the relative difficulty of delivering it. The latter was referred to as a "lift" charge and was based on the elevation of one's home within the Tucson basin. These proposals went into effect in July, 1976.

The economic impact of the new rates had not been correctly anticipated by the city staff nor had the political impact been correctly gauged by the council itself. Because June had been such an extremely hot and dry month (even by Tucson standards), the rate of water consumption was inordinately high. Therefore, while many saw their water bills "only" double, many others in the high lift zones received bills four times higher than those of the previous month (Ingram et al., 1982: I-41).

An immediate effort began to recall the four council members who had voted for the hike. In less than three months more than twice the signatures necessary were gathered for a recall election which would be held in January. The recall forces, especially the Citizens' Recall Committee, spent that time endorsing antihike candidates and campaigning against the incumbents. In a rather belated effort, the incumbents turned to the print and broadcast media ᴛo explain why the rate hikes were necessary.

Their efforts were in vain; all three of the incumbents (one had resigned) lost. Turnout was heavy. Ingram and her associates found that those whose rates were most increased tended to vote for recall (1982: I-48).

Interestingly, the new city council chose not to revoke the rate hikes. They found, as had the recall victims, that revenues would have to be increased through the use of rate hikes in order to continue the water delivery system. Unlike the previous council, however, they removed the lift charges and conducted both a massive public education campaign and several public hearings on the water issue prior to acting.

In a very limited sense, the actions of the Tucson City Council can be deemed a success. After the rate hike went into effect, per capita use of water in Tucson went from a high of 204.6 gallons per day in 1973-1974 to only 139.5 gallons per day in 1978-1979 (Ingram et al., 1982: I-11). In a more general sense, however, the actions of the council did not solve the underlying problem: overdraft of the underground aquifers. To the extent, then, that the council's policy provided only a bandage where a tourniquet was necessary, it was less than successful. In fact, such a partial solution may act to slow other reforms by giving Tucson's residents the feeling that they have achieved a solution.

REFORM OF ARIZONA WATER LAW

Unlike the Tucson rate hike, the 1980 attempt by the state of Arizona to manage its groundwater supplies more completely has been widely hailed as a success. It is, therefore, instructive to analyze these activities.

As noted, Arizona has for several years withdrawn water from ancient underground aquifers at a rate faster than it was replenished by recharge. To some extent, this was caused by what Garrett Hardin (1968) refers to as the "tragedy of the commons." Under Arizona law, water under the land belonged to whoever owned the land. Landowners were allowed to pump as much as they could put to reasonable use with their only cost being the energy required to bring the groundwater to the surface. It is not surprising, therefore, that attempts at groundwater reform were consistently blocked by agricultural and mining interests. Because agriculture consumed approximately 85 percent of the water used in Arizona, farmers were hesitant to open the doors to unknown reforms that might have consequences detrimental to their interests. In the 1970s, however, a series of events broke that barricade and culminated in the passage of the Arizona Groundwater Management Act of 1980.

One of these events was the threat by Secretary of the Interior Cecil Andrus in 1977 to delay and possibly eliminate the Central Arizona Project (CAP) if the state did not adopt a comprehensive, effective groundwater management code. The CAP, the most massive water project in U.S. history, was originally authorized in the 1940s and has long been seen in Arizona as the solution to its water worries. This project, when it eventually goes on line in 1989, will transfer water from the Colorado River to water-short central Arizona. In 1945, however, the Bureau of Reclamation threatened to withdraw its support of CAP unless the state adopted a method of reducing "agricultural consumption of groundwater" (Ingram et al., 1981: 9). The results of this threat were the Groundwater Act of 1945 and the Critical Groundwater Areas Code of 1948, neither of which provided effective groundwater management.

Since President Carter had unsuccessfully placed the CAP on his "hit list" of water projects earlier in his administration, it should have come as no surprise to Arizona that Secretary Andrus would revert to the original requirements of the CAP authorization. Apparently the state was surprised, however, since the dual threats from Carter's hit list and from Andrus acted as a spur to the development and passage of the 1980 act.

A second event spurring that passage came from the Arizona Supreme Court in the 1976 case, *Farmer's Investment Company (FICO)*

v. *Bettwy*. In that case, the courts held that groundwater underlying agricultural lands could not, under the 1948 Critical Groundwater Area Code, be transported for municipal or mining use. This decision threatened the groundwater supply for the city of Tucson and the future operations of five mines in the area. As a stop-gap measure, the Arizona legislature in 1977 amended the 1948 act to allow such transportation on a selective basis.

A third force that pushed for reform was the increasing urban population of the state. Whereas in the past agricultural interests could block groundwater reform in the state legislature, the 1970s saw an unprecedented influx of new residents into the state's two urban centers. Given that 75 percent of Arizona's 2.5 million residents lived in Phoenix and Tucson, agricultural interests knew that the day would not be far off when urban and industrial interests would be able to rule the allocation of water within the state and thus impose their own solutions on the agricultural users. Agricultural users, as a result, saw it in their interests to negotiate at this time rather than to wait until some future date when the urban users would hold the upper hand.

These three events led to the creation in 1977 of the Groundwater Management Commission. Given the need to have the commission's work accepted in all quarters, it was made up of legislators, water experts, and members of the urban, agricultural, and mining interests. The commission reported its recommendations in June 1979 and held statewide hearings on them. However, because the recommendations were "found to be too potentially damaging to agriculture," new negotiations were held among the three major user interests, and a resettlement was tentatively agreed upon (Ingram et al., 1981: 10). Once again, however, agricultural interests were unhappy with the settlement, and the impasse was not resolved until Governor Babbitt intervened personally and steered the negotiations over a six-month period.

On June 11, 1980, the governor convened a special session of the legislature and, after seven hours of debate, the Arizona Groundwater Management Act of 1980 was passed. Governor Babbitt then proceeded to sign the bill into law on the following day.[2]

Although the details of the act are not particularly important here, the act changed the nature of water resource use in Arizona from distribution to regulation. Whereas in the past landowners were allowed to pump all the water they could reasonably use, the groundwater act placed limits on pumpage. Under the provisions of the act, the state will be divided into "active management areas" or AMAs. The goal within all but one of the AMAs is to reach safe yield, or "a long-term balance between groundwater withdrawals and natural and artificial recharge" by the year 2025 (Johnson, 1980: 4). Note the strong similarity between this term and Ophuls's definition of the sustainable state.

In order to achieve safe yield, the groundwater act provides for mandatory conservation by all users of groundwater including urban, agricultural, and mining interests. Once the act is implemented, trade-offs will have to be made within each of the AMAs. For example, within the Tucson AMA, the Department of Water Resources will establish a rate of acceptable per capita use.[3] Should the city wish to build a golf course and use part of its water assets to water the greens, all other users will be forced to diminish their usage in order to meet the city's per capita quota. Similarly, increased numbers of new users will require present users in the area to cut back accordingly so that the per capita goal can be met. Additionally, the act allows for the "permanent withdrawal of irrigated lands, imposition of a use tax on all groundwater withdrawals, prohibition of development of subdivided property without an assured water supply, and augmentation programs to balance uses and supply in groundwater basins" (Ingram et al., 1981: 12).

Although the implementation of the act has only just begun, the act itself is highly praised as an example of effective resource management. Indeed, the Area Manager for the Tucson AMA, Michael McNulty, predicts that the TAMA will achieve safe yield by 1995, fully thirty years before the act's legal mandate requires it. The optimism of McNulty and others is good news. While it is true that the Arizona Groundwater Management Act of 1980 is innovative and deals directly with the aquifer overdraft issue, we remain unconvinced that it truly solves Arizona's water problems.

In the concluding sections we shall analyze the Tucson rate hike case and the Groundwater Management Act in light of Ophuls's call for a social vision to guide change. We shall begin with an analysis of conservation as an important guide to frugality and conclude with a consideration of similarities and differences between the two cases by examining them on the basis of other concerns of Ophuls.

IMPLICATIONS OF CONSERVATION
AS A GUIDE TO FRUGALITY

These two legislative attempts to change water management policy in Arizona support Ophuls's concern that achieving change requires a social vision about where we do and do not wish to go. Water policy particularly requires "viable preachment." Symbolic appeals and commonly held ideologies are especially crucial for the majority coalition building necessary for legislative action (Ingram et al., 1982: III-1).

Appeals for conservation based on fears of water scarcity seem to have been a common factor in both Arizona cases. Yet there has been little consensus historically about the meaning of the term "conservation." The two main branches of the conservation movement, the utilitarians and the preservationists, have disagreed about its implications for resource use. These differences plagued the movement in the early 1900s and continue today to weaken the impact of conservation as a guide to making difficult social and resource choices.

Gifford Pinchot, Chief U.S. Forester and one of Theodore Roosevelt's prominent lieutenants, was one of the first to articulate the utilitarian position. Pinchot argued that the first principle of conservation was development—using resources to benefit mankind (McConnell, 1965). The second principle was the prevention of waste. Resources should not be squandered, but, at the same time, failure to use resources was equally wasteful. The third principle of the utilitarians was that resource management should be for the many, not for the few. Resources were to be managed to provide "the greatest good for the greatest number for the longest time" (McConnell, 1965: 193).

The appeal of conservation is powerful, yet its shortcomings are evident in the Arizona examples. Ingram et al. (1982: III-5) have identified four ways in which the conservation ideology fails as a guide for deciding difficult natural resource questions. The two utilitarian weaknesses will be discussed first, followed by the two preservationist ones.

Utilitarian weaknesses. To begin with, utilitarian conservation systematically overemphasizes development. As a result, the basic desirability of programs is seldom questioned and negative social and environmental consequences are seldom fully taken into account.

In Tucson and in Arizona as a whole, decision makers' attitudes reflect this utilitarian overemphasis on development. Note that the most important reason for the Tucson rate hikes was financial, not water, conservation. The city needed to raise rates to pay for an extremely expensive program of capital improvements. Shaving the peak water usage delayed the need for these capital improvements and allowed time for revenues to build. "Conservation" as practiced here really provides for further development and use. "Development, however, will be staged to match the availability of funds, and water demand will be managed so as not to outstrip available water supplies" (Ingram et al., 1982: III-4). Prices were raised to increase the capital needed to develop. But marginal cost prices that might have more accurately signaled the true costs of water-consuming growth were not chosen. Instead, average cost pricing allowed Tucson rates to remain relatively low, a situation that "may actually encourage growth [and] generate pressures for further water development" (Ingram et al., 1982: III-4). Ironically, Tucson's widely publicized success at water conservation coupled with the state legislation emphasizing "safe yield" may purvey an image to investors and builders that there will be no water problem in the future (Ingram et al.. 1982: III-4, 5).

Second, utilitarian conservation fails to address successfully problems of equity. Water allocation decisions are particularly difficult, and exhortations to provide "the greatest good for the greatest number for the longest time" are not really helpful. The argument is that value choices about who benefits are being made without any guidance.

In the Tucson basin, for example, irrigated agriculture accounts for 56.7 percent of total aquifer pumpage while municipal users pump only 12.8 percent. The 1980 Groundwater Management Act envisions reduction of agricultural pumping over time, but some believe such a rich farming area should get more, not less, water. And in the meantime, Tucson's residents are urged to save water, while most of the overdraft is created by agriculture.

Other decisions are equally vulnerable to equity criticisms. Present and future water users in Tucson are forced to bear costs, while housing developers and their newcomer customers reap benefits (Ingram et al., 1982: III-8). Advertising campaigns such as "Beat the Peak" urge water customers to use less so that new water development can be delayed. Some doubt the efficacy or the equity of this approach, since the campaign would ultimately encourage further growth while delaying the costs that growth creates.

Preservationist weaknesses. The preservationist strand of the conservation movement was led by John Muir and George Perkins Marsh. Preservationists believe generally that nonuse of resources is often the highest purpose and that all wild things have an importance beyond their usefulness to man. Present resource use should be rationed to provide for a reasonable resource base for the future.

Although the main force of Arizona water development has clearly been utilitarian, the preservationists have been represented in both city council actions and the 1980 Groundwater Act. Restricting pumping to "safe yield" levels clearly evidences the preservationist outlook. And for the city council, this philosophy was reflected in water rates that penalized persons who planted "jungles" around their homes instead of natural desert vegetation or who built homes in the foothills that destroyed mountain vistas (Ingram et al., 1982: III-13).

The preservationist conservation strain has shortcomings, however. As Ingram and her associates persuasively argue, the preachment of nonuse may be useful as a strategy to sensitize the public to its natural surroundings and to inculcate the value of frugality. But in some situations it delivers few real benefits. When water is in a stream, for example, it may be reused numbers of times on its way to the ocean. Foregoing use at any particular point along the stream can be a sacrifice that makes no one better off, unless there is a shortage downstream and uses there would be of a higher value. Since groundwater is recharged, nonuse is rarely justified, and even mining ground water beyond natural replenishment levels may not necessarily be bad. "It can be argued that leaving the same amount of water in the aquifer forever is like leaving money in the bank forever, without collecting interest. Neither action produces any benefit" (Ingram et al., 1982: III-13).

A second shortcoming of preservationist conservation is a tendency to put ideology above political feasibility. According to preservationists, ecological balance is more important than are human preferences; therefore, preservationists should do what is right even if it is unpopular. This element of self-righteousness was evident in the surprising disregard by elected Tucson officials for political feasibility. Not only did city council members place serving their moral values above the job of mirroring their constituents; they also failed to communicate to voters their beliefs in a higher morality.

IMPLICATIONS FOR THE POLITICAL DIMENSION

Thus far, our analysis of two Arizona water policies has reaffirmed Ophuls's concern that attaining a frugal sustainable state would require a definite social vision to guide policymakers and to assist in building supportive publics. We have seen that appeals to conservation may be dysfunctional unless the inconsistencies inherent in its meaning can be resolved.

But there are also other implications from these two examples of water resource management that reflect Ophuls's concerns. Initially, two similarities can be noted. First, both cases illustrate the interlocking nature of energy and water and the reasons why one problem's solution may only exacerbate other problems. In the case of Arizona, the CAP has long been touted as the savior for the dry central Arizona desert. However, because the elevation of Tucson is higher than that of Phoenix, it will be necessary to use increased energy resources in order to pump the CAP water uphill and deliver it to the Tucson basin. Furthermore, increased energy will be needed once the water reaches central Arizona because treatment plants will be required to clean the "dirty" water of the Colorado River.

Similarly, Tucson has also experienced this interconnection of two problems. After the Arab oil embargo of 1973-1974 led to increased energy costs, Tucsonans began to economize by using evaporative or "swamp" coolers, rather than the more energy-consumptive refrigerated air-conditioning. Unfortunately, however, evaporative air-conditioning uses an "average of 200 gallons [of water] per day when in use" (Ingram et al., 1982: VI-2).

A second similarity between the two cases is that of leadership. In both cases members of the political structure provided leadership in order to get the new policies adopted. In the Tucson rate hike case, this leadership was provided by the four "new politics Democrats," and in the Arizona groundwater controversy, the responsibility for leadership was shouldered by Governor Babbitt. In both instances the leadership was effective at least in the limited sense of gaining legislative passage.

We have identified three differences between these two policymaking instances. The first of these is the difference between a market solution and a regulatory one. The Tucson rate hike involved a modified market solution designed to bring home to consumers some sense of the cost of water use in the desert. However, as Ophuls would have predicted, this solution was not a complete success. He argues that "rising prices are not likely to induce timely and appropriate responses to ecological scarcity, and they will certainly not preserve resources from exhaustion and degradation." The reason that the price mechanism is not likely to preserve resources, claims Ophuls, is that consumers make their decisions based on the more than simply price (Ophuls, 1977a: 169-170). For example, the sheer enjoyment provided by a lush lawn or a swimming pool often outweighs the economic costs of water to the consumer. Furthermore, consumers may be locked into high water consumption practices from which they cannot easily extract themselves due to prior investment decisions. For instance, the homeowner who has chosen an evaporative cooler prior to water rate hikes or who has moved into a home where the previous owner had cultivated a green lawn may find it too costly to install refrigerated air conditioning or to replace an existing lawn with desert landscaping. Additionally, such rate hikes would lead to selective effects and result in inequities.

Conversely, the Groundwater Management Act embodies a regulatory approach of which Ophuls apparently would approve. Indeed, in its attempt to create an equilibrium between water demand and water supply without engaging in overdraft, the act seems to match Ophuls's definition of the sustainable state. We must, says Ophuls, "restrain individual self-seeking and legislate social temperance." In order to do this, the state would have to limit individual access to certain resources but would not necessarily obtain "dictatorial control" over one's everyday life (Ophuls, 1977a: 155-156).

A second major difference between the two policies is the area of political acceptability and public awareness. As we have seen in the Tuscon rate hike case, very little concern was expressed by the majority of the council over the acceptability of their proposals. For the most part, the public was left in the dark over the meaning of the plan. Very little space was given to the issue in the two local newspapers, and only a few public hearings were scheduled to warn residents of the forthcoming changes. Additionally, a $50,000 public education program was postponed until *after* the rate hikes had gone into effect. Such public education did not begin until the incumbents resurrected it to defend themselves from the recall. Even more important, however, was the fact that the council majority ignored the pleas of the "godfather" of the "new politics Democrats" and their own mentor, Ron Asta, who urged them to act more slowly on the rate changes in order to gain political acceptability. Instead, they forged ahead believing that they were making tough but "right" choices (Ingram et al., 1982: I-30).

In the negotiations over the groundwater code, however, members of all the major user groups were encouraged to participate. Thus, not only were the members of the legislature and their water experts involved in the process (as had been the case in Tucson), but individuals representing the interests of mining, agricultural and urban users were also active participants. Not only was the Groundwater Management Study Commission carefully selected in an "attempt to legitimize whatever recommendations were made," but also recommendations that were made were subjected to intense scrutiny in multiple statewide hearings. When various portions were found to be unacceptable to agriculture, the commission met for three separate sets of negotiations (Ingram et al., 1981: 10). Because the act was such a precise balance of interests, the code includes a nonseverability clause, which provides that if one part of the act is found unconstitutional, the entire act must be declared unconstitutional.

A third area of distinction between the two policies is that of policy timing. This area can be seen dually as one of when the policy becomes effective and the amount of time given for implementation. The Tucson rate hikes were voted on in June and scheduled to go into effect the following month. Therefore, no time was given for softening the blow or allowing the water department to develop implementation strategies. In addition, the summer months are the peak periods of water use over the course of the year. Had they increased the rates during the less consumptive winter months and given consumers time to adjust to them, the public outcry would have been less vociferous. For instance, many of the incumbents found while campaigning to hold their seats in the January recall election that residents "would often refuse to believe" that the increased rates were still in effect (Ingram et al., 1982: I-44).

The Groundwater Management Act conversely provided members of the Department of Water Resources with a three-year period over which to adopt implementation strategies and promulgate regulations. The act, which was adopted in 1980, will not officially place limits on water use until January 1983. Additionally, the goal of safe yield does not have to be attained until the year 2025, giving the state 45 years to reach it. The result has been to soften the effects of the required frugality by providing incremental steps toward the goal rather than mandating one large lurch.

CONCLUSIONS

The usual perceptions of these two policy efforts are that the city rate hike was a failure, while the state groundwater act is a success. We would point out, however, that even though Ophuls might share this view for the reasons we have given, we remain doubtful.

It is clear that water rate increases, at least as they were undertaken by the 1976 Tucson City Council, are not the answer. Not only were they politically disastrous; they were only intended to postpone capital improvement costs while revenues grew for future improvements. Misperceived as a method to limit growth, council actions actually made further growth easier.

The 1980 Arizona Groundwater Management Act also provides no panacea. Four concerns are paramount. First, "safe yield" levels have yet to be set. Technical experts, not elected officials, will make these decisions. Yet the levels are the key to how much water will be left in the aquifers. In many respects the safe yield levels will provide the teeth for the new law or expose its lack of them.

Second, the act provides for an extensive buy-out of farmers' water rights to provide for urban growth. This is not a clear shift toward frugality. It looks very much like a continuation of past subsidy policies but with a different group of beneficiaries.

Third, implementation problems seem likely. Economic hard times have already forced state budget cutbacks, which mean less money, fewer staff, and delays in meeting implementation goals. Agriculture is expected to bear much of the cost of implementation, yet there are few incentives for farmers to participate. Moreover, success of the act is based on somewhat questionable assumptions: that the CAP will be completed and will provide the amounts of water anticipated, that the farmers will sell out, and that population projections for the future will prove accurate.

Finally, it is our view that the Arizona Groundwater Act, even if implemented, will not resolve the underlying conflict inherent in

Southerwestern water policy between development and finite rsource limits. By itself, the Act may even be self-defeating for precisely the same reason Ophuls gave for rejecting the maximum sustainable state. If growth limits are not directly addressed, eventually the urban numbers will again cause aquifer imbalance, and water limits will be reached.

Policy goals are seldom attainable in the real world and, as we have shown, trying to solve some problems creates others. Wildavsky (1980) argues that we should only ask whether the new problems are more tractable than are the previous ones. We are concerned that Tucson's future difficulties may be far worse than are its present water problems. State population projections anticipate 1.8 million people living in Tucson by 2035. On the basis of presently projected supplies, the aquifer will be stabilized only if residents reduce their per capita water use to 100 gallons per day. Quality of life may decline. As Ingram et al. conclude:

> At some point population growth will have to stop, and it may be more difficult to construct a steady-state economy with 1.8 million rather than .5 million. Should the overdraft continue, eventually the aquifer will be completely depleted. Locating additional surface supplies or dismantling the city would pose no simple problem. It will be a curious turn of events if water conservation in Tucson will leave the future worse off, but that seems a clear possibility [1982: III-10].

Ophuls (1977b: 170) has urged us to project social visions that "can warn us against some actions, even though they seem intuitively reasonable, and push us toward others, even though they are counterintuitive. . . . We can thus, in part at least, help to create the future we want." So to conclude, we would like to speculate on the counterintuitive.

If water conservation may leave the future worse off, what if we were to choose not to manage water, but merely to mine the aquifers and allocate the water as equitably as possible in the short run. Let people enjoy life in a desert oasis until the water runs out, then let them move on.

In a sense this alternative is unthinkable, yet the West is replete with gold and silver mining ghost towns. Even today, across the West the rush is on to build energy boom towns that we know will not outlast the nearby strippable coal or oil shale deposits. The economic and social dislocations that will result when these places are emptied will be massive, but they are apparently acceptable.

This social vision may not be attractive but it is nowhere written that people must continue to live in the middle of the Sonoran desert in perpetuity. At the very least it seems to us more useful to face these questions directly rather than to act as though we can continue forever to promote growth, balance the aquifer, and lead the "good life" all at the same time. With Ophuls, we hope that our highlighting of these various water-related social visions—historic and future—will at least continue to fuel the debate, for we agree that the issues are serious ones that merit wider attention.

NOTES

1. An acre-foot is the amount of water required to cover one acre of land to a depth of one foot. This is approximately 325,851 gallons.

2. In a 1982 case (*Chino Valley* v. *Prescott*) the Arizona Supreme Court held that the groundwater act was constitutional. The U.S. Supreme Court has refused to hear the case on appeal because it did not raise a substantial federal question.

3. The current rate of water use in the city of Tucson is approximately 150 gallons per person per day.

REFERENCES

BUCKLEY, K. E. (1981) "Water awareness in Tucson, Arizona—a pilot study." M.A. thesis, University of Arizona.

DAVIDSON, E. S. (1973) Geohydrology and Water Resources of the Tucson Basin, Arizona. Geological Survey Water Supply Paper 1939-E. Washington, DC: Government Printing Office.

DETTLOFF, J. A. and N. K. LANEY (1978) Nuclear Fuel Reprocessing Plant Siting, Attitudinal Survey Results. Fuel Cycle Facility Environmental Impact Topical Report. Draft.

HARDIN, G. (1968) "The tragedy of the commons." Science, 162: 1243-1248.

INGRAM, H. et al. (1982) "Saving water in a desert city." Office of Water Research and Technology.

——— (1981) "Arizona groundwater reform: The forces of change." Presented at the 17th annual conference of the American Water Resources Association, Atlanta, Georgia, October 4-8.

——— (1980) A Policy Approach to Political Representation: Lessons from the Four Corners States. Baltimore: Johns Hopkins University Press.

JOHNSON, J. W. (1980) Summary of the Arizona Groundwater Management Act. Monograph.

MANN, D. (1963) The Politics of Water in Arizona. Tucson: University of Arizona Press.

McCONNELL, G. (1965) "The conservation movement—past and present," in Ian Burton and Robert W. Kates (eds.) Readings in Resource Management and Conservation. Chicago: University of Chicago Press.

MEADOWS, D. H. et al. (1972) The Limits to Growth. New York: Universe.

MEISSNER, S. (1981) "Southern Arizona running dry." Arizona Daily Star (November 22): 1.

OPHULS, W. (1977a) Ecology and the Politics of Scarcity. San Francisco: Freeman.

——— (1977b) "The politics of the sustainable society," pp. 157-172 in Dennis Clark Pirages (ed.) The Sustainable Society: Implications for Limited Growth. New York: Praeger.

PASZTOR, A. (1982) "The pork-barrel politics of western water pose a dilemma for Reagan's budget plans." Wall Street Journal (February 11): 27.

PEREIRA, H. C. (1973) Land Use and Water Resources. Cambridge: Cambridge University Press.

SAARINEN, T. F. and R. U. COOKE (1971) "Public perception of environmental quality in Tucson, Arizona." Journal of the Arizona Academy of Science 6: 260-274.

WILDAVSKY, A. (1980) Speaking Truth to Power. Boston: Little, Brown.

10

THE POLITICS OF
COAL SEVERANCE TAXATION

UDAY C. DESAI
OSBIN L. ERVIN

Southern Illinois University at Carbondale

During the 1970s, coal severance taxation became a salient political issue, in large part due to the widespread perception of energy resources scarcity. The 1974 Arab oil embargo and the subsequent formation of the Organization of Petroleum Exporting Countries (OPEC) drew attention to the national security problems posed by the dependence on foreign oil and signaled the end to cheap energy. When attention then focused on increased development of domestic energy sources, coal was widely viewed as having the most potential, at least in the short run, for contributing to national energy sources. The result has been increased domestic coal production, increased attention to the value and exhaustability of the resource, and new or higher state taxes on coal severance.

The recent implementation of new or higher state taxes on coal severance has raised interesting questions about state utilization of this tax base. The intergovernmental and interregional conflict accompanying this issue may be illustrative of policy conflict over scarce resources more generally.

Issues in state utilization of the tax include the matters of rate, yield, and revenue use. Such matters are especially important because they are the fodder of political conflict and, furthermore, because the rapid rate of change in severance tax legislation has resulted in a great deal of conflicting information about these and similar aspects of the tax. The interregional and intergovernmental conflict, at times quite heated, has pitted East against West and the federal government against the western states. Much of the conflict concerns the appropriate rate of taxation and the issue of who pays and who benefits.

This chapter has two major parts. First, current goal severance tax policies and practices in major coal-producing states are discussed in light of the recent history and present rationales for the tax. Second, the resultant political conflict arising from state policies and practices is described and analyzed.

Much of the discussion and analysis in each of these parts focuses on ten states that utilize a coal severance tax.[1] Five of the states (Montana, Wyoming, Colorado, New Mexico, and North Dakota) are in the West. Four (Kentucky, Tennessee, Alabama, and Arkansas) are in the South and Southeast. The remaining state is Ohio.

COAL SEVERANCE TAXES IN SELECTED STATES

The taxation of mineral severance is not a recent innovation. Michigan enacted the first such tax in 1846, and Texas has had a severance tax on oil since 1907. However, the tax has attracted public attention and has been a focal point of political controversy only since the 1974 oil embargo. In the period since 1974, most major coal-producing states have either enacted severance taxes or substantially increased the rates on existing taxes. Some of the chronology of the postembargo severance taxation in the ten states of our study is indicated in Table 10.1.

Most of the criticism of coal severance taxation has been directed toward the western states. All five of the western states included in this analysis have enacted severance tax laws or steeply increased rates during the post-1974 period. In particular, the current severance tax laws of Montana, North Dakota, and Wyoming—the three states that have been most frequently criticized—were enacted in the mid-1970s. The current laws of Colorado and New Mexico were also passed in 1977.

The post-embargo passage or amendment of coal severance tax legislation has not been restricted to western states. Alabama, Kentucky, and Tennessee have also made important changes in their severance tax laws during this period. Nonetheless, the more dramatic enactments and rate increases have occurred in the West.

The four most important issues in describing current severance laws and policies of state governments are: (1) rationale of the tax, (2) tax rates, (3) revenue yield, and (4) distribution and use of revenues (Ervin et al., 1980).

RATIONALE FOR THE TAX

The legislation and related materials of states implementing a coal severance tax indicate that three reasons are used most frequently to justify the tax: (1) irretrievable loss of state wealth, (2) exportability of the tax burden, and (3) socioeconomic impacts of coal resource development. This last justification is the one to which most attention has been directed, and it will be given the most complete elaboration here.

The first rationale is that once coal is removed from the earth and consumed its value is irretrievably lost to the state. The idea of "natural heritage" is frequently applied (Starch, 1979), in which it is argued that no individual has the right to exploit resources for private property without compensating the rest of the community for using what is the natural heritage of all (Verrecchia, 1981).

A second rationale for a state severance tax on coal is that the tax burden would be borne by persons and organizations who are actually benefiting from the use of coal, wherever they may be located. The idea is that users in other states should compensate the state and community from which the coal is extracted, and an assumption is, of course, that the tax would be shifted from the producing company to the buyer or consumer. Thus an argument of energy-rich states is that the tax burden can and should be in large part exported to other states. Griffin and Shelton (1978) note that this rationale has played an important role in the severance tax debate and legislation of western states, and Gillis (1979) argues that this rationale is a major influence in state decisions about tax rates.

The rationale of the local socioeconomic impact has two dimensions—one concerned with immediate socioeconomic and fiscal dislocations and the other focused on long-term economic well-being.[2] Although these two aspects have a great deal in common, they are distinguishable and can be discussed separately.

TABLE 10.1 Chronology of Coal Severance Tax Legislation

	Alabama	Arkansas	Colorado	Kentucky	Montana	New Mexico	North Dakota	Ohio	Tennessee	Wyoming
1974						Increased rate to .5%			Increased rate to $.20 per ton	Increased rate to 3%
1975					Enacted current law, set rate at 30%		Enacted 1st law, set rate at $.50 per ton with CPI escalator			Increased rate to 4%
1976				Increased rate to current 4.5%						
1977	Enacted additional CST law, bringing rate to current 33.5%		Increased rate to $.60 per ton with CPI escalator			Changed to volume (per unit) tax. Set rate at $.38 per ton with CPI escalator	Increased rate to $.65 per ton with CPI escalator			Enacted additional levies, bringing tax to current 10.5%

1978	Expanded taxable base	
1979	Amended CST law to return 50% of revenues to local governments	Increased rate to $.85/ton with CPI escalator
1980		
1981		Increased rate to $.29 per ton, effective 7/1/82

The argument regarding short-term socioeconomic dislocations is that quickened coal extraction or processing activities increase employment opportunities and, consequently, result in rapid population growth in the host community. This new population of coal industry workers brings an increased demand for local public services and facilities. Workers and their families require housing, sewage and water services, leisure activities, and various social services. The local jurisdiction, the argument goes, frequently does not have the fiscal resources for meeting these demands. Consequently, there is a deterioration of local fiscal health and quality of local public services. This phenomenon of rapid population growth and associated socioeconomic and fiscal dislocation is sometimes characterized as a "boomtown" syndrome. Another concern expressed in this argument is that the coal extraction and processing activities themselves provide additional demands on services such as road maintenance, water supply, and fire protection.

The second dimension of the local impacts argument shows less concern about immediate needs and greater concern about the local economy that future generations will inherit. It is noted that the coal resources of the community are limited and nonrenewable, and the question raised is: What will be the economic base for provision of jobs and tax revenues when the resource is exhausted? The answer frequently advanced is that the community must begin early to invest in an infrastructure of public services, facilities, and amenities that will render the community attractive to other industries at some future time. Capital development in the areas of education, water and sewage facilities, transportation, and recreation are frequently emphasized.

Both of these dimensions of the local impacts argument proclaim a need for new or additional revenues in the coal community, and both posit severance taxation as an important source of such revenues.

These three arguments in justification of coal severance taxation— irretrievable loss of wealth, exportability of the burden, and local socioeconomic impacts—have become common in state legislative debate and in the defense of the tax in the face of challenges from coal-importing states, electric utility companies, and the federal government. However, this leaves unanswered the question of to what degree any of these justifications are actually implemented in tax policies and practices. This question will be addressed in the discussion of state distribution and use of severance tax revenues.

TABLE 10.2   Coal Severance Tax Rates, 1982

State	Base	Rate
Montana[a]	Value	30% of Gross (2.32 per ton)
Kentucky	Value	4.5% of Gross (1.19 per ton)
Wyoming[b]	Value	10.5% of Gross (1.16 per ton)
North Dakota	Volume	$1.00 per ton
New Mexico	Volume	$.835 per ton
Colorado	Volume	$.79 per ton
Alabama	Volume	$.335 per ton
Tennessee	Volume	$.20 per ton
Ohio	Volume	$.04 per ton
Arkansas	Volume	$.02 per ton

SOURCE: Current statutes of the respective states and telephone interviews with revenue officials in each state. The rates are effective as of May 1982.

a. For Montana, Kentucky, and Wyoming the value-based rate has also been calculated on a volume, or per-ton, basis and is indicated in parentheses. This was accomplished by means of data on total coal production and total coal severance tax revenues for 1981.

b. The 10.5% Wyoming rate does not include a 6.5% production tax that is levied in lieu of local property taxes. This tax is similar to a severance tax and is considered a state severance tax by some observers. It is not clear whether or not the 6.5% levy would be considered in application of a proposed 12.5% federal cap on state coal severance taxes. The 10.5% levy is the rate used for calculations throughout this chapter.

TAX RATES AND BASES

As in other taxes, the base and rate are the two major elements of a coal severance tax, and it is the interaction of these two elements that determines revenue yield and taxpayer burden. Severance tax rates and definitions of the taxable base have changed so frequently in coal-producing states that there is often confusion as to the actual level of taxation among the various states. Table 10.2 indicates the rates and bases effective in ten states in May 1982.[3]

As indicated in Table 10.2, three of the ten states—Montana, Wyoming, and Kentucky—use a value base, while the other seven states tax on the basis of volume. This raises an important issue in the comparison and discussion of state severance tax rates. Levy of the tax on the basis of tons produced is very straightforward, and the level of taxation is easily understood. In contrast, when the tax is levied on *values,* a decision must be made as to the point in the production process at which value is to be assessed and as to allowable exemptions. States using the value base vary in these decisions and, therefore, simple observation of tax rates may be misleading. For this reason, Table 10.2 shows the approximate unit, or volume, rates for the three states taxing on the basis of value.

The rate of the severance tax varies greatly across the ten states. The three states with value-based taxes have the highest rates on a per ton basis, with Montana's rate of $2.32 per ton being the highest. These three are followed closely by North Dakota, with a rate of $1.00 per ton. The other rates range from $.83 per ton (New Mexico) to $.02 per ton (Arkansas). The high rate of the Kentucky tax, when considered on a volume basis, reflects the high market price of Kentucky coal compared to the coal of western states. These data generally support the widely held perception that coal severance is taxed more heavily in the West than it is in the East, with Kentucky as an exception. A 1978 study of the total production tax burden imposed on coal companies by state and local governments also supports this propostion (West Virginia Research League, 1978). Montana and Wyoming ranked first and third among ten states studied; Pennsylvania ranked second.

The central question in the coal severance tax debate is whether the rates are too high, and further, whether the federal government should intervene to set a maximum coal severance tax rate. The first part of this question cannot be answered by the political scientist or policy analyst. The most one can do is provide information on the consequences of various tax rates; this is done in the next section of this chapter. The second part of the question—intervention of the federal government— is more amenable to treatment, and we shall argue that such intervention does not appear necessary or justifiable.

TAX YIELD

The yield of the coal severance tax reflects differences in rate and base across the various coal-producing states. Montana, Kentucky, and Wyoming all have large taxable bases (high coal production) and

TABLE 10.3   Yield of the Coal Severance Tax, FY 1981

State	Coal Severance Tax Revenue[a]	Total State Tax Revenue[b]	Coal Severance Taxes as % of Total State Tax Revenue
Montana	70,415,022	469,955,000	15.0
Wyoming	60,129,097	469,316,000	12.8
Kentucky	178,759,379	2,276,492,000	7.8
North Dakota	15,829,552	451,959,000	3.5
Colorado	10,641,794	1,431,940,000	0.7
New Mexico	14,373,693	1,202,376,000	1.2
Tennessee	1,955,561	1,956,674,000	>0.1
Alabama	7,598,931	2,026,038,000	0.4
Ohio	1,500,000	5,242,309,000	>0.1
Arkansas	3,984	1,189,014,000	>0.1

a. SOURCE: Telephone interviews with officials in each of the ten states.
b. SOURCE: U.S. Department of Commerce (1981).

comparatively high tax rates, and these three, as would be expected, show the highest coal severance tax yield among the ten states studied (see Table 10.3). The highest yield of revenues in FY 1981 was the $178,759,379 collected in Kentucky. Montana and Wyoming collected about $70 and $60 million, respectively. In contrast, Arkansas collected only a few thousand dollars. All of the western states included in the survey realized significant revenues from the tax.

The importance of the coal severance tax in state tax systems can be assessed by comparing this tax with total state tax collections. As Table 10.3 indicates, the coal severance tax is quite important to the tax structures of Montana and Wyoming—accounting for about 15 and 13 percent of state tax collections, respectively, and it accounts for about 7.8 and 3.5 percent of tax revenues in Kentucky and North Dakota, respectively. The remaining two western states, Colorado and New Mexico, derive about 1 percent of their tax revenues from the coal tax, and in the remaining four states (Tennessee, Alabama, Ohio, and Arkansas) the tax appears rather significant when viewed as a component of state tax structure.

DISTRIBUTION OF REVENUES

State distribution of coal severance tax revenues is pertinent to a number of issues in severance tax politics, but especially to the tax rationales advanced earlier. The question is, do states distribute and use severance tax revenues in ways that reflect state justification of the tax? The most revealing way to conceptualizing state distribution appears to be in terms of return of revenues to local producing jurisdictions as opposed to retention of the monies in the state treasury (see Table 10.4). There is a further important distinction in each of these categories. For monies retained for state use, the distinction is that of deposit in the general fund versus trust funds; for monies distributed to local coal-producing jurisdictions the question is that of allocation by formula versus allocation for specific local projects.

Tennessee returns virtually all coal severance tax revenues to its local coal-producing jurisdictions, while New Mexico and Ohio retain all revenues in the state treasury. The other seven states vary between these two extremes. The three states having the highest coal severance tax revenues—Kentucky, Montana, and Wyoming—return 3.7, 8.75, and 19.0 percent, respectively, to local jurisdictions, depositing the remainder in their state treasuries. The two remaining western states included in the analysis, North Dakota and Colorado, divide revenues about equally between state use and local distribution.

Regarding monies retained in the state treasury, the five western states place significant amounts in trust, while the five nonwestern states do not place any monies in such funds. Montana, Colorado, and New Mexico place half or more of these revenues in trust. Kentucky and Arkansas, on the other hand, place about 75 percent of state monies in the general fund.

A pattern also emerges with regard to formula versus project allocations to local jurisdictions. The four western states returning monies to local jurisdictions make heavy use of the project approach, while the other states that distribute severance tax revenues locally do so only by formula. One of the four western states, North Dakota, makes significant use of both the formula and project approaches.

These data suggest that, first, the five energy-rich western states included in the study place large amounts of severance tax revenues in trust, creating an accumulation of wealth that may in part compensate for the loss of wealth in energy resources. Second, the western states (with the exception of New Mexico) distribute significant amounts of money to local coal-producing jurisdictions for projects related to socioeconomic impact; they show little inclination to distribute monies

TABLE 10.4 State Distribution of Coal Severance Tax Revenues[a]

State	State Government				Local Coal-Producing Jurisdictions		
	General Funds	Trust Funds	Earmarked Funds	State Total	Formula Allocations	Project Grants	Local Total
Montana	19.0	60.0	12.25	91.25		8.75	8.75
Wyoming	19.0	23.8	38.20	81.00		19.0	19.00
Kentucky	74.6		21.70	96.30			3.70
North Dakota	30.0	15.0		45.00	20.0	35.0	55.00
Colorado		50.0		50.00		50.0	50.00
New Mexico		50.0	50.00	100.00			0.00
Tennessee	3.0			3.00	97.0		97.00
Alabama	34.0		6.00	40.00	60.0		60.00
Ohio			100.00	100.00			0.00
Arkansas	75.0			75.00	25.0		25.00

a. Disposition of coal severance tax revenues in terms of state accounting entities is, of course, mandated in the CST legislation of the particular state. However, utilization with respect to the categories in this table, which are thought to be the most meaningful, is not as clear cut and requires considerable research beyond study of state statutes. The data are based on state statutes, unpublished materials of state offices, and telephone interviews with state officials. One point about these figures is particularly noteworthy. That is, the data in the right half of the table reflect only monies directed toward *coal-producing* local jurisdictions for purposes related to coal development. Other monies represented by the numbers on the left side of the table may also be distributed to local governments, but without reference to coal production or coal development impacts.

TABLE 10.5   Percentage of the Coal Production of Ten Coal Severance Tax States Utilized by Steam-Electric Units (25 MW or greater), 1980

Producing State	1980 Calendar Year Production (tons of coal)[a]	1980 Distribution to Utilities (tons of coal)[b]	Percentage of Production Used by Utilities
Kentucky	150,143,973	112,379,800	74.8
Tennessee	10,569,395 (Est.)	7,643,000	72.3
Ohio	40,950,667	34,324,000	83.8
Alabama[c]	24,636,201	15,826,100	64.2
Arkansas[d]	224,655	10,900	4.9
Colorado	18,770,318	13,566,300	72.3
Wyoming[d]	71,445,178	68,800,500	96.3
Montana	29,837,728	27,924,700	93.6
North Dakota	17,009,453	15,404,800	90.6
New Mexico	19,480,820	16,973,400	87.1
Totals	383,068,388	312,853,500	81.7

a. SOURCE: Information obtained from state agencies.
b. SOURCE: Energy Information Administration (1981: 79-92).
c. 1980 calendar year production was obtained by averaging FY 1980 and 1981 production figures.
d. 1979 production figures were used.

for unrestricted local use. The 8.75 percent returned by Montana does, however, appear small considering the severe local impact thought to be associated with energy development in isolated western communities.

INTERGOVERNMENTAL AND INTERREGIONAL CONFLICT

Most (about 82 percent) of the coal produced in the United States is consumed by the electric utilities. Table 10.5 shows, for 1980, the total amount of coal produced and, of that, the amount used by the electric utilities for each of the ten major coal severance tax states.

Over 80 percent of the coal produced in the western states is sold to and burned by electric utilities in other parts of the country. It is the large percentage of coal exported by the western states to the other parts of the United States that has created intense interest in coal severance tax policy among the lawmakers and officials in the Midwest and East.

COAL SEVERANCE TAXATION AND THE COURTS

In early 1978 three utilities—Commonwealth Edison of Chicago, Detroit Edison, and the Lower Colorado River Authority in Texas— filed a suit against Montana challenging the state's 30 percent severance tax on coal. The tax was challenged principally on the grounds that it violated the commerce and supremacy clauses of the Constitution. The Montana trial court and the state supreme court upheld, by a vote of 6 to 3, the state's tax. The case was decided in Montana's favor on July 2, 1981, by the U.S. Supreme Court. In upholding the constitutionality of Montana's severance tax, the U.S. Supreme Court rejected the argument that the 30 percent severance tax levied by Montana was an unconstitutional burden on interstate commerce. The Court, in rejecting the challenge based on the supremacy clause, also pointed out that neither the federal Mineral Lands Leasing Act of 1920 nor the federal Powerplant and Industrial Fuel Use Act of 1978 prohibited or placed any limit on a severance tax levy (Beck, 1981). The Court, making it clear that questions about the appropriate rate of a severance tax should be resolved through the legislative process, wrote: "The appropriate level of taxation is essentially a matter for legislative and not judicial resolution" (Congressional Quarterly, 1981: 1238).

COAL SEVERANCE TAXATION AND CONGRESS

Coal severance taxation began attracting serious attention in Congress in 1980. In that year, S.2695 was introduced in the Senate by a bipartisan group of senators from coal-consuming states. The bill sought to limit to 12.5 percent all the severance taxes levied on "any coal mined or produced on Indian lands or lands owned by the Federal Government which is destined for shipment in interstate commerce for use in any powerplant or major fuelburning installation" (U.S. Congress, Senate, 1980a: 1-3). A similar bill, HR6625, was introduced in the House, also by a bipartisan group of representatives from coal-consuming states. The major difference between the House and Senate bills was that while the Senate bill limited state severance taxes levied on coal produced on federal or Indian lands, the House bill limited severance taxes on all coal, regardless of where it was mined. Relatively lengthy hearings were held by both houses. The House Interstate and Commerce Committee, after the hearings in late 1980, favorably

reported out a bill limiting state severance taxes to 12.5 percent of value
on any coal shipped in interstate commerce for use in powerplant or
major fuel burning installations (U.S. Congress, House, 1980a). However, the bill died on the House floor. In the Senate, S.2695 was never
reported out of committee, and in late 1980, the Senate Judiciary
Committee held hearings on Preemption of State Energy Policies, to
provide a sympathetic platform to opponents of the federal limit on
state coal severance taxes (U.S. Congress, Senate, 1980b).

A bill similar to HR6625 was introduced early in the 97th Congress.
Congressman Sam Gribbons (D-Fla.), introducing HR1313 in January
1981, proposed to limit state severance taxes on any coal shipped in
interstate commerce. Representative Tom Corcoran (R-Ill.) introduced
a bill (HR4841) in October 1981 that would have limited to 12.5 percent
state severance taxes on coal produced on federal lands. A similar bill
(S.178) was introduced in the Senate by Senator David Durenberger
(R-Minn.) in January 1981. Hearings on HR 1313 and on S.178 were
held in 1981 with no action taken. No hearings have been held on any of
the three bills in 1982, and no action is likely on any of them in this
Congress.

ACTORS IN THE CONFLICT

As the prices and tax revenues generated by the energy-rich states
from the production of fuels have increased, congressional interest in
the consequences of uneven natural distribution of energy resources
among the states has also increased. Members of Congress from the
energy-consuming states have formed the Northeast-Midwest Congressional Coalition to focus attention on the severance taxes levied by
energy-rich states. Its more than 200 members represent a broad bipartisan coalition of members from northeastern and midwestern energy-
consuming states. The Congressional Sunbelt Council, a coalition of
sunbelt, energy-rich states, was created to counter the Northeast-
Midwest Coalition, even though there is no unanimity of view on state
coal severance taxes among the energy-rich states. For example, Senator Lloyd Bentsen of Texas was the leadoff witness at the hearings on
S.2695, arguing in favor of a 12.5 percent federal cap on the coal
severance taxes.

The Western Governors' Policy Office (WESTPO), representing
governors of thirteen western states, has been very active in opposing

any federal cap on state coal severance taxes.[4] In 1981, WESTPO unanimously adopted resolutions opposing federal limitations on state severance taxes. Western governors also directed WESTPO to lobby actively against any federal cap on state severance taxes and to engage in public education activities concerning state severance taxes. Western governors and state officials have also been active in testifying before the congressional committee considering a cap on state coal severance taxes (U.S. Congress, House, 1980b; U.S. Congress, Senate, 1980a).

One of the major arguments used by the proponents of a federal limit on state coal severance taxes is that these taxes are passed on to the utility consumers in their states and, thus, that these consumers bear the brunt of these taxes. Thus, at least implicitly, reduction in state coal severance taxes will result in reduction of consumers' utility bills. However, it is noteworthy that consumer groups have shown little support for the effort to cap coal severance taxes.[5] Indeed, Robert McIntyre of Public Citizen (a Ralph Nader citizens' group) testified against the federal cap on the severance tax and called such a bill "a boondoggle for the coal companies" (U.S. Congress, House 1980b). Electric utilities, on the other hand, have been working aggressively to limit state coal severance taxes. In addition to challenging Montana's coal severance tax in the courts, they have been lobbying Congress very hard. An electric utility trade organization, Edison Electric Institute, "has hired a top-flight Washington law firm, O'Connor and Hannan, to lobby" (Congressional Quarterly, 1982: 320) for federal legislation. The coal-burning utilities have formed a group, National Coal Consumers Alliance, dedicated to imposing of a federal cap on coal severance taxes (Congressional Quarterly, 1982: 320). The utilitizes have joined hands with other groups, such as mayors and governors of coal-consuming states, in forming coalitions such as the National Coal Consumers Alliance Steering Committee to lobby for federal cap legislation (U.S. Congress, Senate, 1980a: 172). Utilities have also put pressure on the representatives and senators from their states to support federal legislation (Congressional Quarterly, 1982: 138). Individual utility companies have also been very active in testifying before the Congress in support of proposed federal cap legislation.[6]

Clearly, the major actors in the coal severance tax controversy favoring the federal cap include elected politicians from coal-consuming states and electric utilities. The major actors opposing the

federal cap include the officials from coal-producing states, particularly
the western states. Consumer and labor groups and coal companies
have been only minor actors. Therefore, the western coal-producing
states have been successful in fighting off federal legislation limiting
coal severance taxes. However, the battle has just begun. It promises to
be a long and bitter one.

ARGUMENTS IN THE CONFLICT

The major arguments reflect the justifications and rationales outlined above. The proponents of a federal cap on coal severance taxes
argue that a large transfer of money is taking place from energy-poor
states to energy-rich states. Energy-rich states received over $5.6 billion
in 1981 from state severance taxes and royalties on oil, gas, and coal
production (Congressional Quarterly, 1982: 319). Coal severance taxes
generated about $400 million of this $5.6 billion total. Even more
important than current severance tax receipts is the potential increase in
them due to oil and gas price decontrols. The Northeast-Midwest
Institute has estimated that "state severance tax revenues on oil alone
will be $128 billion between 1980 and 1990" (U.S. Congress, Senate,
1980a: 553). Comparable revenues are expected to be generated from
gas severance taxes as well. The price of coal is not expected to rise as
rapidly as are the prices of oil and gas and, therefore, coal severance tax
revenues are likely to be an even smaller percentage of total state
severance tax revenues in the future than they are today.

The billions of dollars collected by energy-rich states in fossil fuel
severance taxes and the potential for even more revenues collected from
fossil fuel severance taxes have raised fears of massive transfer of
income from energy-poor to energy rich states. The fear, at its extreme,
is that "we are witnessing the creation of a kind of United American
Emirates— a group of superstates, with unprecedented power to beggar
their neighbors in economic and fiscal terms" (U.S. Congress, Senate,
1980a: 554).

The western coal-producing states argue that their antagonists have
picked the wrong target. They point out that very little (only about 8
percent in 1980) of total fossil fuel severance tax revenues are accounted
for by coal (Cuciti et al., 1982: 14). They point out that in 1980 about 84
percent of the severance tax revenues were accounted for by oil and gas
(Cuciti et al., 1982: 14). Since the federal cap of 12.5 percent would
affect current rates of only a very few coal-producing states (Montana

and, possibly, Wyoming and North Dakota) it seems that the impact of such a law on total state severance tax revenues would be miniscule. A federal cap on state coal severance taxes is not likely to have any noticeable impact on the transfer of economic resources from energy-poor to energy-rich states, given current tax rates. However, it is a concern about the possibility of further state rate increases that has, in large part, prompted proposals for a federal cap.

Energy-poor states of the Midwest and Northeast have feared that the energy-rich states of the West and Southwest will be able to reduce their business and personal taxes and thereby lure industry away from the older industrial regions of the Midwest and Northeast (U.S. Congress, Senate, 1980a: 553). It is true that in 1981 seven energy-rich states—Alaska, Louisiana, Texas, Oklahoma, New Mexico, Montana, and Wyoming—received over 20 percent of their total tax collection from mineral severance taxes, with Alaska receiving 50 percent of its total state revenues from oil severance taxes. However, we found that there is no evidence on the extent of reduction in other state taxes in Montana and Wyoming, two main targets of a coal severance tax limit. There is also very little evidence available to substantiate the claim that low nonserverance tax rates in coal severance tax states have played a significant role in luring industry away from the Northeast-Midwest industrial regions.

It has been argued by the supporters of a federal cap on state coal severance taxes that utility customers in coal-consuming states are paying large sums of money to coal-producing states with high coal severance taxes. This argument assumes that the coal severance tax is passed on to the customer by the utility company and that the reduction in the tax will result in corresponding reduction in customer utility bills. Interestingly, many of the supporters of state coal severance taxes in the western states earlier used the same argument—that the coal severance tax is largely exported to consumers in other states—to justify levying or raising their coal severance tax. Understandably, the proponents of a federal limit on coal severance taxes have argued that since the tax is exported to other states, the voters in Montana or Wyoming are not likely to act as a brake on the tax rate (U.S. Congress, Senate, 1980a: 406-407).

The supporters of federal limitation also argue that Montana and Wyoming contain such a large percentage of the nation's low sulfur coal reserve that they may levy coal severance taxes at almost any level without having market forces acting as a corrective. There is also a suggestion by the proponents of federal limitations that Montana and Wyoming may act as a cartel and thus escape any discipline whatsoever of the marketplace on their coal severance tax levies (U.S. Congress, Senate, 1980a: 406-407). However, economic analysis has shown that "the possibilities of substantial exporting of severance taxes on coal exports to nonresidential consumers would be exceedingly slim" (Gillis, 1979: 63). In the short run, higher coal severance taxes would be borne by recipients of rents, in this case any quasi-rents accruing to labor and capital in the taxed industry, and resource rents received by owners of coalmining rights (Gillis, 1979: 63). In the long run, higher coal severance taxes would be "largely borne by resource rents" (Gillis, 1979: 63). Thus the tax would be exported only to the extent that these rents are received by out-of-state capital or resource owners. Even if Montana and Wyoming were to form a coal cartel "full exporting of taxes [is] not likely to be realized" (Gillis, 1979: 63).

The effect on consumers' utility bills is likely to be hardly significant even if the state coal severance tax were fully passed on to the consumer. Table 10.6 shows the effect of Montana's coal severance tax on an average monthly electric utility bill of a resident customer in major coal-importing states in the Midwest. Table 10.6 also shows the effect of other utility taxes on the resident customer's monthly bill in those states. Clearly, elimination of Montana's coal severance tax would at a maximum reduce a customer's electric bill by less than $4.00 per year in Minnesota, and by much less in Illinois, Iowa, and Wisconsin (State of Montana, n.d.: 12). It has also been shown that Montana and North Dakota coal severance taxes amount to between 0.2 and 2.2 percent of the average annual residential electric bill of consumers in other states (Conrad, 1981: A1-A2). Thus both the absolute average number of dollars paid by consumers in monthly electric bills for Montana or North Dakota coal severance taxes and the percentage of their bill going to pay for the coal severance taxes seem rather small. It must be added that the total amount of coal severance taxes do add up to millions of dollars per year. There has been no evidence presented, however, to indicate that savings from reduction in state coal severance taxes would indeed be passed on to consumers, and consumer groups have been skeptical of that claim (U.S. Senate, House, 1980b: 363-371).

TABLE 10.6   Utility Taxes, 1980

Taxpayer (Utility)	State and City Sales Taxes	State Income, Property and Other Taxes	Federal Taxes on Fuel and Utilities	Montana Severance Tax
Illinois (Commonwealth Ed.)	$1.72	$3.58	$1.85	15¢
Iowa (Interstate Power)	$1.03	$1.62	$1.98	06¢
Michigan (Detroit Edison)	$1.20	$1.52	$0.91	10¢
Minnesota (Northern States)	$1.23	$1.49	$1.69	31¢
Wisconsin (Wisconsin P&L)	$1.35	$1.17	$2.18	29¢

SOURCE: State of Montana (n.d.: 12).

Most of the legislation proposed in Congress to put a federal limit on state coal severance taxes has been restricted to coal mined on federal lands.[7] Senator Lloyd Bentsen (D-Texas), testifying at a hearing on S.2695, argued that federally owned coal in Montana and Wyoming "belongs to the people of San Antonio as well as to the people of Laramie and Wyoming" (U.S. Senate, Hearings on S.2695: 1980b 8).

The federal government owns considerable mineral rights in western coal-producing states, particularly in Montana and Wyoming. For instance, 75 percent of Montana's coal is federally owned. Thus legislation limting coal severance taxes on federally owned coal would be targeted on Montana and Wyoming in particular. Whether some states should be targeted for such a law because of historical bargains struck when they joined the union remains debatable. However, there seems to be increased recognition among Northeast-Midwest Coalition members that to reduce signficantly the transfer of wealth from energy-poor to energy-rich states would require a much broader attack on state energy taxes than would be represented by a 12.5 percent limit applied to federally owned coal (Congressional Quarterly, 1982: 323-324).

Proponents of a federal limit on state coal severance taxes, particularly electric utility companies and their consultants, have argued that

high severance taxes result in reduced production of much needed low
sulfur coal (U.S. Congress, Senate, 1980a: 406-408, 550). This is clearly
not in the national interest, it is argued, and is contrary to congressional
intent as expressed in the Powerplant and Industrial Fuel Use Act of
1978. Actual production figures for coal show an increase in the production of coal from 613 million short tons in 1970 to 835 million short tons
in 1980 (Cuciti et al., 1982: 16). Production of Montana coal has nearly
tripled since 1973 and has increased from 1.3 million tons in 1970 to an
estimated 34.5 million tons in 1981 (State of Montana, n.d.: 15). There
seems to be very little evidence that the coal severance taxes have
reduced either production or demand for low sulfur western coal.[8]
Indeed, there is a surplus of coal in the United States at the present time
(State of Montana, n.d.: 15).

The opponents of a federal limit on state coal severance taxes have
argued that such legislation would seriously undermine the federal
system. They argue that it would threaten the basic right of state
government to use a tax that it finds suitable to raise necessary revenues.
It would be "an ill-advised incursion into state taxing authority" to use a
tax (Muniz, 1981: 1). The proponents of federal limitation point out
that the legislation limiting coal severance taxes on federally owned coal
is strictly limited and does not unduly impinge on states' taxing authority. The constitutionality of federal limitation does not seem doubtful
since it was the Supreme Court itself that all but invited Congress to
resolve the issue of what is a reasonable coal severance tax (Beck and
Runyon, 1981).

SUMMARY AND CONCLUSION

Perception of energy resources scarcity has clearly had an impact on
state coal severance taxation, and both the perceptions and the changes
in state tax policy have acted as catalysts for a political issue of national
dimensions. The facts pertinent to the debate are not easily separated
from myth and misunderstanding, but they are available. States have
indeed significantly increased their taxation of coal severance in recent
years, and the rationale for increases has focused on tax exportability,
irretrievable loss of wealth, and local socioeconomic impacts. Evidence
on exportability is somewhat mixed. But data from the states do clearly
indicate state utilization of tax revenues for purposes related to the

latter two justifications: The states, particularly those in the West, return a great deal of the tax revenues to affected local governments and place other amounts in trust for the benefit of future generations. Regarding the magnitude of state revenues from the coal severance tax, the tax is an important revenue source in perhaps four states— Kentucky, North Dakota, Montana, and Wyoming. It is of little signficance in the others. State government revenues from coal severance taxation are very small compared to revenues from severance taxes on other minerals.

Issues in federal limitation on state coal severance taxes are both highly complex and highly emotional. Firm and objective data are hard to find. This is partly a result of an understandable proclivity of partisans in a policy debate to pick and choose data that support their particular positions. It is also partly a result of the highly complex nature of the issues involved. Computation of the cost of coal development to the local and state governments is very complex. The computation of the effect of different levels of coal severance taxes on coal production is equally difficult. And so is the computation of the extent to which the taxes are passed on to the consumers under different market conditions.

State sovereignty and federal incursion into state taxing authority are highly emotional issues. Energy-rich states beggaring their neighbors and profiteering at their expense are equally emotional issues not easily resolved by objective analysis. They are the stuff of political rhetoric. The issues in the coal severance tax debate have been joined. The arguments have been bitter at times. The western coal-producing states, feeling unfairly singled out and outnumbered, are fighting back hard. They have been successful, so far, in preventing any federal legislation getting to the floor of either house of Congress. But the battle of severance taxes has just begun, as the nation attempts to adjust to a painful transformation from an energy-abundant to an energy-scarce economy.

NOTES

1. These are the ten states identified as having a coal severance tax and actually collecting from the tax in a 1976 publication of the Council of State Governments

(Council of State Governments, 1976). However, several additional states do have coal severance tax laws, and a few others have provisions for taxing coal in ways closely approximating a severance tax. In the 1980 U.S. Senate Hearings, 17 states were identified as having a coal severance tax. We have chosen to restrict our discussion to the ten states identified by the Council largely because we have monitored developments in these states for the past three years.

2. The literature on socioeconomic and fiscal impacts of energy resources development has become voluminous in recent years, and no attempt will be made here to provide a representative bibliography. Some of the most illustrative and theoretically interesting papers in this literature are those by Nellis (1978), Baldwin et al. (1977), Ervin (1979), Leistritz et al. (1975), and Krebs (1975). Papers by the U.S. Department of Housing and Urban Development (1976) and Denise and Ervin (1979) attempt to summarize and synthesize some of the case studies in this literature.

3. Current information on tax rates was obtained by study of state statues and documents and updated and verified through telephone conversations with officials in each of the ten states. This approach was also used in collection of information on severance tax reveneues and revenue distribution.

4. Thirteen states are: Alaska, Arizona, Colorado, Idaho, Montana, Nebraska, Nevada, New Mexico, North Dakota, South Dakota, Utah, Washington, and Wyoming.

5. Michael Podhorzer, legislative director of Consumer Federation of America, testified in favor of HR6625, but his testimony emphasized the need for limiting severance taxes on oil and gas (U.S. Congress, Senate, 1980a: 187).

6. Electric utilities and related electricity providers formed the largest single group testifying in support of S.2695 (U.S. Congress, Senate, 1980a).

7. HR1313 and HR6625 are exceptions. They would put a federal coal severance tax cap of 12.5 percent on all coal regardless of where it is mined.

8. Ms. Sally H. Streiter, vice president of National Economic Research Associates, Inc., a consulting firm, conducted a study of the Montana coal severance tax for electric utility companies and testified for federal legislation to limit state coal severance tax. However, she gives no evidence that Montana's coal severance tax has reduced either the national production or demand for low sulfur coal (U.S. Congress, Senate, 1980a: 399-435). Also see Mr. Robert McIntyre's testimony in this regard (U.S. Senate, House, 1980b: 363-371).

REFERENCES

BALDWIN, B.T.E., J. E. METZGER, and E. J. STENEHJEM (1977) "Local socioeconomic impacts of coal development in the Midwest." Presented at the Fifth Annual Energy and Environment Conference, Cincinnati, Ohio, November.

BECK, R. and C. RUNYON (1981) "Montana's coal severance tax survives constitutional challenge." Coal Policy Review Series 81-2. Southern Illinois University, Carbondale: Coal Extraction & Utilization Research Center.

Congressional Quarterly Weekly Report (1982) "Severance taxes on energy seen widening gap between rich, poorer areas of nation." 40, 8: 317-324.

CONRAD, K. (1981) "Testimony before the Senate Subcommittee on Intergovernmental Relations on fiscal disparities, state energy taxation and tax competition." (August 31): Tables A1, A2. (mimeo).

Council of State Governments (1976) State Coal Severance Taxes and Distribution of Revenues. Lexington, KY: Council of State Governments.

CUCITI, P., H. GALPER, and R. LUCKE (1982) "State energy revenues: a potential intergovernmental problem." (unpublished)

DENISE, P. and O. ERVIN (1979) "Energy resources development and the local community: a secondary analysis of impacts and policy options," in Harold Wolensky (ed.) The Small City and Regional Community. Stevens Point: The University of Wisconsin Press.

Energy Information Administration, Department of Energy (1981) Energy Data Report: Cost and Quality of Fuels for Electric Utility Plants, 1980 Annual. Washington, DC: Government Printing Office.

ERVIN, O. L. (1979) "Local fiscal effects of coal resource development: a framework for analysis and management," in Robert Lawrence (ed.) New Dimensions to Energy Policy. Lexington, MA: D.C. Heath.

ERVIN, O. L., U. C. DESAI, and J. L. FOSTER (1981) Policy Issues in Coal Severance Taxation. Coal Policy Review Series 80-1. Carbondale: Southern Illinois University, Coal Extraction and Utilization Research Center.

GILLIS, M. (1979) "A tale of two minerals: severance taxes on energy resources in the U.S.." Growth and Change 10 (January): 55-71.

GRIFFIN, K. N. and R. W. SHELTON (1978) "Coal severance tax policies in the Rocky Mountain states." Policy Studies Journal 7 (Autumn): 29-40.

KREBS, G. (1975) "Technological and social impact assessment of resource extraction: the case of coal." Environment and Behavior 7 (September): 307-329.

LEISTRITZ, L. F., A. G. LEHOLM, and T. A. HERTZGAARD (1975) "Public sector implications of a coal gasification plant in Western North Dakota," pp. 493-500 in proceedings of the Fort Union Coal Field Symposium, Vol. 4. Billings: Eastern Montana College.

MUNIZ, F. (1981) "Written statement of Fred Muniz, secretary, New Mexico Taxation and Revenue Department: submitted for the record of the hearings of October 28 of the fossil and synthetic fuels subcommittee of the House Energy and Commerce Committee." (unpublished)

NELLIS, L. (1978) "What does energy development mean for Wyoming." Human Organization 33: 229-236.

State of Montana (n.d.) State Tax Fairness: Montana's Coal Tax in the Context of State Resource Taxation in our Federal System.

STARCH, K. E. (1979) Taxation, Mining, and the Severance Tax. Information Circular 8788. Washington, DC: U.S. Department of the Interior, Bureau of Mines.

U.S. Congress, House of Representatives (1980a) Committee on Interstate and Foreign Commerce. Limitation on Coal Severance Taxes. HR96-1527, part I to accompany HR6625, 96th Cong., 2d sess. December 4. Washington, DC: Government Printing Office.

U.S. Congress, House of Representatives (1980b). Hearing Before the Subcommittee on Energy and Power of the Committee on Interstate and Foreign Commerce on HR6625, HR6654 and HR7163. 96th Cong., 2d sess. Washington, DC: Government Printing Office.

U.S. Congress, Senate (1980a) Hearing Before the Committee on Energy and Natural Resources on S.2695. 96th Cong., 2d sess. Washington, DC: Government Printing Office.

U.S. Congress, Senate (1980b) "A bill to amend the Powerplant and Industrial Fuel Act of 1978 to further the objectives of national energy policy of conserving oil and natural gas through removing excessive burdens on production of coal." S.2695, 96th Cong., 2d sess. Washington, DC: Government Printing Office.

U.S. Department of Commerce, Bureau of the Census (1981) Quarterly Summary of State and Local Tax Revenue (October). Washington, DC: Government Printing Office.

U.S. Department of Housing and Urban Development (1976) Rapid Growth from energy Projects: Ideas for State and Local Action. Washington, DC: Department of Housing and Urban Development.

VERRECCHIA, STEPHEN A. (1981) Coal Severance Taxation: Issues and Perceptions Research Report. Carbondale: Southern Illinois University. (unpublished).

West Virginia Research League, Inc. (1978) A Comparison of State Tax Burdens Imposed Upon the Coal Industry in West Virginia and Selected States. (A report prepared for the Taxation Subcommittee of the Legislature's Joint Committee on Government and Finance).

11

THE SAGEBRUSH REBELLION:
UTILIZATION OF PUBLIC LANDS

ALLEN R. WILCOX

University of Nevada, Reno

In a nation whose imagery has shifted from resource abundance to resource scarcity, a predictable target of increased utilization is the land still managed by the federal government. Although millions of acres acquired by the United States through purchase and conquest have been transferred to state and local governments or to private ownership, vast expanses still remain under federal jurisdiction. Most of the public lands, totaling some 636.4 million acres, lie west of the 100th meridian. Large percentages of the land mass in these western states are consequently subject to federal control, ranging from 29.2 percent in Washington to 89.5 percent in Alaska. The federal agencies charged with land management responsibilities are many, but the Bureau of Land Management (in the Department of Interior), with 254.9 million acres, and the U.S. Forest Service (in the Department of Agriculture), with 189.0 million acres, are easily the predominant land managers (Culhane, 1981).

The doctrine that has long governed the operations of the Forest Service, and more recently, the Bureau of Land Management (BLM) is that of multiple use (see the Multiple Use and Sustained Yield Act, 1960; the Classification and Multiple Use Act, 1969; the Federal Land Policy and Management Act, 1976). This approach to resource management is concisely summarized by Culhane (1981: 126).

> The philosophy of multiple use—and it is a philosophy, not a precise management formula—is that any use should be carried out to minimize interference with other uses of the same area and, if possible, to complement those other uses. In economists' terms, the goal is to minimize external diseconomies of the use and maximize the use's external economies (net benefits), even if the cost of producing the primary output is increased. The concept of sustained yield reinforces this approach to multiple use; sustained yield is the long-run result of multiple-use management. The optimal level of a use is the highest level sustainable in the long run that does not diminish (and ideally increases) the sustained yield of other resources.

Appropriate uses identified under this doctrine include outdoor recreation, range, timber, watershed, fish and wildlife, mining, and wilderness (see Dana and Fairfax, 1980, for a guide to the relevant literature).

The doctrine, although somewhat vague, is far from meaningless (Culsimple matter of bureaucratic routine. Uses often conflict in ways that are not easy to accommodate. In particular, conflict is often itense over the designation of additional wilderness areas, for other forms of multiple use are typically completely incompatible with wilderness preservation.

This conflict epitomizes the changes in public lands politics brought about by the environmental movement in the United States. Environmentalism has contributed an additional dimension to the traditional orientation of the earlier conservation movement. The distinction is one of emphasis: "Conservationists worry about a depletion of resources that would affect human consumption; and environmentalists worry about the future of the biosphere, including the human race" (Culhane, 1981: 9).

Despite their differences, both conservationists and environmentalists face common antagonists. Traditional economic interests, particularly the lumber industry on Forest Service lands and the cattlemen on BLM territory, have reacted strongly to restrictions that they perceive to threaten their livelihood. The recent "energy crisis" and the less publicized "minerals crisis" have created new and intense pressures. The scarcity of resources, both nationally and internationally, has fueled efforts to extract from the public lands known and suspected reserves of coal, oil and gas, and geothermal energy. In like fashion, a wide range of mineral deposits have become targets of extraction and exploration. In many cases, these are deposits that have become economically feasible targets only through the increased demand stimulated by the "new scarcity."

THE SAGEBRUSH REBELLION

All of these pressures on the public lands have become nationally salient throught the political movement that has become known as the Sagebrush Rebellion. The major impetus for the rebellion came from the state of Nevada, which, with 87 percent of its land under federal control, has long been a focal point of such political unrest. In 1979, Assembly Bill 413 laid claim to the state's BLM lands and proposed their transfer into state ownership. The sagebrush "rebels" followed this legislative action with both political and legal thrusts. The legal arguments are too complex to be summarized here, and the political moves approach the same level of complexity (see Cawley, 1981; for legal arguments see State of Nevada ex. rel. Nevada State Board of Agriculture v. United States of America et al., 1981).

It must be noted, however, that the rebellion spread to other western states, and strong emphasis has been placed on building a coalition spanning all states with large percentages of land under federal management. These efforts have achieved only mixed success, and it has become clear that the rebellion's attack on federal "domination" has far from unanimous support even within its strongest citadels (see Francis, 1982). Recent proposals by national leaders to dispose of federal property to reduce the national debt have led to further redrawing of the battle lines. Many supporters of the original rebellion, which stressed devolution of federal lands to the states, are not nearly as enthusiastic about "privitization." Among other issues, this latter process raises the possibility that outside private interests may outbid indigenous state interests.

THE CURRENT STUDY

The constellation of philosophies, interests, and forces sketched above make current public lands politics an intriguing and informative example of the complexity surrounding developing struggles over scarce resources. One opportunity to explore this complexity arises from a survey conducted in Nevada among individuals believed to be especially knowledgeable about public lands.[1] The particular focus of the analysis that follows is on the relationships between general attitudes toward resource scarcity and specific preferences concerning the utilization of public lands. The policy implications of these relationships will be explored in the concluding remarks.

METHODOLOGY

SAMPLING

The analysis that follows is based on the results of a 36-page mail questionnaire sent, in the summer of 1981, to over 1600 individuals throughout the state of Nevada. The sample was purposive: All respondents were selected because of their potential expertise in or knowledgeability about the management and use of Nevada's public lands. Three broad categories of respondents were: (1) individuals in legislative or administrative positions in federal, state, or local government; (2) individuals in relevant interest groups who either occupied key positions or were known to be active on public lands issues; and (3) the approximately 400 memebers of the state's task force reviewing the Draft Environmental Impact Statement for the deployment of the MX missile system.

Legislative officials included all members of the state legislature, the county commissions, and the city councils. Administrative personnel were taken from federal land management agencies (notably the BLM, Forest Service, and Soil Conservation Service), state agencies related to land use, city and county managers, school district superintendents, and local planning agencies. In addition, respondents were included from quasi-legislative bodies: grazing boards, multiple-use advisory boards, conservation district supervisors, and planning commissions.

Interest groups represented in the sample spanned the range of organizations contributing to the public lands debate: for example, chambers of commerce, the mining association, the cattlemen's association, the Sierra Club, and the Inter-Tribal Council. Finally, individuals were selected from two general lists—a compilation kept by BLM of individuals expressing interest in its activities and a list of the membership of the MX task force.

This last source of respondents, as well as several of the others, notably legislative bodies, provides one explanation for the rather low response rate (492 usable questionnaires or 30 percent). To respond, individuals typically had to see themselves as knowledgeable about the public lands. Many members of the task force had specialized knowledge relevant to MX review but were not necessarily acquainted with public lands issues in general. On that basis they "removed themselves" from the sample. Another reason for the response rate was the length of the survey instrument. Authorities on mail questionnaires unanimously counsel against excessive length, but in this case the need for comprehensiveness outweighed the risk of refusals.[2]

The nature of the original sample, as well as possible response biases, make generalizations to any population problematic. The survey results are probably roughly representative of the views of Nevadans knowledgeable about public lands, but interpretations based on this assumption must be treated carefully and regarded as tentative. Fortunately, the present analysis is concerned more with relationships among variables than with generalization to populations, and conclusions can therefore be treated with greater confidence.

SCALE CONSTRUCTION

The questionnaire included almost 300 forced-choice items, many of which are used in this analysis. Most of these items were subparts of general questions. Consequently, to make interpretations manageable as well as substantively more meaningful, the number of potential variables was reduced through scale construction. Similar items were first grouped together and then factor analyzed. Items that loaded highly on each resulting factor were subjected to reliability analysis using Cronbach's alpha coefficient as a criterion. The result is a much more parsimonious set of variables that can be used to explore relationships between general attitudes and views on the utilization of public lands.[3]

The single exception to this procedure is the variable used to operationalize attitudes toward the aims of the Sagebrush Rebellion. It was constructed from a set of three questions asking about preferred changes

TABLE 11.1   Scale Means and Midpoints

	Mean	Midpoint	High Value
Liberalism-Conservatism	2.08	3	liberal
Environmentalism	2.79	3	antienvironment
Technology	3.12	3	antienvironment
Growth	2.77	3	antienvironment
Tradeoffs	2.97	3	antienvironment
Waste Disposal	2.60	3	antienvironment
Rural Development Use	1.61	2	nonsupport
Multiple Use	1.46	2	nonsupport
Preservation Use	1.65	2	nonsupport
Sagebrush Rebellion	2.17	3	more federal

in the proportion of land in the state owned by the federal government, the state government, and the private sector. Respondents were placed in one of five categories: (1) less federal, more state and private; (2) less federal, more private but state same or less; (3) less federal, more state, but private same or less; (4) remain the same; (5) more federal.

FINDINGS

ENVIRONMENTAL ATTITUDES AND ATTITUDES TOWARD THE SAGEBRUSH REBELLION

Our first concern is to determine the extent to which attitudes toward the aims of the Sagebrush Rebellion are related to environmental attitudes generally and to overall political stance. Scales were created to measure liberalism and views about pollution and resource depletion, the benefits of technology, the effect of population growth, the problems of waste disposal, and the tradeoffs between economic and environmental values.[4] Table 11.1 indicates that the mean point for this sample is considerably to the right of the ideological middle of the road, but slightly on the proenvironmental side of the midpoint in four of the five general environmental scales. The group is well toward the less federal ownership side on attitudes toward the Sagebrush Rebellion.

We might expect positive attitudes toward the aims of the Sagebrush Rebellion to be highly related to general antienvironmental attitudes

TABLE 11.2 Correlations Among General Attitude Scales

	Libcon	Env	Tech	Growth	Trade	Waste
Liberalism- Conservatism[a]						
Environmentalism	−.62					
Technology	−.66	.81				
Growth	−.45	.79	.55			
Tradeoffs	−.58	.83	.81	.54		
Waste Disposal	−.25	.53	.37	.48	.36	
Sagebrush Rebellion	.52	−.46	−.43	−.41	−.44	−.12

a. High score equals greater liberalism, less commitment to environmentalism, greater belief in technology, growth, the advantage of sacrificing some environmental values for economic growth and a belief that waste disposal is not a problem, and more commitment to federal ownership in the Sagebrush question.

and to an overall conservative stance. Indeed, as Table 11.2 indicates, those in favor of the rebellion are more likely to be conservatives, have a negative attitude toward environmentalism, believe environmental problems are exaggerated (ENVIRONMENTALISM), have confidence in the benefits of technology to solve environmental problems (TECHNOLOGY), believe that growth in housing and population poses no serious problems (GROWTH), believe that we should be willing to trade off environmental damage in return for more energy and prosperity (TRADEOFFS), and believe that neither toxic nor nuclear waste are serious problems (WASTE DISPOSAL). While the correlations are moderately strong (.35 to .46) in each case except WASTE DISPOSAL, it is clear that attitudes toward the aims of the rebellion are far from perfectly predictable from overall ideological orientations or general environmental attitudes. Further, no one attitude seems a better predictor than the others. Thus while a conservative ideological orientation and antienvironmental position are related to support for the aims of the Sagebrush Rebellion, other factors also are shaping this support.

Table 11.2 also shows us that the beliefs concerning environmentalism, technology, growth, and tradeoffs are very strongly related, as one might expect in this group of environmental activists and policymakers. Only the waste disposal issue is not closely tied with the other environmental beliefs, and even it has a moderate relationship. The correlation of liberalism with these values is also quite substantial (.45 to .66) except in the case of the attitudes toward dangers of waste disposal.

In general, then, Table 11.2 reveals that environmental attitudes and attitudes toward the aims of the Sagebrush Rebellion array themselves along a liberal-conservative dimension. They exhibit a closer relationship with traditional liberalism than one may have anticipated. On the other hand, one must remember that this is a very select sample of activists and public officials, and that this rather tight bond between economic conservatism and environmental conservatism may not obtain among the general public.

SPECIFIC LAND USE ISSUES

We next turn to a consideration of more specific issues relating to land use and ownership. While the questionnaire asked about dozens of land use options, perceptions of conflict, and related issues, we will focus here on only a few issues concerning preferred uses of land:

(1) *multiple use* (including recreation, grazing, wildlife, agriculture, and fisheries)
(2) *preservation use* (including wilderness, wildlife, and historical preservation)
(3) *rural development use* (including energy, mining, grazing, agriculture, oil, and gas)

Table 11.1 indicates that there is support for each of the three types of uses: rural development use, multiple use and, most significantly, preservation use are all supported. Thus the high levels of changes in land ownership away from the federal government are not paralleled by similarly high levels running in the antifederal direction either on general attitudes toward the environment or on specific types of resource utilization associated with federal "interference" (i.e., preservation use). It is not possible, then, to make simple and direct predictions from distributions of responses on land ownership preferences or general ideological orientations to distributions of responses on land use. This being the case, how do specific land use and ownership issues relate to the more general ideological and environmental stances and to attitudes toward the aims of the Sagebrush Rebellion?

First, perhaps surprisingly, attitudes toward the aims of the rebellion are not strongly related to these land use options. The Sagebrush Rebellion adherents seem much more agreed on who should own the

TABLE 11.3 The Relationship of General Attitudes to
Specific Land Use Beliefs

	Preservation Use	Multiple Use	Rural Development Use
Liberalism-Conservatism	−.32	.29	.38
Environmentalism	.37	−.28	−.45
Growth	.34	−.28	−.40
Tradeoffs	.36	−.25	−.43
Waste Disposal	.26	ns	ns
Sagebrush Rebellion	−.19	.26	.37

land (or more precisely, who should not) than on what should be done with it. Table 11.3 demonstrates that those favoring the aims of the Sagebrush Rebellion are not much more likely than are others to oppose preservation use or support multiple use or rural development use. Those who favor less federal ownership are only slightly less likely to favor preservation use and slightly more likely to favor multiple use. The relationship to rural development use is somewhat stronger (.37) but still not of an extremely high magnitude. Thus it is somewhat easier to categorize land ownership preferences by general ideological and environmental orientations than by attitudes on specific land uses.

This lack of relationship may be best explained by considering that when rather specific decisions have to be made, the question of *who* is deciding typically becomes less important than the question of *what* is to be decided. In public lands politics, this means that a whole range of uses may become the focus of debate and discussion, from a variety of developmental uses through the multiple uses mandated by BLM and USFS legislation to waste disposal and military uses.

In Nevada, a rather special planning process has been quite successful in resolving such disputes involving the public lands. Coordinated Resource Management and Planning (CRMP) procedures bring together all parties that have an interest in the utilization of a specific parcel of real estate. If the process works properly, the result is a consensus among *all* original participants that is formalized by a signed agreement detailing a plan for utilization. The signatories or their substitutes remain on the planning group to monitor the implementation of the plan.[5] In this way, positions that might ordinarily be dictated solely by liberal-conservative views or by environmental attitudes are moderated by the necessity of dealing with a specific set of land use alternatives. Ideological posturing tends to be submerged by a process of mutual understanding and accommodation.

The most significant contextual feature of CRMP is that it operates within the confines of the multiple use doctrine that governs management of the public lands. This significance can be illustrated by Table 11.3. The correlation between LIBERALISM-CONSERVATISM and MULTIPLE USE is .29 and rural use is .38. The more conservative (or antienvironmental) an individual is, the more likely he or she is to support MULTIPLE USE and RURAL DEVELOPMENT USE, including mining, oil and gas, grazing, and other activities. On the other hand, the correlation between LIBERALISM-CONSERVATISM and PRESERVATION USE is negative (-.32). The more conservative and antienvironmental an individual is, the less likely he or she is to support preservation. However, the correlation between PRESERVATION USE and MULTIPLE USE is also positive (.31), indicating that those who support preservation are also more likely to support multiple use.

Although conservatives and nonenvironmentalists support multiple use because many of those uses (e.g., timber and grazing) benefit private economic interests, liberals and environmentalists also support multiple use through the mediating influence of the preservation uses that they support and that are now part of the multiple use roster. Consequently, the multiple use doctrine is difficult to attack ideologically. It helps to defuse the potential conflict in a process such as CRMP because it leads all participants to a more pragmatic discussion of specific cuts to be made in the multiple use pie. As long as this central doctrine of BLM/Forest Service management remains intact, it is unlikely that any movement such as the recent Sagebrush Rebellion will result in major changes in land ownership. It is likely that such shifts could occur only if all major interests were convinced that state or private ownership would protect multiple uses at least as well as would federal ownership. There are few signs that any such convincing has taken place.

CONCLUSION

With the continuing pressures of population and economic growth, the public lands will provide an arena of conflict over the utilization of scarce resources for some time to come. General attitudes held by the population and, more important, by the politically active and knowledgeable will continue to be influential. The above analysis indicates that both liberalism-conservatism and environmentalism permeate the debate over the public lands, at least among Nevada knowledgeables. However, the magnitude of the correlations, although high, leaves plenty of room for other influences, not the least of which are the specific facts, problems, and issues applicable to each relatively isolated controversy over public land use.

The relative importance of these various influences on attitudes will depend in part on the social, economic, and, above all, political context. In the context of legislative debate, executive proclamation, or interest group pronouncement, general attitudes will be most salient and decisive. In the context of shirt-sleeve planning sessions and other less ideologically charged arenas, myriad less grandiose considerations will often be dominant. The fate of the public lands may ultimately depend on which of these contexts become the predominant sites of choice among policies, plans, and projects.

Interestingly, supporters of the aims of the Sagebrush Rebellion differ widely on land use issues. They appear to be only slightly more antipreservation or prodevelopment than are other respondents. Clearly, being united in the belief that the federal government should own less of the public lands does not imply agreement on more specific issues.

NOTES

1. The survey was part of a larger research project funded by the Nevada Attorney General's Office. The purpose of the project was to acquire any nonlegal information that might support the attorney general's legal arguments to the effect that federal ownership of land in Nevada constituted an unreasonable impairment of sovereignty. The researchers were given complete freedom in the design, implementation, and analysis of the survey.

2. There were at least two other reasons for losing respondents: (1) some individuals in politically sensitive positions were reluctant to respond even with guarantees of confidentiality, and (2) not all of Dillman's (1978) procedures for maximizing response rates (especially extensive followups) could be used because of funding limitations.

3. SPSS statistical routines were utilized for the analysis. Requests for copies of the questionnaire and other inquiries should be directed to the author at the Nevada Public Affairs Institute, University of Nevada, Reno, Nevada, 89557.

4. The liberalism-conservatism items and many of the environmentalism items were taken from Ingram, Laney, and McCain (1980). The remaining items were created for this study. See Appendix for a fuller description of the items.

5. The process has considerable support. Of those responsdents who considered themselves informed about CRMP, 70.4% agreed with the statement: "The CRMP program in Nevada provides a real opportunity for private citizens to take the initiative in developing plans to meet local needs," while 16.1 percent were uncertain, and only 13.6 percent disagreed.

APPENDIX

The questionnaire items that comprise the scales mentioned in the text are listed below. They have been abbreviated to save space but in a way that conveys their basic content. In parentheses after each item of a particular type are the extremes of the response categories and an indication of the number of categories. The number in parentheses after each name for a scale is Cronbach's alpha coefficient of reliability. Scores on some items were reversed in order to construct the scales.

GROWTH (.77)

(1) Environmental problem—destruction of land and townscapes (very serious to no problem—5)
(2) Environmental problem—population growth
(3) Environmental problem—housing development in rural or undeveloped areas
(4) Environmental problem—water shortages
(5) Environmental problem—depletion of natural resources (trees, minerals, wildlife)

TECHNOLOGY (.80)

(1) A certain amount of environmental damage in this state will have to be tolerated as the price for economic prosperity (strongly agree to strongly disagree—5).
(2) Scientific research and technological developments can solve most environmental problems.
(3) We should be willing to accept more air and water pollution in order to insure plentiful supplies of energy.
(4) The possible benefits from a nuclear powered electrical plant far outweigh the possible hazzards.
(5) The seriousness of environmental problems in this state has been greatly exaggerated.
(6) Solutions to environmental problems depend on . . . (from "changing our lifestyle" to "developing better technologies"—5).

ENVIRONMENTALISM (.89)

(1) A certain amount of environmental damage in this state will have to be tolerated as the price for economic prosperity (strongly agree to strongly disagree—5).

(2) Ground water should be considered public property rather than private property.

(3) Industry should pay a severance tax on nonrenewable resources (coal, copper) taken from this state.

(4) We should be willing to accept more air and water pollution in order to insure plentiful supplies of energy.

(5) The possible benefits from a nuclear powered electrical plant far outweigh the possible hazards.

(6) This state should not permit environmental damage in order to produce energy for use in other states.

(7) The seriousness of environmental problems in this state has been greatly exaggerated.

(8) Preference for land use (no to very strict planning and control—4)

(9) Environmental problem—air pollution (very serious to no problem—5).

(10) Environmental problem—water pollution

(11) Environmental problem—destruction of land and townscapes

(12) Environmental problem—open pit mining

(13) Environmental problem—soil erosion

(14) Environmental problem—depletion of natural resources (trees, minerals, wildlife)

WASTE DISPOSAL (.82)

(1) Environmental problem—toxic wastes (very serious to no problem—5)

(2) Environmental problem—radioactive wastes

TRADEOFFS (.77)

(1) A certain amount of environmental damage in this state will have to be tolerated as the price for economic prosperity (strongly agree to strongly disagree—5).

(2) Industry should pay a severance tax on nonrenewable resources (coal, copper) taken from this state.

(3) We should be willing to accept more air and water pollution in order to insure plentiful supplies of energy.

(4) This state should not permit environmental damage in order to produce energy for use in other states.

(5) The seriousness of environmental problems in this state has been greatly exaggerated.

(6) The possible hazards from a coal-powered electrical plant far outweigh the benefits.

(7) Preference for land use (no to very strict planning and control—4)

LIBERALISM-CONSERVATISM (.88)

(1) The federal government is interfering too much in state and local matters (strongly agree to strongly disagree—5).

(2) The government has gone too far in regulating business and interfering with the free enterprise system.

(3) Social problems here in this country could be solved more effectively if the government would only keep its hands off and let people in local communities handle their own problems in their own way.

(4) Generally speaking, any able bodied person who really wants to work in this country can find a job and earn a living.

(5) We should rely more on individual initiative and ability and not so much on governmental welfare programs.

RURAL DEVELOPMENT USE (.84)

(1) Preferred uses of public lands—mining (should to should not—3)

(2) Preferred uses of public lands—energy facility siting

(3) Preferred uses of public lands—recreation

(4) Preferred uses of public lands—industrial development

(5) Preferred uses of public lands—grazing

(6) Preferred uses of public lands—nonelectrical geothermal developments

(7) Preferred uses of public lands—agriculture

(8) Preferred uses of public lands—oil and gas

(9) Preferred uses of public lands—timber

MULTIPLE USE (.08)

(1) Preferred uses of public lands—recreation

(2) Preferred uses of public lands—grazing

(3) Preferred uses of public lands—nonelectrical geothermal developments

(4) Preferred uses of public lands—wildlife

(5) Preferred uses of public lands—agriculture

(6) Preferred uses of public lands—fisheries

(7) Preferred uses of public lands—timber

(8) Preferred uses of public lands—water conservation and development

PRESERVATION USE (.60)

(1) Preferred uses of public lands—wilderness

(2) Preferred uses of public lands—wild horses

(3) Preferred uses of public lands—cultural (archaeological, historical preservation)

(4) Preferred uses of public lands—wildlife

REFERENCES

CAWLEY, R. M. (1981) "The sagebrush rebellion." Ph.D. dissertation, University of Wyoming.

CULHANE, P. J. (1981) Public Lands Politics: Interest Group Influence on the Forest Service and Bureau of Land Management. Baltimore: Johns Hopkins University Press.

DANA, S. T. and S. K. FAIRFAX (1980) Forest and Range Policy: Its Development in the United States. New York: McGraw-Hill.

DILLMAN, D. (1978) Mail and Telephone Surveys. New York: John Wiley.

FRANCIS, J. G. (1982) "The west and the prospects for rebellion: an analysis of state legislation responses to the public lands question, 1979-1981." Presented at the 24th Annual Conference of the Western Social Science Association, Denver.

INGRAM, H. M., N. K. LANEY, and J. R. McCAIN (1980) A Policy Approach to Representation: Lessons from the Four Corners States. Baltimore: Johns Hopkins University Press.

STATE OF NEVADA, EX. REL. NEVADA STATE BOARD OF AGRICULTURE v. UNITED STATES OF AMERICA ET AL. (1981) 81-45-4, U.S. Court of Appeals, Ninth Circuit.

12

AGRICULTURE AND SCARCE RESOURCES

DON HADWIGER

Iowa State University

The politics and vigorous technology of America's food system have been based on the presumption of cheap water, cheap energy, and relatively cheap land, leading some critics to predict that we will need a radically different technology for this age of limits. Yet this system may be adjusting well to an environment of scarce resources.

Although the food system displays a lack of commitment to resource conservation in its tolerance of soil erosion and in its aversion to studying human nutrition and alternative agricultural systems, it still is meeting the nation's nutritional needs to a superior degree, even as it releases land and water for other uses. It is becoming more efficient both in production and in consumption.

Governmental programs written by producer interests have been notably influential in the development of the food system, a fact that makes its current resilience all the more surprising. In this century, a comprehensive framework of supportive federal programs was implemented by powerful industry groups seeking the industry's convenience and profit. They displayed hostility toward goals such as good human nutrition and resource conservation. The behavior of these interest groups dominant in agriculture sparked Theodore Lowi's (1969: 101-115) pessimism about the outcome of American liberalism.

The food system has become resource conserving despite its failure to provide voice or equity to many of its participants. Notwithstanding the complexities of agriculture's political bargaining, benefits from farm programs have not been distributed well among farmers and laborers, which seems to illustrate Charles Lindblom's (1982: 15) observation that manifest conflict among groups—in this case, the struggle among commodity groups—may exclude attention to conflict between the advantaged and disadvantaged. Consumer political groups, such as they were, were ignored until the 1960s although, as it is argued here, consumers have ended up as major beneficiaries in terms of the wide choices available to them from among moderately priced foods, as well as through the achievement of both good nutrition and resource conservation.

Improved nutrition and resource conservation are explainable as second-order outcomes, largely unintended. In some economic theory such benefits from unintended outcomes are relied on, as when self-interest in the marketplace produces economic development, or when capitalism—in Marxist theory—lays the groundwork for socialism.

Unintended results that override the intended ones are characteristic of U.S. farm policy. Agricultural interests have frequently enacted policies in pursuit of immediate economic or political objectives, the end results of which were sometimes predictably contrary to their objective. Federal programs to control crop acreage, supported by farm groups as a way to create scarcity, instead spurred farmers to produce more crops on fewer acres. Price supports, intended to sustain farm family incomes and thereby perpetuate the family farm, provided large profits and reduced risks for a few farmers, encouraging them to invest in labor-saving technologies, which in turn drastically reduced the total number of farm families. Most income and estate tax provisions that were intended to serve family farmers have had perverse results (Davenport and Boehlje, 1982).

Indeed, the structure of family agriculture, so prized in political rhetoric and romantic literature, has been undermined by policies ostensibly designed to protect it. Moreover, the structural effects of these policies were often predicted quite well by experts before enactment. Publicly supported agricultural research is an example. Farm groups and agribusinesses realized that such research would likely bring in its wake a consumer windfall of lower meat prices by allowing the control of rampant animal diseases. Again and again, industry groups have been unable to resist the temptation to enact policies that provide them with short-range relief and middle-range agony. This chapter details some of these results, which have made agriculture adaptable within an environment of scarce resources. It also suggests further study of the mechanisms that shape such second-order results as resource conservation.

THE CONSERVATION OF
RESOURCES IN AGRICULTURE

The farm is a major marketplace for millions of tons of synthetic fertilizers and pesticides, and for advanced machinery and the fuel required to run it. The modern superfarm, large and highly capitalized, is resource dependent compared with the diversified small farms that were once dominant. On diversified farms, major energy needs may be supplied by resident humans and animals. Soil fertility may be maintained by alternating cash crops and restorative crops, and also by returning animal manure to the soil. This farming model of relatively self-sufficient agriculture, and the way of life associated with it, are still economically viable, as demonstrated by prosperous Amish farmers and other practitioners of "alternative" agriculture. Particularly relevant to today's mainstream agriculture are the energy-saving practices on large "organic" farms, which are thoroughly mechanized but which minimize the use of pesticides and synthetic fertilizers.

By comparison, mainstream American agriculture has until lately been careless in its use of energy, water, and land. When fossil energy was cheap, applications of fertilizers and pesticides paid large dividends, so farmers were encouraged to use these products. Soon most farmers used too much fertilizer and pesticide. Farmers in arid regions enjoyed an era of cheap water, obtained from publicly subsidized irrigation systems or from pumping groundwater using inexpensive energy. The soil too was expendable as demand grew for U.S. agricultural products.

The period of extraordinary profligacy in the use of soil, water, and fossil fuels may well be at an end. The new structure of large farms is quite sensitive to cost factors. These adaptive farms, whose development was inadvertently assisted by public tax, subsidy, and research policies, have access to capital, technologies, and management skills, enabling them to switch relatively quickly to resource-conserving practices—for example, to a low-tillage system that requires less fuel, that shepherds soil moisture, and that may reduce soil erosion. It seems likely that federal programs that have enlarged our farms, therefore, have had a further result of creating the potential for a more conserving agriculture. With respect to energy use, for example, energy costs per unit of output are lower for large farms, mainly because these farms quickly economized on energy as costs rose. In the future, according to one authoritative assessment, "agricultural production is likely to use capital and land more intensively but energy, fertilizer and labor less intensively" (Van Dyke et al., 1979: 205).

It should be noted, for perspective, that agriculture is a relatively large user of land and water and a relatively small user of fossil energy. The use of energy in agriculture accounts for as little as 2 percent (the high estimate is 6 percent) of total national energy use, although by adding other segments of food production including processing and preparation of food in the home, the food system may account for as much as 17 percent of total energy use (Paarlberg, 1980: 176).

For land and water too, resource-conserving adjustments are being made. Prominent in the earlier development of the United States was the expansion of farming onto new lands. When there was no frontier beyond which to expand, and as population continued to grow, serious concerns were voiced that this nation would not be self-sufficient in the production of basic foods. But these concerns eased as production per acre increased, in large part as a result of technology produced by the public research institutions, and also due to federal acreage control programs that challenged farmers to increase their income from a restricted acreage. Today, a large percentage of U.S. farm acres are devoted to the production of commodities for export. Except for the pressure of exports, land would be available for conversion to many nonfarm uses. But the demand for major nonfarm uses is stable or declining. For example, land to be used for roads and transportation will very likely decline over the next several decades (Raup, 1980: 49-52). Currently, only about 3 percent of all land is built up in urban areas, highways, roads, railroad rights of way, and airports, and by comparison, about 21 percent of all land is devoted to crop land (Bills and Didriksen, 1980: 113).

There is disagreement as to whether per acre yields will continue to increase, in effect making land more abundant. Responding to concerns that per acre yields may be leveling off, economist Earl Heady (1982: 35) concluded, "Except for cotton, available time series data provide no firm evidence of yield plateaus." Assuming continuing support for public agricultural research, the history of agricultural technology encourages optimism about the prospects for major breakthroughs in areas such as genetic manipulation, and in improving photosynthate accumulation. Developments of these types and their widespread application even offer the ultimate possibility of worldwide land abundance.

In contrast to the availability of land, water is becoming a scarce resource, particularly for agriculture in the arid West. In the mid-1970s, about 58 million acres were irrigated—an area roughly equal to the total built-up acreage referred to earlier. Many of these irrigated acres were converted into cropland as a result of the Reclamation Act of 1902, which, as Helen Ingram (1982) has pointed out, established a government program that quite definitely achieved its objectives. Vast deserts have become agricultural heartlands as a result of public works delivering surface water for agricultural irrigation.

Now water supplies for irrigated agriculture are being constricted. Some groundwater reservoirs used for irrigation are being depleted. Irrigated agriculture faces competition in the marketplace from higher-value uses such as industry and mining. In this competition, agriculture, which now consumes 86 of the 107 billion gallons for off-stream uses, retains a favored political position under regulatory law and has strong support among local publics. However, agriculture's adjustment to diversion of water to higher value uses is already under way, in some cases resulting in a return to lower-yielding, but viable, dryland farming, in other cases changing to a more conserving irrigation technology, such as drip irrigation. In still other cases, water scarcity signals an end to production, or more accurately, a movement of production to regions in which both rainfall and water for irrigation are abundant, including the north-central, middle-Atlantic, southeast, and New England regions.

To summarize, there is a growing consensus that modern American agriculture is quite adaptive to a resource-conserving environment, though this adaptability may have come at considerable cost to the social fabric of rural America. Nor is there any question that public policies have played an instrumental role in the creation of this prolific, adaptive agriculture.

There may be less agreement that changes in consumption are another principal means for adjusting to resource scarcity. I argue that indeed, such changes in diet are occurring. Furthermore, these changes, like those in production, are coming about in considerable part as an inadvertant result of public policies.

NUTRITION AND CONSERVATION

Up to now, concerns that our food resources might not support our increasing population have been eased by production revolutions. Meanwhile, another powerful food revolution has waited in the wings. This revolution may change what Americans choose to eat, allowing them to make better use of the wide choices now available among both "natural" and manufactured foods. Such a diet revolution will contribute in a major way to the conservation of soil, energy, and other natural resources. Its benefits will also include generous reductions in health care costs and food budgets.

"If we were really intent on saving energy in the food system and having a low-energy form of agriculture," said economist Don Paarlberg (1980: 178), "we could accomplish this by changing our diets. We could consume grain directly rather than feeding these crops to livestock and then eating the resulting meat, milk and eggs." It should be granted that there are some grounds for pessimism that the diet revolution will occur, let alone that it may leave us notably healthier and wealthier. For one thing, dietary behavior is ingrained, and past changes have usually been glacial. People eat what they have learned to eat, which is the food that their cooks take pride in preparing and which the food system has learned to produce and deliver. Food habits are built into the cultural status system, and, of course, the food industry has worked hard to reinforce or even create some of the status distinctions that favor the use of such traditional foods as butter and beef.

A sharp change toward resource-conserving diets would be a heavy blow to some segments of our food industry, which, however, would be better able to bear it than would the family agriculture of the past. Agricultural groups have always understood the implications of dietary change. Because nutrition research and education was mainly lodged within institutions that producers controlled, they were able to monitor and circumscribe it thoroughly.

Thus, another reason for pessimism about diet revolution is that major responsibility for improving human nutrition is vested in the U.S.

Department of Agriculture and the agricultural experiment stations, which have mainly answered to producers. Within these institutions, however, there was an early commitment to nutritious, safe foods. A. O. Atwater, a founder of the experiment stations, was also a pioneer of research on human nutrition, he believed that adequate nutrition should be a major goal. However, farm groups beat back subsequent efforts to establish nutrition as a public policy goal because of concern that a nutritious diet might not include enough of their own products. In the Great Depression, for example, Department of Agriculture surveys found "one-third of the nation ill-nourished," and Secretary Henry A. Wallace began planning to increase food consumption with a view to meeting real food needs. Wallace asked his nutrition research bureau, the Bureau of Home Economics, to specify the minimum food requirements for a human being and also to indicate the maximum diet for good health. In response, Dr. Hazel K. Stiebeling, who had organized the USDA's nutrition surveys, prepared recommendations for four diets at different levels of costs and nutritive content, including a minimum diet that would be adequte in emergencies. Some farm groups were angered by Stiebeling's minimum diet because it included only small amounts of sugar, meat, and animal products. A "rider" aimed at Stiebeling was attached to a USDA appropriations bill, denying a salary to "anyone who advocated less use of a farm commodity." The rider was removed after nutritionists at the land grant colleges came to Stiebeling's aid (Stiebeling, 1977).

Building on Stiebeling's work, another USDA official, Howard Tolley, director of the Bureau of Agricultural Economics, ordered a study that converted Stiebeling's diets into production goals. According to historian Richard Kirkendall (1966: 79-80), Tolley and others in the department "publicized a conclusion of the study, which indicated that when prosperity and better knowledge of nutrition allowed Americans to consume the diet recommended as best, the U.S. would need more, not less, land in production."

Some farm leaders brushed aside Tolley's optimism, resentful that "their" department should have given any attention to urban consumers and the poor in its food goals and rural development program. A rural-oriented Congress "reorganized" Tolley's agency following World War II, then terminated it. In the next 30 years, the concept that nutrition policy should guide production was completely reversed: That is, production policy was presumed to result in good nutrition. For example, the Department of Agriculture, in its product feasibility studies, was allowed to ask only whether a new food product would sell, not whether it was nutritious.

During these years in which production interests exercised a tight grip on food policy, that policy still made striking contributions, inadvertent for the most part, to the goal of improved nutrition. As one contribution, a body of regulatory laws was created, and administrative agencies were established within the Department of Agriculture, seeking to assure the safety of our food. Food safety had come to the national agenda at the turn of the century through the journalistic exposures of serious problems, and through the flamboyant leadership of a career civil servant within USDA, Harvey Wiley. The agency established by Wiley—the Food and Drug Administration—initiated a second round of food safety reforms during the 1930s. Other regulatory efforts, largely within the Department of Agriculture, included extensive meat inspection activities that helped producers maintain quality standards and combat animal diseases. In recent years, the Food and Drug Administration and the Environmental Protection Agency, now with their own supportive clienteles and decision processes largely differentiated from those of the Department of Agriculture, were often involved in controversy with the agricultural industry about regulations intended to prevent harmful additives or agricultural residues in food (Hadwiger, 1982). Such pressure from other agencies and constituencies obliged the Department of Agriculture to accept some nutrition goals. During the 1960s and 1970s, civil rights, antipoverty, and environmental lobbies became influential in agricultural policy agenda setting and then became important allies of agricultural interests in forming congressional coalitions on farm bills.

A major impact of the new, nonindustry participants was in converting several minor surplus disposal programs—particularly food stamps and school lunches—into major nutrition programs to which more than half of the Department of Agriculture budget became committed. Priority was also given to nutrition research and education, the funding for which had previously languished under the oversight of rural legislators. Senator George McGovern's Senate Select Committee on Nutrition and Human Needs, which had prompted food stamps and school lunches, also produced a set of specific dietary guidelines. Other authoritative groups, including the American Medical Association and the National Cancer Institute, then followed with dietary recommendations.

More nutritious, resource-conserving diets will depend on new knowledge, and on the capacity of the food industry to provide a variety of food choices at low cost and on the pliability of consumer tastes. The American food industry has gone far in making food accessible and in making consumers manipulable. Outstanding examples are the fast-food establishment and the modern supermarket, which at first glance seem to be achievements of the private sector. In fact these delivery systems have benefited enormously from agricultural programs, some of which have contributed to resource-conserving nutrition as well as resource-conserving production.

First, production research and extension, although usually aiming to solve specific problems of specific producers, has had the cumulative effect of reducing the price of foods and also making available a wide variety at the grocery stores. Second, price supports and other subsidy programs providing profits to innovative farmers have brought about the creation of more effective food production systems. There is simply no question that consumers, particularly low-income consumers, are the major beneficiaries of price support and production research programs for agriculture.

Third, there has been some public research on nutrition within the agricultural research institutions, providing important findings about the nutritional needs of the human body, the components of our food, and the general nutritional condition of the population. The land-grant universities support departments of food and nutrition, which undertake research, teach nutrition, and prepare nutrition professionals for a variety of roles. Although nutrition may have been underfunded in comparison with other agricultural research ares, it has at least had a home in a research establishment that has received generous institutional support for more than a century.

Fourth, there is a considerable disease control effort by the Animal Plant Health Inspection Service that is intended to prevent diseases in plants and animals, some of which are transmittable to humans. APHIS take its greatest pains to control such diseases.

COMMENTARY

Our food system is resource conserving and, in this respect, currently viable. This viability was unintended, unexpected, and, one may say, undeserved. It was achieved in part through public policies that were reckless in the pursuit of short-range clientele interests.

Of course, there were many other unintended results from government's developmental role in agriculture, not all of which are likely to be perceived as benefits. For example, farm interests refused for several decades to accept rural industrialization programs because these were possible competitors to the commodity price support programs, although industrialization programs might have helped to forestall the waves of regional migration, at first out of the rural South during the 1950s and 1960s, and then back to it during the 1970s and 1980s. The demise of the small and medium family farm was abetted by federal policy, and this result has been viewed generally as unfortunate.

The unintended effects of agricultural policies were not always unpredictable. Agricultural economists designed measures for predicting and even achieving second-order effects. Political scientists might do more to understand those political mechanisms that achieved specific second-order results. These conclusions should be offered to those who would manipulate the second-order effects. An appreciation of second-order effects should also be incorporated into evaluations of our political system such as those by Lindblom (1982) and Lowi (1969), referred to earlier.

A list of mechanisms which might produce second-order results include the following:

(1) Agenda setting by public interest groups is feasible. The formal agenda for agricultural policies was established with the creation of the Department of Agriculture and the experiment stations in nineteenth-century laws, which were statements of the need for these institutions. These "agenda" laws were secured by public interest groups such as newspaper editors and horticultural organizations that expected no direct return to the sponsors, and by legislators who were seeking support from these groups. Subsequently, public-spirited federal bureaucrats such as Harvey Wiley and his successors in the Food and Drug Administration were important in agenda setting. Senator McGovern's Select Committee on Nutrition and Human Needs, like the earlier agenda setters, cultivated a concerned public outside the agricultural clientele with which policymakers were obliged to deal.

(2) The prospect of unintended benefits is useful in developing coalitions in support of a continuation of programs. Thus the food stamp program, which served nutritional objectives, was originally resisted by the agricultural coalition and then embraced as a way to

obtain adequate votes for commodity programs in Congress. Even a relatively tiny voting block may be crucial, as in the case of proponents of organic farming and proponents of nutrition research, each of whom were provided some satisfaction in order to gain their support for passage of the 1977 and 1981 farm bills.

(3) In a pluralist system, decisions in each functional area may be made by subsystems composed of interested elites whose monopoly of power extends over the particular process but not over the range of possible outputs. The agricultural subsystem tried to monopolize decisions on pesticides. Yet it was unable to prevent passage of amendments to pure food laws that prohibit agricultural residues, nor could it prevent the creation of an Environmental Protection Agency that gained authority to initiate and administer pesticide regulations.

(4) Vital institutions seek to preserve their momentum, adding or changing objectives when earlier objectives are fulfilled or no longer possess adequate political support for institutional growth. The Department of Agriculture in particular has found additional support by exploiting unintended results such as agricultural surpluses useful in food assistance overseas and domestically. Now, agricultural research agencies can be justified in terms of the development of resource-conserving agriculture.

Thus there are opportunities to achieve results other than those sought by current actors. Some opportunities exist at the time of agenda setting that may give institutions and statutes an *esprit* that interested groups can not easily obliterate. Also, unintended results can be obtained from pluralist politics. So the achievement of a resource-conserving yet prolific food system need not be attributed wholly either to a self-interested elite or to accident. Such an achievement was anticipated in the conception of many public policies, and as a result, was unintended only by the elites seeking immediate benefits from these policies. Favorable middle-range results from these policies were magnified in a number of recognizable ways.

REFERENCES

BILLS, N and R. DIDRIKSEN (1980) "Land and water base: historical overview and current inventory,"in Farm Structure: A Historical Perspective on Changes in the

Number and Size of Farms. Committee Print. U. S. Senate Committee on Agriculture, Nutrition and Forestry. Washington, DC: Government Printing Office.

DAVENPORT, T. C., M. BOEHELJE, and D.B.H. MARTIN (1982) "Taxes and the Family Farm," in D. Hadwiger and R. Talbot (eds.) Food Policy and Farm Programs. New York: Academy of Political Science.

HADWIGER, D. (1982) "Nutrition, food safety and farm policies," D. Hadwiger and R. Talbot (eds.) Food Policy and Farm Programs. New York: Academy of Political Science.

HEADY, E. (1982) "The adequacy of agricultural land: a demand-supply perspective," in P. Crosson (ed.) Crop Land Crisis: Myth or Reality. Baltimore: Johns Hopkins University Press.

INGRAM, H. (1982) "Water rights in the western states," in D. Hadwiger and R. Talbot (eds.) Food Policy and Farm Programs. New York: Academy of Political Science.

KIRKENDALL, R. (1966) Social Scientists and Farm Politics in the Age of Roosevelt. Columbia: University of Missouri Press.

LINDBLOM, C. (1982) "Another state of mind." American Political Science Review 76 March: 9-21.

LOWI, T. (1969) The End of Liberalism. Boston: W. W. Norton.

PAARLBERG, D. (1980) Farm and Food Policy: Issues of the 1980s. Lincoln: University of Nebraska Press.

RAUP, P. (1980) "Competition for land: the future of American Ariculture," in S. Batie and R. Healy (eds.) The Future of American Agriculture as a Strategic Resource. Conservation Foundation.

STEIBELING, H. K. (1977) Interview held on October 13.

D. VAN DYNE, R. REINSEL, T. LUTTON, and J. BARTON (1979) "Energy use and energy policy," in Agricultural Economic Report 438, Structure Issues of American Agriculture. Washington, D.C.

13

CHOOSING DEPLETION?
SOIL CONSERVATION AND
AGRICULTURAL LOBBYING

Central Michigan University

KENNETH J. MEIER

University of Oklahoma

Among the prominent and important issues related to the long-term productivity of American agriculture are soil conservation, land use, water depletion, environmental contamination, overuse of chemical fertilizers and pesticides, and right-to-farm questions. Although different in content, these issues are related in their focus on protection for the most basic farm resources: land and water. In pursuit of this end, all have been the subject of extensive legislation or legislative proposals at either the state or national level.

The most politically notable of these issues remains soil conservation with its emphasis on preventing soil loss. It was addressed earliest and, dating from the activist period of the Great Depression, has the longest history of government involvement (Rasmussen, 1981). As a result, soil conservation has the greatest number of programs, administrative experts, and most extensive system of local delivery. Both the Soil Conservation Service (SCS) and Agriculture Conservation Program

(ACP) of the Agricultural Stabilization and Conservation Service (ASCS) are well institutionalized within the U.S. Department of Agriculture (USDA). In addition, powerful congressional supporters such as Representative Jamie L. Whitten (D-Miss.), chairman of the House Appropriations Committee and its subcommittee on agriculture, frequently intercede on behalf of soil conservation. Were it not for the committee's differences with presidents, Whitten said at its 1981 hearings (part 5: 655), "about half the country would be a dust bowl today." Following committee recommendations, the Congress has appropriated more to the SCS than the president requested 29 times.

Despite nearly 50 years of government attention, a leading soil scientist (Wittwer, 1978: 375) complains that "soil erosion continues unabated." Only 25 percent of U.S. farmlands are managed with approved conservation practices, and severe farm problems through loss of production capacity are predicted. A government watchdog, the National Agricultural Research and Extension Users Advisory Board (1980: 5), warns of such losses because farmers "continue to increase use of intensive production practices." A private national research effort, the Cornucopia Project (1982: v), states more dramatically: "To provide our food abundance, we are burning up natural resources. . . . In the midst of plenty, we seem bent on devastating our potential for future productivity. With over five tons of topsoil lost per acre annually (USDA, SCS, 1980a: 8), the nation's yearly loss totals 6.4 billion tons (USDA, 1980a: 101). In heavy loss areas, an inch of topsoil that takes perhaps a thousand or more years to produce is lost every 10 to 20 years (USDA, SCS, 1980b: Table 16). In all, one-third of U.S. topsoil has been lost in 200 years (Pimentel, 1976: 154).

Neither are these losses abating. Some analysts claim that today's annual losses exceed those of dust bowl days (Reding, 1981: 162). At best, only some erosion reductions have been identified (Ogg and Miller, 1981: 8). Even these marginal gains are threatened by farmers using soil depleting practices as plowing up pastures and grassland, halting strip farming and contour plowing, and reverting to continuous production of a single crop (Rasmussen, 1981: 18).

This chapter will examine the question of why the problem of soil depletion has gotten worse, and why conservation efforts are decreasing at a time when the need for them is increasing. After a description of the major soil conservation programs, we will attempt to answer these

questions through consideration of interest group activity and its influence on soil conservation policy.

SOIL CONSERVATION PROGRAMS

Because the soil loss concerns of the 1930s were heavily influenced by
dust bowl conditions, soil and water have always been inextricably
linked (USDA, 1980b: 209). New programs, especially since the 1950s,
have aimed at conserving both soil and water as tandem resources.
Watershed and river basin protection programs are two examples. The
dual emphasis, however, has added complexity to the formulation and
administration of public policy. In addition, other new programs that
are marginally directed toward conservation practices such as habitat
protection have been included with soil conservation.

ADMINISTRATION

This complexity is heightened by the administrative fragmentation
that has characterized soil conservation for over 45 years. Two principal
USDA agencies (the Soil Conservation Service and ASCS's Agriculture
Conservation Program) have soil and water protection as their mission;
but a variety of others participate in and operate these and other
programs. This overlap has resulted in a history of multiple jurisdictions, fragmented policy control, interagency competition, conflict over
research and services, and competition for support (Baker, 1976; Rasmussen, 1981).

The oldest of the two USDA major agencies, the Soil Conservation
Service (SCS), was created in 1935 by bringing the existing Soil Erosion
Service of the Department of Interior into USDA. Although SCS's
workload of programs has expanded throughout the years, its primary
emphasis remains much the same. Most of its efforts go to making
payments and grants directed toward "farmer requested conservation
analysis" and planning (O'Rourke, 1978: 20). Drainage studies, irrigation investigations, and soil surveys have been added to SCS and are
consistent with the agency's self-perception as a research agency.

The Agriculture Conservation Program (ACP), in contrast, is more
service oriented. Authorized in 1936, ACP shares costs with farmers for
soil- and water-related projects designed to improve the quality of their
land. To receive ACP funding, the farmer must be eligible for other

ASCS programs (e.g., price supports). Although only approved practices are funded, the approval is fairly broad with traditional fundable measures including small reservoirs, strip cropping, terracing, shrub and tree planting, and liming. A 1980 amendment to the enabling legislation emphasized energy security and authorized such additional practices as installation of minimum tillage systems, energy-efficient irrigation systems, integrated pest management systems, and waste product storage facilities. SCS provides technical and planning assistance for ACP projects where necessary at a cost of 5 percent of ACP's budget (USDA, 1980b: 212).

SCS and ACP do not have a monopoly on soil conservation even in USDA. Seven other USDA agencies including the Farmers Home Administration (FmHA), Economic Research Service (ERS), Agricultural Research Service (ARS), Extension Service, and Forest Service both independently and cooperatively sponsor 34 programs with soil and water projects related to SCS and ACP efforts.[1] Their expertise is applied to such various responsibilities as making and servicing loans, developing rural areas, enhancing fish and wildlife habitat, providing recreational opportunities, and increasing forest productivity.

Compounding the difficulty of coordinating several agencies and numerous programs is the regulative role played by non-USDA agencies. The Occupational Safety and Health Administration (OSHA) and Food and Drug Administration (FDA) have been drawn into soil programs to ensure safe and healthy operation for producers and consumers. But neither these nor other agencies have had the impact of the Environmental Protection Agency (EPA), with its jurisdiction over air, soil, and water pollution abatement. EPA, as a result, has general responsibilities in soil and water matters related to erosion, water sedimentation, resource conservation and recovery, surface mining, and chemical and toxic substance use in soils and water. All are related to SCS and ACP operations.

Beyond these earlier assignments, the Soil and Water Resources Conservation Act of 1977 gave EPA additional specific soil conservation linked duties (Paarlberg, 1980: 122). The 1977 act has proven difficult to implement because conservation and environmental protection concerns frequently have operated at cross-purposes rather than as complements. EPA, for example, views soil erosion as a problem of water pollution rather than of soil loss (Hildreth, 1978: 4). To soil

Wind erosion	Water quality
Pasture and range productivity	Irrigation and water management
Cropland productivity	Drainage
Land reclamation	Waste management
Flood Plains management	Habitat development
Watershed protection	Outdoor recreation
Water supply	

Figure 13.1 Types of Activity to Which Soil and Water Conservation Are Directed

SOURCE: U.S. Department of Agriculture (1980) Appraisal, Part II, Soil, Water, and Related Resources in the United States: Analysis of Resource Trends. Washington, DC: Government Printing Office.

conservationists, this approach defeats the purpose of soil programs, but the agency can do little without first responding to EPA dictates. Accordingly, many projects lose their effectiveness in meeting USDA goals.

PROGRAM EXPANSION

The enabling acts of 1935 and 1936 creating SCS and ACP were only two of the twenty pieces of authorizing legislation establishing soil and water conservation programs. Three of these, such as the Smith-Lever Act of 1914, which created the Extension Service and empowered it to conduct soil-based educational programs, preceded the 1930s legislation. The remainder, along with a host of periodic amendments, simply expanded the number of soil and water conservation programs. Other legislation, such as the Soil Bank provisions of the Agricultural Act of 1956 and voluntary set-aside or land retirement features of later farm bills, had direct soil conservation implications.

The resulting programs have enlarged the scope of soil conservation policy and made it difficult to pinpoint its meaning. Conservation activities sponsored by USDA fall in several categories as noted in Figure 13.1. The reasons behind this expansion, as might be expected, go beyond a simple concern for minimizing soil and water loss on farmland. Over the years, those interested in soil conservation have made several strategic observations. First, conservation efforts can be extended and improved on if they are made to dovetail with programs providing benefits beyond just soil conservation. For instance, soil scientists applied their expertise to timber productivity in order to address water runoff and erosion difficulties. Second, soil conservation programs can win increased politicial support by providing program benefits to a broader constituency. By 1968, for example, charges were made that SCS was more concerned about recreation groups and municipal officials than it was with farmers (Talbot and Hadwiger, 1968: 300). Third, information obtained through conservation research and technological applications can be used to produce better use of soil and water resources even though loss is not an appreciable problem. Irrigation and waste management processes were developed in response to such beliefs. These strategic considerations, combined with regulatory responses to such agencies as EPA and FDA, have shifted the emphasis of soil conservation beyond food and fiber production into a multipurpose, multiconstituency effort.

LOCAL DELIVERY OF PROGRAMS

While administration of soil and water programs is housed in USDA agencies, their delivery is distinctly local. Local implementation serves to fragment further the already complex operation of soil programs. ACP activities, on the one hand, are managed from county ASCS offices. SCS programs, on the other hand, are administered by a unit of local government established in the enabling legislation. Organized as a subdivision of state government, soil conservation districts (or SCDs) operate on their own to assist in the introduction of federal as well as state conservation programs.

By 1947, all states had organized SCDs under their own enabling powers. With 3000 districts exercising jurisdiction over nearly all private U.S. rural lands, local district officials, usually elected, actually govern decisions made by SCS to fund landowners and undertake projects. To exercise these responsibilities, SCD officials work closely with appropriate agency officials of USDA in their county offices. These contacts, which also bring SCS and SCD officials together with state agriculture department and county extension personnel, establish a broad and wide-ranging base of political support for local activities and the federal programs that fund them.

SUPPORTING SOIL CONSERVATION

Political support for soil conservation has been portrayed, with some frequency, as obviously strong. The key explanation for this support has always been given in terms of the issue's internal characteristics. Soil conservation has "strong emotional appeal." This emotional appeal has recently been reinforced by the public's concern for the environment (O'Rourke, 1978: 88). Coupled with the tangible benefits of soil conservation, these more abstract values generate support for soil conservation policy.

Meier (1978) has found that SCS and ASCS were among the most supported agencies in appropriations hearings for both 1963-1965 and 1974-1976. This was true for both interest groups and anxious legislators who wanted to secure funds for districts back home. Similarly, Talbot and Hadwiger (1968: 153) noted the effective intervention of clientele groups when SCS has been threatened. Soil conservation clientele exhibit substantial diversity: the National Association of Conservation Districts (NASCD), Soil Conservation Society of America, and National Limestone Institute represent soil conservation officials, professionals, and agribusiness suppliers, respectively. Other advocates include land grant universities, whose research funding is heavily soil related, and municipal and recreational users.

The expansion of programs, importance of the issue, and array of those who benefit from conservation spending make it likely that soil conservation would receive strong support in the policy process. Yet the lack of progress in combating soil loss and the relatively small number of acres operating under approved conservation practices that were noted earlier causes some skepticism about this presumed support. The reports of political observers cast additional doubt. A USDA survey (Bowers, 1981) of interests affecting food and agricultural legislation fails to list conservation measures as a likely issue to be pressed by interest groups or agribusiness in the 1980s. Soil conservation clientele are notable by their absense from the report's list of groups likely to affect legislation and appropriations. *The Food Lobbyists* (Guither, 1980), a complete compendium of food organizations, make no note of any particular visibility or influence of any of the above clientele. Nor does it single out soil conservation as any more highly contested or endorsed as an issue than any of the other nonincome maintenance programs. In fact, Guither (1980: 56) notes that the greatest amount of interest in ACP relates to its close relationship to income supports rather than to its conservation importance.

Available research on farm organizations offers findings that reinforce these beliefs. An analysis of farm groups and agribusiness lobbies (Browne, 1982) shows that the focal point of primary interest has clustered around price supports, disaster payments, loan guarantees, acreage allotments, and market orders. All are income maintenance issues. In examining the priority issues of the general farm organizations, pricing issues were identified by the staffs as the single issue that members would not allow them to neglect (Browne and Wiggins, 1978). General farm organizations generally neglected the debate in the late 1970s over farm structure (even though structure affected their political resources) for a focus on price maintenance issues (Meier and Browne, 1983). In looking for an explanation, Graham Wilson (1981) concluded that farm interests have no other option in setting priorities because the approximate $6 billion in annual subsidies dwarfs all other programs. The nature of the industry makes production planning to balance demand and supplies impossible. As a result, farming has become dependent on government supports. Soil conservation, therefore, does not have the priority among interest groups that other farm programs do.[2]

EXAMINING INTEREST SUPPORT

While past research about the actual influence and power of interest groups demonstrates mixed findings, the prevailing sentiment among political scientists is that these lobbies indeed do matter. Some recent research and analysis suggests they may matter on soil conservation programs. Sabatier and Mazmanian (1979) provide a model of variables affecting the implementation process. If groups or firms see an issue as salient, have some degree of solidarity on expectations about the intended results, have access to policy channels and information, and can somehow aid the efforts of implementing agencies and meet some specific needs of intended program beneficiaries, they can work to structure agency responses in a manner consistent with their policy goals.

Kirst and Jung (1982), moreover, have operationalized these concepts and demonstrated that involved groups, over a period of several years have had positive influence in shaping the delivery of educational programs in desired directions. Since soil conservation programs have been operated and refined in a similar manner over a period of nearly 50 years, lobbies interested in food and fiber production have had substantial opportunity to further their interests.

Four sets of lobbies were identified as having a history of direct involvement in soil conservation policy through either testimony at legislative hearings or visible public action on a particular program.[3] The sets include: (1) soil conservation organizations and related associations of professionals and businesses, (2) general farm organizations, commodity groups, other farm organizations, and agribusinesses that manufacture agricultural products or process agricultural commodities, (3) nonagricultural groups and firms who are the recipients of soil conservation programs, and (4) nonagricultural organizations who do not directly receive soil conservation programs but who, nonetheless, are concerned with product availability, product cost, and means of production (see Figure 13.2).

Each of these lobbies, during the decades of the 1960s and/or 1970s, expressed support for well-developed, well-funded, and effective soil conservation programs. First, soil conservation organizations were essentially one-issue interests that became politically active to protect programs that they organized and administered; they can be termed "clientele." Second, farm groups and agribusiness received material benefits because they gained appreciably from soil programs that led to increased productivity; they can be termed "recipients." Farmers were able to produce more effectively; agribusiness gained more sales as a result. Both, however, stood to lose from drops in production capacity as a result of soil and water loss.

Third, directly benefiting nonagricultural groups received some specific, non-farm-related benefits from soil conservation expenditures. Included were groups with primary interests in municipal programs, forestry, and wildlife conservation (termed "nonagricultural recipients"). These interests had received the rewards of expanding soil conservation efforts and wanted to protect these policy gains. Fourth, the remaining nonagricultural interests were less obviously motivated. For the most part, those in this set were consumer and environmental

Occupation	Research	Projects
Agriculture	Set 1 Clientele (e.g., conservation professionals)	Set 2 Recipients (e.g., farmers)
Nonagriculture	Set 4 Interested Others (e.g., environmentalists)	Set 3 Nonagricultural Recipients (e.g., cities)

Figure 13.2   Groups Interested in Soil Conservation

public interest groups (termed "interested others"). Their specific goals were mixed and included: conservation efforts that furthered the production of inexpensive and plentiful food supplies, nutritious and/or chemically free food products, and nonpolluting farm practices.

PRIMARY EMPHASIS OF SUPPORT

The clustering of groups into four sets reflected the differing interests of the lobbies and produced fragmented demands on soil conservation policy.[4] This fragmentation was reminiscent of the complex delivery system that supplied soil programs and was consistent longitudinally from group to group. Groups exhibited surprisingly narrow concerns on a broad issue.

The clientele groups of soil conservation agencies emphasized research contributions and the specialized knowledge products that contributed to specific conservation gains. Even limestone producers, whose product was supported as an approved soil conservation practice, and soil project contractors addressed these topics. In contrast, because they represented recipients rather than specialized providers, farm groups and agribusiness lobbies were all project oriented and more inclined to speak well of ACP benefits rather than SCS contributions.

This agency distinction, however, was only true of appropriations hearings. On major conservation bills affecting soil and water services, both SCS and ACP programs were endorsed vigorously. The research versus project distinction was still evident, though, in that farm groups were more inclined to address individual user benefits than technological proficiency.

Project support was also evident among the nonagricultural recipients, but they endorsed even more narrow program benefits than did the agriculturalists. Their focus was on specific projects that benefited them whether in appropriations activity or major environmental and conservation bills. This project focus distinguished them from the interested others (the fourth group), most of whom were environmentalists. These were research oriented but lobbied on behalf of environmental protection rather than traditional soil and water research. As such, they were reform oriented.

DIRECTION OF SUPPORT

Although interest groups rarely criticize agencies in hearings (Meier, 1978), activity on soil and water conservation was both positive and negative. All four types of groups made positive statements of support as would be expected where individual benefits are concerned. The two most frequent negative comments concerned inadequate funding or inappropriate program goals (e.g., environmentalists).

Interests who received funding wanted more. Interests who were dissatisfied with the present emphasis on preventing soil loss or the regulations attendant with the process wanted a reorientation toward a more national or centralized implementation system. The "interested others" expressed discontent with the direct payment of funds for projects undertaken by recipients. They attacked the shortsightedness of projects and abuses in implementation services. They also questioned conservation successes. Similar arguments, although less critical, were advanced by some farm interests. However, they directed their opposition toward soil conservation district practices and their lack of accountability. On major soil and water bills, in contrast to appropriations, farm interests (both clientele and recipients) also opposed reforms that would interfere with past soil and conservation program practices.

FREQUENCY OF SUPPORT

Of approximately 100 groups and firms identified, recipients—farm interests and related agribusiness—constituted fully 60 percent.[5] Soil clientele numbered about 15 percent. Each of the two nonagricultural sets of interests were represented by about the same number of groups or firms. Together they included about 25 percent of the total lobbies addressing soil conservation over the 22-year period.

The soil and water conservation clientele organizations were the most continuously involved of the four sets on both appropriations and substantive legislation. Environmental groups, which included about two-thirds of the "interested others," were involved with near equal frequency on substantive bills after 1970. At least some of the farm and agribusiness lobbies were always involved.[6] Except for the American Farm Bureau Federation (AFBF) and to a much lesser extent the National Farmers Union (NFU) and the Grange, however, none were involved with any ongoing frequency. Chemical agribusiness was an exception on the substantive bills. Because of the threat posed by environmental interests, many individual chemical firms and trade associations were active on these particular issues. As one spokesman noted, "Velsicol opposed everything the EPA did in the early 1970's" (Schneider, 1982: 104).

INTENSITY AND COMMITMENT

Relative to other USDA agencies, SCS received strong positive support in legislative hearings in the 1960s and 1970s (Meier, 1978: 65). But this intensity of support measure did not translate into increased budgetary resources for the agencies. As a result, a new measure of intensity was sought for this research. Participating groups were considered to be intensely committed to the issue if lobbying was reported or observable beyond mere legislative testimony.

When such a control was applied, group or firm participation fell by nearly three quarters. The most involved groups were soil program clientele; these interests continued to lobby on both appropriations and substantive legislation. Beyond that, however, participation among each of the other three sets declined significantly. Some general farm organizations were evident, especially AFBF. A number of environmental groups were also considered committed, but only on substantive legislation. General farm organization involvement was most likely on the same bills. In fact, the differing emphasis of the general farm organizations and the environmental groups on this legislation produced what could be seen as the primary conflict on soil-and water-related legislation. With the exception of forestry groups on substantive matters of the 1978 act, no other nonagricultural groups appeared committed.

EVALUATING INTEREST SUPPORT

"You have to understand," responded one long-time observer of agricultural politics, "that this [soil conservation] is the priority issue of almost no one." If soil conservation clientele are discounted, the available data on interest group support for soil and water programs confirm that interpretation. A distinct and rather sharply drawn division of interests characterizes the expectations about the program. Four different sets of groups have four often very different agendas in mind, often with further fragmented concerns evident within each set. At no point are any of the sets especially supportive of the whole array of programs or total operational system by which programmatic benefits are delivered. Different preference lists and even some conflict exists. Moreover, much of the support for soil conservation efforts, in whole or in part, is episodic and without much commitment. Support for soil conservation, except from soil clientele, is mainly symbolic. Groups such as those representing farms and municipalities are looking to side payments of land improvement or recreational projects for the group members they represent. For pork barrel reasons, therefore, they endorse soil conservation. Or, as with the farm and environmental groups, they are involved in a far broader conflict over how and for what purposes the land should be used.

Any interest group emotionalism about soil conservation, therefore, relates either to the issues' pork-barrel attraction or the hidden agenda of those discussing it, but not to any real commitment to soil loss as a priority farm problem. The limited support of those who benefit most from soil programs—farmers and businesses dependent on farm income—is particularly noteworthy. These groups and firms apparently are untroubled by unabated soil loss, limited use of approved conservation practices, and whatever relationship loss and use have to sustaining long-term agricultural productivity. Their members also must be untroubled since the groups seem to feel no grass-roots pressures motivating their staffs to give soil conservation priority status. Interest groups generally respond to such pressures to keep their members' dues and support (Moe, 1980; Browne, 1977: 56); obviously no such pressures are applied here.

Based on the apparent lack of progress in implementing an effective national soil conservation policy over a period of 50 years,[7] the Sabatier and Mazmanian model leads to the additional conclusion that interest groups have mattered most for soil programs in a negative way. By focusing narrowly on specific conservation projects, they have diverted attention away from the national issues of soil and water conservation. The aggregated demands of the recipients fail to add up to a comprehensive national effort to conserve soil and water resources.

The issue's lack of salience seems evident, as does the lack of solidarity about the desired outcome of the programs. Many groups claimed benefits for those they represent, both directly as payments from soil programs and indirectly as the satisfactions of environmental protection; but these benefits are largely unrelated to one another or to any established national goal of soil conservation. Agencies likewise have received ongoing interest group support—which was provided at minimal group cost—for expanding their efforts; but this support has further fragmented program goals and diffused government's ability to articulate a national soil policy. The inadequacies and lack of resources of interest groups, rather than their strengths, have contributed to the agency responses that resulted in plentiful programs and projects with minimal policy direction.

EXPLAINING INTEREST SUPPORT

The relative inattention of interests—especially those in the agricultural set—to soil conservation issues may seem rather paradoxical. That is, the policy area has obvious importance but still remains largely neglected. That assessment, however, omits the explanation for the inattention and overstates the situation as a result. What appears as narrow and self-defeating behavior from a perspective of what is of interest makes more sense when the problem is examined from the viewpoint of the interests. Interest groups, because of both external and internal limitations, cannot attain or attempt to attain all policies that might be desirable (Meier and Brudney, forthcoming).[8]

EXTERNAL FACTORS INFLUENCING GROUP POSITION

The position taking of established interests occurs in relationship to policymakers and other interests involved in the policy arena. Over time, given the need to work with others and the scarcity of the resources used in lobbying (Truman, 1951), lobbyists must recognize that all options are not open and all issues cannot be addressed. With regard to soil and water conservation and any reforms proposed for sustaining productivity, the existence of two institutionalized conditions in the total agricultural policy process restricts interest demands. These two conditions include (1) the income maintenance or the pricing emphasis driving agricultural policy and (2) the fragmentation of the delivery system for USDA programs in general and soil conservation programs in particular.

Pricing policy. Farm prices, from 1973 to present, have consumed the attention of the agricultural interests as a result of economic conditions. That period was a continuing downturn of prices that has pushed them below actual production costs for many farmers. Beginning with the 1973 farm bill and its encouragement of fence row to fence row planting to increase production, the supply of food and fiber products generally has outstripped demand. However, the growing export market envisioned by policymakers and cultivated by farm producer associations did not expand rapidly enough to absorb this demand. The results of production incentives lowered prices and also made individual producers acutely aware of marketplace instability (Spitze, 1976).

This period preceded a number of years, from the late 1960s through the early 1970s, when both total net farm income and farm prices were high. They were so high, in fact, that the intersectional income gap that had always characterized American agriculture was temporarily eliminated, while important efforts were made to permanently reduce it (Mayer, 1976: 21). Profits during this period, however, were not returned to capital improvement efforts to sustain production over the long range. Instead, throughout the nation, profits were directed toward farm expansion, land purchases of nearby smaller farms, and new equipment purchases for larger-scale farming (Penn, 1979).

Expansion during these high-income years came easily since farm credit was readily available from public and private institutions. For that reason, the price decline of the 1970s was particularly disastrous to agriculture. Many farmers had purchased on credit during highly inflationary periods when land and equipment costs were rapidly escalating. Equipment was bigger and more technologically advanced. Land was more valuable because farm speculators saw additional financial incentives for buyouts.

With declining farm prices, however, came higher interest rates. Many farmers were forced to borrow in order to plant because available cash reserves had gone to increase production capacity. As interest rates doubled and continued higher, government price-related policy became even more important to farm producers and farm suppliers than it normally would have been during a period of instability. Accordingly, the usual problems of oversupply that had characterized farm dependency on government in the 1950s and through the mid-1960s were exacerbated by an unprecedented cost-price squeeze.

All this was critical both to determining the farm group policy emphasis on pricing and to a declining producer interest in soil conservation. Funds earmarked for matching payments for soil conservation projects were directed by producers to, first, farm expansion and, later, to paying the costs of production. In addition, soil conservation practices frequently were ignored, and some projects were reconverted to earlier conditions. Stripcropping, for example, became impractical as farmers were forced to make planting decisions on the basis of greatest financial return. Terracing was inconsistent with the operation of many of the larger pieces of farm equipment. Habitat, erosion-prone pastureland, and forested property were only some of the prior soil conservation efforts that were diverted to raise income. In addition, the larger scale of production intensified soil and nutrient loss as well as water depletion (Cornucopia Project, 1981).

These economic conditions, however, did not cause the resulting interest response by themselves. Since the 1930s, even with the concern for dust bowl conditions, the federal government allocated most of its agricultural assistance to income maintenance and pricing programs through a complex system of price supports, disaster payments, and loan guarantees. When a crisis situation emerged in the late 1960s, the combined attention of program administrators and congressional supporters along with agricultural interests gravitated toward adjusting the dominant features of farm policy to ongoing conditions. Exactly the same responses had resulted from economic instability in the 1950s and early 1960s. During the years of higher prices, these combined forces— all well versed in and well identified with pricing policy—worked to adjust pricing and support mechanisms to better reflect their own strategies for increasing farm income as an aid to a more productive agriculture. Related issues of taxes and estates also consumed large amounts of time.

In essence, existing programs dominated the attention of both policymakers and involved interests throughout the last 22 years. After developing an interventionist farm policy to which farmers had adjusted and to which government devoted its time and attention as well as most of its agricultural funding, agricultural interests could not seriously propose any radical restructuring of total farm policy and be viewed as credible.

Fragmented programs. Since pricing and support policies were dominant, most agricultural interest attention went there. By nature of funding, these programs produced the greatest amount of benefits directed toward farm members and industrial producers. Only selectively on items of potentially high member benefit or high member cost do agricultural interests gravitate to support or oppose the other programs of USDA. Agribusiness, for example, contested soil bank policies in the mid-1950s because of lost sales through land retirement (Bonnen, 1981). In 1981, the National Agriculture Chemical Association and related firms advanced an interest in promoting "no till," chemically intensive planting as a means of developing a sustainable agriculture.[9] Similarly, the Farm Bureau and other groups worked hard on soil and water conservation bills where it appeared that EPA involvement might jeopardize ongoing farm practices and seriously burden producers.

But for routine matters of lesser consequence to the group or firm, farm interests relied on the soil conservation clientele groups to make demands and exert the necessary influence to secure funds and modify programs. These groups developed the necessary expertise and cultivated ties with the appropriate policymakers. The general farm organizations, in particular, backed them up, as did nonfarm recipient groups who often were contacted for coalition support.

The complexity of agricultural policy created a division of labor with resulting specialization. As a result, soil and water issues seldom became a matter of broader agricultural interest for either groups or firms. "Those programs are not really our business," responded a general farm lobbyist. "We're involved, but others do a good job on the matter without much need for assistance. Besides the issue and the process are a bit too complicated for our organization to be effective." Farm interests and farmers, in other words, depend on the technical skills of USDA and on the combined support of soil program clients and Congress to actually sustain agriculture. The short-term emphasis of support programs and the priority of pricing policies lead agricultural groups and firms to a different arena, and a sufficient number of trusted partners in the external policy environment of agriculture allow them to be comfortably absent. In brief, the relationships developed with others within the agriculture system, and the resulting role differentiation makes it unlikely for comprehensive policy on long-term conservation to emerge from even a coalition of agriculture interests. Even if the others produce inadequate programs, there is little these interests can do to take corrective action.

INTERNAL FACTORS INFLUENCING GROUP POSITION

Research has consistently shown that interest groups must devote a large portion of their efforts to organizational maintenance (Browne, 1977; Salisbury, 1969). Olson (1965) showed that collective policy benefits were rarely sufficient to induce members to join a group, and without members interest groups lose their policy relevance. As a result, a large proportion of interest group activities must be devoted to providing material incentives (insurance, information, publications, and so on) to retain members. This emphasis means interest groups have only limited resources to use in their efforts; the rational interest group, therefore, must set priorities.

Member expectations about the groups to which they belong, as well as corporate expectations about their firm's lobbying staffs, determine the priorities of group lobby efforts (Browne, 1977: 56). Washington staffs are constrained in their lobby actions by the expected judgment of their employers/members. Given the importance of price supports, therefore, lobby efforts will focus there.

As shown elsewhere (Browne and Wiggins, 1978), even the eclectically interested general farm organizations have had to emphasize pricing issues due to member expectations and demands. More recently, the American Agriculture Movement's (AMA) emergence and national protests (Browne, 1979) demonstrated the commitment of farmers to support programs. Since their earlier protests, AMA members have worked to gain grass-roots control of other farm groups. At least two state affiliates of AFBF and NFU have been taken over, and plans are in effect to do the same with the National Cotton Council of America. Each of these efforts have been made to generate organizational demands for even higher price supports.

Farm groups, however, need no member surveys to know which programs matter most to their members. Farm groups have annual legislative conferences, usually at state and local levels as well as nationally, to assemble platforms for their lobbying demands. The greatest member pressure comes for pricing and government support programs within almost every organization.[10] Soil conservation receives comparatively little support. Additional information about member preferences comes from program usage. Price supports, loans, and disaster payments are highly used while even valued SCS-ACP projects are received by a much smaller proportion of farmers.

As a result, agricultural interests with limited staff time and money find that member priorities define their lobbying territory. Even if external environmental conditions favored it, which they do not, the presence of dues-paying members prohibits interest group attention being directed to agricultural issues other than pricing policy except on short-term, short-duration matters.

CONCLUSION

This research examined the role of interest groups in soil conservation policy. Two questions have troubled soil conservation analysts. Why with all the efforts devoted to soil conservation, has the problem gotten worse? Why, when the need for soil conservation is greater than ever, are we spending fewer resources on soil conservation? The answers to these questions are found in the group process. Interest groups have been able to generate large numbers of supporters for specific conservation programs but have been unable to generate among groups a long-term commitment to conserving farm resources. For the most part, groups are attracted to the specific project that benefits them, not to any general preference for soil conservation. As a result, an administratively fragmented delivery system implements soil conservation projects that are not linked to each other or any national plan. Soil conservation efforts, therefore, undertake many individual projects but fail to protect the nation's soil resources.

The answer to the second question also reflects the interest group process in agriculture. The overriding issue for farmers in an industry where over 10 million people have left the farm in this century is, "Will I make enough money this year to farm next year?" Short-run profits dominate because these profits are uncertain and highly volatile. Farmers and the groups that represent them, therefore, will focus on income maintenance policies—price supports, disaster payments, and the like. Where conservation policies compete for attention with price support policies, conservation policies will be short-changed. Similarly where conservation practices conflict with income maximization, conservation projects will be plowed under. The result is fewer resources committed to soil conservation and a magnification of the future problems of agricultural productivity.

NOTES

1. The Agricultural Research Service and the Extension Service are now part of the Science and Education Administration, and the Economic Research Service is now part of the Economics and Statistics Service. The older titles are used because the programs known to most readers are identified with the old agency title.

2. One explanation for the difference in findings exists. Meier (1978) and others focused on agency-level activities generally through the appropriations process. Price support issues are resolved in a different arena. Price supports concern the entire Department of Agriculture and are resolved through substantive legislation passed every three to five years. When this macrolevel struggle takes place, all other agricultural issues by definition must wait.

3. The time frame for analysis included the years between 1960 and 1982. Annual appropriations as well as the five major substantive bills affecting soil and water were considered. The latter included: the Food and Agricultural Act of 1962 (PL 87-703), the Rural Development Act of 1972 (PL 92-419), the Clean Water Act of 1977 (PL 95-217), the Surface Mining Conservation and Reclamation Act of 1977 (PL 95-97), and the Cooperative Forestry Assistance Act of 1978 (PL 95-313). Only soil and water conservation program components of these complex acts were considered for inclusion in this analysis (USDA, 1980a: 229-230). Group or firm testimony was observable by reading the hearings. However, that method was imperfect for drawing conclusions since the subject of interest or intent of the testimony was sometimes unclear. In such instances, the groups were not counted as participants. Participation at hearings is not the only measure of a group's interest, so other methods were used as well to determine involvement. Groups or firms were also counted as active if their involvement was (1) reported in journalistic accounts of the *Washington Post* in news items related to the legislation issue included, (2) cited in farm, social science, and other indexed journals or related books, or (3) noted by long-term observers of agriculture policy employed by the Congress or USDA and interviewed for their research.

4. These were not the only topics addressed by groups in each set. They do include, however, the topics of most frequent concern. In all four sets, the primary topic was addressed in at least 75 percent of all instances in which a group or firm referred to a specific interest.

5. In total, 104 groups or firms were identified. This figure was rounded to 100 because of the limited accuracy of the procedure. Percentages were simply rounded for the same reason.

6. This related to frequency of testimony and written reports. There almost seems to be a randomness about which lobbies in this set testify at hearings. Perhaps, because of the frequency of interaction among these lobbyists, they have advanced and we have discovered the "your turn principle" of allocating appearance before congressional committees.

7. The amount of concern for effective policy also can be seen in the new simultaneous commissioning of four major studies related to soil conservation (Rasmussen, 1981: 19). One was instituted by the Congress, another by the president, a third by the Economics, Statistics and Cooperatives Service (ESCS) or USDA, and the fourth was done by a multi-agency USDA team.

8. Most of the conclusions from this section were taken from interviews with agricultural lobbyists. These, for the most part, were done in conjunction with research by the authors as cited in the references.

9. The nontraditional nature of the proposal can be seen in the sources used to advance the idea. Rather than being able to work with generally acknowledged sources of influence within Congress and USDA, chemical lobbyists needed to look for assistance from Representative Aron Strangeland (1982) and special project personnel in the agencies.

10. Exceptions have existed in such commodities as soybeans when it was considered necessary to be free of government support to gain economic trade advantages in Europe.

REFERENCES

BAKER, G. L. (1976) "Land use: American dream or political football." Presented at the District of Columbia Chapter meeting of the Soil Sciences Society of America.

BONNEN, J. T. (1981) "Observations on the changing nature of national agriculture policy decision processes, 1946-1976," pp. 309-327 in T. H. Peterson (ed.) Farmers, Bureaucrats, and Middlemen: Perspectives on American Agriculture. Washington, DC: Howard University Press.

BOWERS, D. E. (1981) "The setting for new food in agriculture legislation," pp. 120-134 in Agricultural-Food Policy Review: Perspectives for the 1980s. Washington, DC: USDA, Economics and Statistics Service.

BROWNE, W. P. (1982) "Farm groups and agribusiness." Proceedings of the American Academy of Political Science (Spring).

——— (1979) "The American agriculture movement: what is it and why?" Presented at the Hendricks Policy Symposium, Lincoln, Nebraska.

——— (1977) "Organizational maintenance: the internal operation of interest groups." Public Administration Review 37 (January-February): 48-57.

——— and C. W. WIGGINS (1978) "Resolutions and priorities: lobbying by the general farm organizations." Policy Studies Journal 6 (Summer): 493-499.

Cornucopia Project (1981) Empty Breadbasket? Emmaus, PA: Rodale Press.

GUITHER, H. D. (1980) The Food Lobbyists. Lexington, MA: D. C. Heath.

HILDRETH, R. J. (1978) "Public policy and regulation." Presented at the Annual Meeting of the Northeast Agricultural Economics Council.

KIRST, M. and R. JUNG (1982) "The utility of a longitudinal approach in assessing implementation: a thirteen-year view of Title I, ESEA," pp. 119-148 in W. Williams et al. (eds.) Studying Implementation: Methodological and Administrative Issues. Chatham, NJ: Chatham House.

MAYER, L. V. (1976) "Discussion of 'agricultural and food policy issues and the public decisionmaking environment,'" pp. 21-24 in R.G.F. Spitze (ed.) Agricultural and Food Price and Income Policy. Urbana: University of Illinois Press.

MEIER, K. J. (1978) "Building bureaucratic coalitions: client representation in USDA bureaus," pp. 57-75 in D. F. Hadwiger and W. P. Browne (eds.) The New Politics of Food. Lexington, MA: D. C. Heath.

————— and W. P. BROWNE (1982) "Interest groups and farm structure," in D. Brewster, W. Rasmussen, and C. Youngberg (eds.) Farms in Transition: Interdisciplinary Perspectives on Farm Structure. Ames: Iowa State University Press.

MEIER, K. J. and J. L. BRUDNEY (forthcoming) "Organization theory and interest groups," in J. Cooper (ed.) Organization Theory and Political Analysis. Westport, CT: Greenwood.

MOE, T. M. (1980) The Organization of Interests: Incentives and the Internal Dynamics of Political Interest Groups. Chicago: University of Chicago Press.

National Agricultural Research and Extension Users Advisory Board (1980) Report (October). Washington, DC: Author.

OGG, C. and A. MILLER (1981) "Minimizing erosion on cultivated land: concentration of erosion problems and the effectiveness of conservation practices." Policy Research Notes 11 (August): 5-12.

OLSON, M. (1965) The Logic of Collective Action. Cambridge, MA: Harvard University Press.

O'ROURKE, A. D. (1978) The Changing Dimensions of U.S. Agricultural Policy. Englewood Cliffs, NJ: Prentice-Hall.

PAARLBERG, D. (1980) Farm and Food Policy: Issues of the 1980s. Lincoln: University Nebraska Press.

PENN, J. B. (1979) "The structure of agriculture: an overview of the issue," pp. 2-23 in Structure Issues of American Agriculture. Washington, DC: US, Economics, Statistics, and Cooperatives Service.

PIMENTEL, D. et al. (1976) "Land degradation: effects of food and energy resources." Science 194 (October 8): 149-155.

RASMUSSEN, W. D. (1981) "History of soil conservation: institutions and incentives." Agriculture History Branch, USDA. (unpublished)

REDING, N. (1981) Statement of the National Agricultural Chemicals Association. U.S. House of Representatives, Committee on Agriculture, World Food Situation Hearings, 97th Congress, 1st Sess. Washington, DC: Government Printing Office.

SABATIER, P. and D. MAZMANIAN (1979) The Implementation of Regulatory Policy: A Framework for Analysis. Research Report 39. Institute for Governmental Affairs. Davis: University of California.

SALISBURY, R. H. (1969) "An exchange theory of interest groups." Midwest Journal of Political Science 13 (February): 1-32.

SCHNEIDER, D. (1982) "The deadly shadow of endrin." Outdoor Life (April): 100-112.

SPITZE, R.G.F. (1976) "Agricultural and food policy issues and the public decision-making environment," pp. 5-20 in R.G.F. Spitze (ed.) Agriculture and Food Price and Income Policy. Urbana: University of Illinois.

STANGELAND, A. (1982) "Planning for a sustainable, profitable, and productive farm future. Congressional Record 128 (February 10).

TALBOT, R. and D. HADWIGER (1968) The Policy Process in American Agriculture. San Francisco: Chandler.

TRUMAN, D. (1951) The Governmental Process. New York: Alfred A. Knopf.

U.S. Department of Agriculture (1980a) Appraisal, Part I, Soil, Water, and Related Resources in the United States: Status, Conditions, and Trends. Washington, DC: USDA.

——— (1980b) Appraisal, Part II, Soil, Water, and Related Resources in the United States: Analysis of Resource Trends. Washington, DC: USDA.

——— Soil Conservation Service (1980a) America's Soil and Water: Conditions and Trends. Washington, DC: USDA.

——— (1980b) Basic Statistics, 1977. National Resources Inventory, Revised. Washington, DC: USDA.

WHITTEN, J. (1981) Comments. Washington, D.C.: Soil Conservation Service Appropriations Hearings, Subcommittee on Agriculture, Rural Development and Related Agencies, Appropriations Committee, U.S. House of Representatives, 97th Congress, 1st session.

WILSON, G. K. (1981) Interest Groups in the United States. London: Oxford University Press.

WITTWER, S. H. (1978). "The next generation of agricultural research." Science 199 (January 27): 375.

NAME INDEX

Anderson, Don, 175n
Andrus, Cecil, 188
Aristotle, 12, 28-45, 61
Asta, Ron, 196
Atwater, A. O., 248
Augustine, 29-45

Babbitt, Bruce, 189, 194
Baden, John, 19, 130
Baker, G. L., 256
Baldwin, B.T.E., 223n
Bardach, E., 138
Barnet, R., 25
Barton, A., 86
Beck, R., 221
Beckerman, W., 15
Beer, S., 145
Bennett, Hugh, 156
Bentsen, Lloyd, 215, 220
Bills, N., 245
Bobbit, P., 11
Boehlje, M., 243
Bonnen, J. T., 269
Bookchin, M., 25
Booth, Alan, 13, 93
Bowers, D. E., 18, 20, 260
Bradley, D., 18, 20
Brady, E., 86-88, 90-95, 101n
Brezhnev, Leonid, 71
Brinkerhoff, David, 13-14
Brown, Lester, 65, 81n
Browne, William, 19, 211, 260-261, 270
Brudney, J. L., 267
Buckley, K. E., 184
Burke, Edmund, 81
Butterfield, F., 65, 75, 80

Calabresi, G., 11
Caldwell, L., 137
Calhoun, J., 93
Carson, R., 25
Carter, Jimmy, 138, 166-169, 170, 174, 188
Castro, Fidel, 71, 73, 78
Catton, W., 85
Cawley, R. M., 12, 228

Cephalus, 36-37
Chang, P. H., 74
Cleveland, Gover, 154
Cole, H., 25
Cook, S., 85
Cooke, R. U., 184
Coolidge, Calvin, 159
Cotgrove, S., 114
Culhane, P. J., 226-227
Cutright, P., 14

Daly, H., 48, 128
Dana, Samuel, 152, 227
Davenport, T. C., 243
Davidson, E. S., 185
Davies, B., 139
Davies, J., 139
Deng, Xiao-ping, 80
Denise, P., 223n
Desai, U. C., 18
Dettloff, J. A., 184
Didriksen, R., 245
Dillman, D., 237n
Dirks, R., 85-86, 88-89, 90-95, 100, 101n, 102n
Douglas, P., 129
Downs, Anthony, 166
Dreyfus, D., 137
Dumont, R., 73
Dunlap, R., 85, 128, 140
Dynes, R., 86

Eckholm, E., 15
Eckstein, A., 80
Ehrlich, A. H., 15
Erlich, P., 15, 25
Eisenhower, Dwight, 159-161, 174
Emerson, Ralph Waldo, 152
Ervin, Osbin, 18, 204, 223n

Fairfax, S., 138, 227
Fischer, F., 12
Fort, Rodney, 130
Francis, J. G., 228
Franklin, Benjamin, 33

Friedman, Milton, 169

Galbraith, John Kenneth, 153, 159
Georgescu-Roegen, N., 128
Gillis, M., 204-219
Glasser, R., 25
Glaucon, 32-33
Goldman, M. I., 72
Gregg, F., 138
Greider, William, 169-170
Griffin, K. N., 204
Guither, H. O., 260-261

Hadwiger, Don, 19, 249, 259-260
Hardin, Garrett, 47-48, 188
Harding, Warren, 159
Harrington, W., 131
Harris, Louis, 140
Hart, D., 13
Hass, J., 85
Hawthorne, Nathaniel, 152
Hays, Samuel, 154
Heady, Earl, 245
Heclo, Hugh, 159
Heilbroner, R. L., 15
Hildreth, R. J., 257
Hill, S., 12
Hirschman, Albert, 85
Hitler, Adolf, 97
Hobbes, Thomas, 12, 28-45, 48-63
von Hoffman, Nicholas, 167
Hofstadter, Richard, 62
Hokanson, J., 102n
Homans, George, 94
Hoover, Herbert, 159
Hume, David, 16

Ickes, Harold, 156
Ingram, Helen, 14, 137-138, 144, 182-193,
    196, 198, 237n, 246

Jefferson, Thomas, 62
Johnson, J. W., 190
Johnson, Lyndon, 167
Jung, R., 262

Kaufman, Herbert, 174
Keys, A., 89

Khruschev, Nikita, 71
Kincaid, J., 12
Kirkendall, Richard, 248
Kirst, M., 262
Kneese, A., 130
Krebs, G., 223n

Laffer, Arthur, 169
Laney, N. K., 184, 237n
Laughlin, C., 85-88, 90-95, 101n, 102n
Leistritz, L. F., 223n
Leopold, A., 63
Lindblom, Charles, 243-251
Lipset, S. M., 14
Liroff, R., 137
Locke, John, 12, 29-45, 49-63, 67
Long, Stephen, 16
Lowery, D., 21
Lowi, Theodore, 242, 251
Loy, J., 102n

Maass, Arthur, 157
McCain, J. R., 237n
McConnell, Grant, 191
Machiavelli, Niccolo, 29
McClelland, L., 85
McGovern, George, 249, 251
McIntyre, Robert, 216, 223n
McNulty, M., 182
McPhee, J., 145
Maddox, J., 25
Majone, G., 133
Mann, Dean, 14, 183-184
Mao Zedong, 71
Marsh, George Perkins, 193
Martin, J., 132
Marx, Karl, 27, 29, 67
Marx, Leo, 152
Marx, W., 25
Mather, Cotton, 30
Mather, Stephen, 154
Mayer, L. V., 268
Mazmanian, D., 138, 261, 266
Mazur, A., 102n
Meadows, D., 25, 84
Medvedev, Roy, 80
Meier, Kenneth J., 19, 260-261, 264, 267,
    272n

Meissner, S., 185
Melville, Herman, 152
Merd, M., 28
Miewald, Robert, 16
Milbrath, Lester, 14, 120
Miles, R. E., 15
Miller, A., 255
Moe, T. M., 266
Muir, John, 154, 193
Muniz, F., 221

Nellis, L., 223n
Neubauer, D., 14
Nienaber, J., 17, 138
Neitzsche, Friedrich, 39
Nisbet, Robert, 15, 20

Ogg, C., 255
Ophuls, William, 12, 15, 25, 48-64, 84-85,
    130, 137, 140-141, 143, 180-181, 190-199
O'Rourke, A. D., 256, 260
Orr, D., 12
Osborn, F., 25
Ostheimer, J., 14

Paarlberg, Don, 245, 247, 257
Paddock, P., 25
Paddock, W., 25
Partridge, E., 126
Passell, P., 15
Pasztor, A., 182
Penn, J. B., 268
Pereira, H. C., 185
Pickens, D., 26
Pimentel, D., 255
Pinchot, Gifford, 62, 154, 191
Pirages, D., 48
Plato, 12, 29-45
Podhorzer, Michael, 223n
Powell, John Wesley, 154
Pugleares, L. 138

Quarantelli, E., 86

Rasmussen, W. D., 254-256, 273n
Raup, P., 245
Reagan, Ronald, 17, 95, 97, 140, 145, 160,
    166-170, 173-174

Reding, N., 255
Richardson, E., 160-161, 174
Rigdon, Susan, 13, 19
Ritt, L., 14
Robbins, Ray, 155
Roosevelt, Franklin, 97, 155-156, 198
Roosevelt, Theodore, 62, 154, 158, 191
Rosa, E., 102n
Rosenberg, Nathan, 10
Ross, L., 15
Rudel, T., 85
Runyon, C., 221
Russell, C., 133

Saarinen, T. F., 184
Sabatier, P., 261, 266
Sahlins, M., 16
Sale, K., 48
Sax, K., 25
Schultze, W., 130
Schumacher, E., 25
Scott, W., 13
Selye, Hans, 88, 102n
Shalins, M., 87
Shelton, R. W., 204
Sigelman, Lee, 21
Simon, J., 15, 20
Singer, P., 25
Sirotkin, P., 175n
Sitting Bull, 27
Smil, V., 65
Smith, F. E., 156
Socrates, 32-33, 36
Southwick, C., 93, 102n
Spitze, R.G.F., 267
Stalin, Joseph, 71
Starch, K. E., 204
Stewart, R., 146
Stiebeling, Hazel, 248
Stiglitz, J. E., 127
Stobaugh, R., 84
Stockman, David, 170, 174
Stone, C., 25
Strangeland, Alan, 273n
Stratton, O., 175n
Streiter, Sally H., 223n
Stroup, R., 19
Sun, S., 64

Talbot, R., 259-260
Taylor, Edward J., 156
Tenenbaum, E., 175n
Thoreau, Henry, 152
Tilly, L., 85
Thurow, Lester, 17-18, 25
Tolley, Howard, 248
Topping, S., 80
Truman, David, 267
Truman, Harry S., 159-161, 174
Turnbull, C., 87
Turner, Frederick Jackson, 26

Ullery, S., 138, 144

Vacca, R., 25
Van Dyke, D., 245
Van Liere, K., 140
Verrecchia, Stephen A., 204

Wallace, Henry A., 156, 248
Ward, B., 15
Watt, James, 171-172

Waxman, C., 12
Webb, Walter Prescott, 26

Weber, Max, 174
White, L., 25
White, Lynn, 13, 14
Whitten, Jamie L., 255
Wichelman, A., 138
Wiggins, C. W., 261, 271
Wilcox, A., 18
Wildavsky, Aaron, 198
Wiley, Harvey, 249, 251
Wilford, John Noble, 15
Wilson, Graham, 261
Wittwer, S. H., 255
Woodham-Smith, C., 85

Yergin, D., 84
Yost, N., 138

Zile, Z., 129
Zinam, O., 26

SUBJECT INDEX

Adaptation (to scarcity), 136
Agribusiness, 260-261
Agonistic behavior, 90-100
Agriculture, 243-252
    Department of, 242-252, 255-273
    Conservation Program, 255-273
    production, 72-76
        in China, 74-75
        in Cuba, 74-76
        in Soviet Union, 72-73
Agricultural Stabilization and Conservation
    Service, 256
Anthropological models of scarcity, 86-101
Alabama, 203-224
Arab oil embargo, 195-203
Arizona Groundwater Management Act,
    184, 189
Arkansas, 203-224
Army Corps of Engineers, 152-176
Australia, 180-121
Authority, subordination to, 96-100
Awareness of scarcity, 92-93, 105-121

Britain, 108-121
Bureau of Land Management, 139, 152-176,
    227-238
Bureau of Reclamation, 152-176, 189

Capitalism and resource management, 65-82
Central Arizona Project, 189
China, 65-82
Christianity, 31, 39
Clean Air Act, 141
Coal, 203-224
Colorado, 203-224
Communalism, 141-142
Communist societies, 13, 26
Conservation, 90-100, 153-176
    of food, 243-252
    of water, 182-199
    movement, 62-64
    society, 113-115
Conservatism, 98-99, 231-232
Cuba, 65-82
Czechoslovakia, 66

Declaration of Independence, 70
Deforestation, 65
Demand, policies to reduce, 133-134
Democrats, 98-100
Diets, resource-conserving, 247-250

East Africa, 87-89
Eastern Europe, 65-82
Economic growth, 72-76
Economic models
    of scarcity, 86
    of water pricing, 184-185
Economic theory
    and agriculture, 244
Education
    and attitudes toward scarcity, 18-121
Electric utilities, 216-218
Energy, 37, 167-168
Enlightenment, 15
Environment, 63-64, 166-167
Environmental Protection Agency, 140, 146, 250
Environmental Impact Statement, 138-139
Externalities, 143

Farm Bureau, 270
Farm prices, 268-270
Farming
    and conservation, 244-252
Fish and Wildlife Service, 152-176
Food and Drug Administration, 250
Food System (in U.S.), 243-252
Forest Service, 152-176, 227
Frontier, 26
Future generations, 127-128

Geological Survey, 151
Germany, 108-121
Gross national product, 81
    China, 81
    Soviet Union, 81
    United States, 81
Groundwater, 183-199, 247
Groundwater Act, 184
Groundwater Management Commission, 190

Holism, 52-53
Hoover Commission, 138

Ik, 88-89
Income
    and attitudes toward scarcity, 108-121
Ireland, 94
Irrigation, 247

Jeffersonian polity, 182

Kentucky, 203-244

Labor mobilization, 77-78
Labour government (Britain), 98
Land use, 231-239
Leviathan (Hobbes), 13, 14, 20, 48-63, 144
Lifeboat ethics, 29
Limits to growth, 110-121

Market economy
    for water, 182-199
Marxism
    and natural resources, 65-82
Mass campaigns (China) 78-79
Michigan, 204
Montana, 203-224
Multiple use (of land), 227-239

National forests, 155
National Park Service, 152-176
Neoclassical economics, 128-129
New Deal, 156-159
National Environmental Policy Act (NEPA), 138, 166
Nevada, 229-239
New Mexico, 203-224
North Dakota, 203-224
Northeast-Midwest Congressional Coalition, 216-221

Occupational Safety and Health Administration, 258
Ohio, 203-224
OPEC, 203

People's Republic of China (PRC), 65-82
Perceptions of scarcity, 135-137, 222
Planning, 70-76
Political structures, 50-52
Population control, 29

Prices
    as regulation of scarcity, 128-131
Prior appropriation (water law), 184
Progressive Era, 153-155
Progress, the inevitability of, 20-21
Proposition 13, 16
Public attitudes on scarcity, 105-121, 184-185
    toward Sagebrush Rebellion, 231-239
Public interest groups, 217, 252-253

Rationality, 19
Rationing, 75-82
Reciprocity, 88-95
Recreational use (of land), 227-239
Regulation, 128-132, 141-144
Reserves, 135-136
Rhesus monkeys, 94
Rights, individual, 67-82
    in Democratic thought, 67-82
    in Marxist thought, 67-82
Rituals, 90-100

Sabebrush Rebellion, 171, 227-238
Severance taxes, 203-224
Scarcity
    as absolute, 10
    and attitudes, 14-16
    beneficiaries of, 16-18
    bureaucratic regulation, 128-130, 141-144
    the concept, 126
    as a cyclical problem, 174
    and demand for goods, 28-45
    and democracy, 14-16, 26, 50-52
    as economic efficiency, 10, 26
    and the future, 127-128
    and market forces, 127-130
    as perceptions, 10
    and policy alternatives, 131-146
    as a political issue, 174
    and property, 50-63

Smith-Lever Act, 259
So (people of East Africa), 87-89
Social networks, 90-100
Social relations, 93-95
Socialism and resource policy, 65-82
Soil conservatism, 255-273
    agencies involved, 2565-260
    political support, 261-271
Soil Conservation Service, 106-111,
    152-176, 255-273
Soil erosion, 157, 255-273
Somerset Trust, 113-115
Soviet Union, 65-82
Steady-state, 48, 50-63
Stress, 89-90
Sunbelt, 216
Supply
    policies to increase, 133-135

Tax, severance, 205-223
    base, 209-211
    federal cap on, 217-219
    yield, 210-211
Technology, 15, 50-63
Tennessee, 203-224
Texas, 204
Tragedy of the commons, 48-63, 189
Tradition
    and coping with scarcity, 95-100
Tucson, Arizona, 186-199

Uganda, 88-89
United Kingdom, 108-112

Water
    scarcity of, 181-199, 247
    pricing of, 184-199
    projects, 160-161, 169-170
Water law, 184
West India, 89-90
Wyoming, 203-224

ABOUT THE CONTRIBUTORS

Alan Booth is Professor of Sociology at the University of Nebraska—Lincoln. He is the author of *Urban Crowding and Its Consequences* as well as articles on housing, sex roles, and family relations. His current interests include the causes and consequences of divorce, the impact of multiple dwelling residences, and scarcity.

William P. Browne is Professor of Political Science and Coordinator of Public Administration Programs at Central Michigan University. He has published five books and over 20 articles, monographs, and essays primarily on the subjects of interest groups, agriculture policy, and bureaucratic decision making.

Michael W. Bowers is a Ph.D. candidate in the Department of Political Science at the University of Arizona in Tucson. He has published in the fields of public law and public policy. His most recent work on resource management and public policy is "The West and Energy Policy: The View From Capitol Hill," with Henry C. Kenski, in *Energy Development in the Western United States*, edited by James L. Regens.

Dorotha M. Bradley is a political science doctoral candidate at the University of Arizona in Tucson. Her particular interests include legislative processes and natural resources policymaking. She has participated in the Lake Powell Research Project considering the role of consultants in the Environmental Impact Statement process and in a study of institutional arrangements for water quality management conducted by the Pima Association of Governments. Most recently she is the co-author with Dr. Helen Ingram of a paper on the Bureau of Land Management.

R. McGreggor Cawley is Assistant Professor of Political Science at the University of Wyoming. In 1981, he received the first Ph.D. in Political Science awarded by Colorado State University. His dissertation, *The Sagebrush Rebellion*, was awarded Honorable Mention by the Western Political Science

Association. His research interests include natural resource and public land policy.

Uday C. Desai is Research Associate in the Coal Research Center and Assistant Professor in the Political Science Department at Southern Illinois University at Carbondale. His major research interests are organizational decision making and natural resources policy, and his published work includes articles in *Administration and Society*, the *ASCI Journal of Management*, and the *Indian Journal of Public Administration*. His current research focuses on implementation of the 1917 Surface Mining Control and Reclamation Act.

Osbin L. Ervin is Research Associate in the Coal Research Center and Associate Professor in the Political Science Department at Southern Illinois University at Carbondale. His major research interests are tax policy and municipal budgeting, and his published work includes articles in *Policy Studies Journal*, the *American Review of Public Administration*, and *Public Productivity Review*. His current research focuses on coal severance taxation and local fiscal effects of coal resources development.

Don Hadwiger has written books on wheat policy, price supports, rural housing, food stamps policy, agricultural research policy, and civil rights. He was a Congressional Fellow with the House Agriculture Committee, and has served as resident political scientist/historian with the Economic Research Service and the Agricultural Research Service. He has served in a civil rights organization, in the U.S. Department of Agriculture's Agricultural Research Service and Economic Research Service, and is currently Professor of Political Science at Iowa State University.

Helen M. Ingram is Professor of Political Science at the University of Arizona. She is a graduate of Oberlin College and received her doctorate at Columbia University. She has written a number of books and articles about public policy, particularly concerning water and natural resources. Her scholarly contributions include *A Policy Approach to Political Representation: Lessons from the Four-Corners States*, with Nancy Laney and John R. McCain (1980). In 1980, she and Dean Mann edited a Sage yearbook entitled *Why Politics Succeed or Fail*. Professor Ingram is President of the Western Political Science Association in 1982-1983.

John Kincaid is Assistant Professor of Political Science at North Texas State University, Associate Editor of *Publius: The Journal of Federalism*, Co-Director of the Workshop on Covenant and Politics, and author of numerous articles in political science.

Dean E. Mann is Professor of Political Science, University of California, Santa Barbara. He has written extensively on the management of natural resources, particularly in the West. His research interests focus on water development, water pollution, natural hazards (seismic safety), and weather modification. He presently serves as editor of the *Western Political Quarterly* and associate editor for environmental policy for the *Policy Studies Journal.* He recently edited two volumes of original articles on environmental policy formation and implementation for Lexington Books.

Kenneth J. Meier is Associate Director of the Bureau of Government Research at the University of Oklahoma. He is the author of *Politics and the Bureaucracy* and *Applied Statistics for Public Administration.* His current research interests include agricultural policy, financial institutions, and the techniques of cost-benefit analysis.

Robert Miewald is Professor of Political Science at the Univerisity of Nebraska, Lincoln. A specialist in public administration, he received his Ph.D. from the University of Colorado, in 1966. Among his publications is *Public Administration: A Critical Perspective* (1978).

Robert Miewald is Professor of Political Science at the University of Nebraska, Center and Professor of Political Science at the State University of New York at Buffalo. Prior to coming to SUNY/Buffalo in 1966, he was on the faculty of Northwestern University, Duke University, and the University of Tennessee. He has twice been a Fulbright Scholar to Norway, a Visiting Professor at the University of Aarhus in Denmark, and a Visiting Scholar at the Center for Resource and Environmental Studies at the Australian National University in Canberra. He has built on past research interests in political beliefs, political participation, and lobbying and has now turned these talents to environmental questions. Current research focuses on environmental perceptions, beliefs, attitudes, and values. He also is interested in public participation in environmental policy decisions; in conceptualizing, measuring and studying environmental quality and quality of life; and in forecasting and planning for environmental futures.

Jeanne Nienaber received a Ph.D. in Political Science from the University of California, Berkeley, in 1973. She is currently an Associate Professor at the University of Arizona, and has been at that institution since 1974. Her publications include two books dealing with politics and resources: *The Budgeting and Evaluation of Federal Recreation Programs* (with Aaron Wildavsky) and *Can Organizations Change? Environmental Protection, Citizen Participation, and the Corps of Engineers* (with Daniel Mazmanian).

Susan Rigdon, Research Associate in the Center for International Comparative Studies at the University of Illinois—Urbana, is co-author with Oscar and Ruth Lewis of a three-volume series on the impact of the revolution on daily life in Cuba—*Living the Revolution: An Oral History of Contemporary Cuba* (1977, 1978). She recently served as Visitng Associate Professor of Political Science at the University of Nebraska—Lincoln, where she taught Chinese and Cuban politics.

Allen R. Wilcox is Chairman and Professor in the Department of Political Science, and Director, Nevada Public Affairs Institute, at the University of Nevada, Reno. He received a B.A. from the University of Chicago and an M.A. and Ph.D. from Northwestern University. He has authored *Legislative Roll-Call Analysis*, edited and co-authored *Public Opinion and Political Attitudes* and *Energy in Nevada*, and published numerous articles. In addition to public land politics, his current research interests include analysis of statistical meaures of qualitative variation, the integration of social impact assessment into planning processes, and the relationships of personality, ethical, and systems theory to policy analysis.

Susan Welch is Professor and Chair of the Department of Political Science, University of Nebraska, Lincoln. Since receiving her degree from the University of Illinois in 1970, she has published widely on state and urban politics. Recent works include *Black Representation and Urban Public Policy* (1981, with Al Karnig) and *Quantitative Methods for Public Administration* (1983, with John Comer).